Conversations in Exile

Conversations

IN EXILE

Russian
Writers Abroad

Interviews translated by
Richard and Joanna Robin

Edited by

John Glad

DUKE UNIVERSITY PRESS   Durham and London   1993

© 1993 Duke University Press
Printed in the United States of America
on acid-free paper ∞
Library of Congress Cataloging-in-Publication Data
appear on the last printed page of this book.
Photo credits: Photo of Joseph Brodsky by Bengt Jangfeldt, © 1987
(p. 101); photo of Igor Chinnov by Ray Studio, Nashville,
Tennessee (p. 31); photo of Yury Ivask by Laszlo Dienes (p. 39);
photo of Vladimir Maksimov by Boris Feldblyum, © 1985 (p. 239);
photos of Maria Rozanova and Andrei Siniavsky courtesy of the
Smithsonian Institution, Washington, D.C. (p. 141); photo of
Sasha Sokolov by Tanya Retinova (p. 174).

Contents

Acknowledgments

In addition to the writers whom I have interviewed, I wish to express my deepest gratitude to Mark Altshuller, Heidi Araya, Susan Ashe, Carol Avins, Abraham Brumberg, Ellen Chances, Maurice Friedburg, Larisa Glad, Valery Golovskoy, Ken Wissoker, Christopher Morris, Charles Moser, Rachel Mott, Dale Peterson, Lev Loseff, Joanna Robin, the late Nikolai Poltoratsky, Richard Robin, Elena Suhir, Boris Taubvurtzel, Josephine Woll, and Eugenia Zhiglevich for their invaluable assistance. The work was made possible in part by assistance from the National Endowment for Democracy and the Graduate School of the University of Maryland.

I apologize to all those—living and dead—whose names do not appear here. My file of Russian writers in exile numbers some 2,500, and it is not an exhaustive list.

It has not always been easy to get interviews. Solzhenitsyn refused, as he almost always does. Leonid Rzhevsky died just before we were scheduled to conduct an interview. I regret the absence in the volume of Nina Berberova, a still-living representative of the First Wave. A prominent critic, prose writer, and poet, she has lived through the entire Soviet period of literary exile and is a unique witness to her time. But conducting interviews is tricky business, and when I told her I had already interviewed Roman Goul, her former friend, later to become a bitter enemy, she abruptly changed her mind and refused to grant an interview.

Russian émigré letters are fraught with such conflicts. As Naum Korzhavin once put it, "that's why we left—to fight with each other." And if that is not the way things should be, it is the way they are. In the long run, we are the richer for having these talented men and women in our midst, although we have often tended to ignore them. They are now returning home, in their books if not in person, to a Russia that wants to listen. Let us hope that we in the West have listened a little too.

Introduction

Glasnost in the Soviet Union has a special meaning for Russia's banished writers, who now find themselves cast in the unfamiliar role of "expatriates." Exile, if not exodus, appears to have come to an end. At the same time millions of Russians outside the Russian Republic now find themselves living "abroad." Thus it is a time to take stock of the past and preserve for future generations the living testimony of those who lived through the experience of separation from their homeland.

In a sense, the very concept of "literature in exile" is a recognition of defeat, granting to a political regime the right to define the victimized writer and his work. If the work is to be judged sui generis, if it is to survive the ages as an Arnoldian "touchstone" to measure greatness in future works, what then is the relevance of its creator's incidental circumstances? When the chronicler of the Gulag Archipelago was deported from the Soviet Union in 1974, a devotee of his work remarked that historians would later write of Brezhnev that he was a bureaucrat who served during the Age of Solzhenitsyn.

Certainly, some Russian writers in exile have attempted to exist on a plane virtually untouched by political vicissitudes—Viacheslav Ivanov might serve as an example, although even his case can be accepted only with reservations. However, the overwhelming majority of Russian writers residing outside the boundaries of Russia have been highly politicized, and the same is true of their works. Russian literature is no exception in this regard.[1]

Russian literature in exile begins as far back as the sixteenth century, with Prince Andrei Kurbsky's enraged letters to Ivan

---

1. See, as an example, *Literature in Exile*, edited by John Glad and published by Duke University Press in 1990.

the Terrible from Livonia and Gregory Kotoshikhin's seventeenth-century tract composed in Sweden and entitled *On Russia in the Reign of Aleksei Mikhailovich*. Russia's literary exiles also could be said to include her "internal exiles"—writers sent into exile within the confines of the Russian empire. These include the seventeenth-century Archpriest Avvakum and such nineteenth-century writers and critics as Aleksandr Radishchev, Aleksandr Pushkin, Mikhail Lermontov, and the "Decembrists"—Aleksandr Bestuzhev-Marlinsky, Pyotr Chaadaev, and Wilhelm Küchelbecker. Then too there were the nineteenth-century Russian expatriates Nikolai Gogol, Ivan Turgenev, and Vasily Zhukovsky, who accepted the Western nature of secular Russian literature and who were—in a strictly literary sense—simply coming home to their roots.

The true forerunners of the writers interviewed in this volume are the Tsarist political émigrés who fled to England, France, and Switzerland: the publisher and memoirist Aleksandr Herzen, his coworker Nikolai Ogaryov, the terrorist Sergei Nechaev, the anarchist Mikhail Bakunin, the revolutionary and literary critic Pyotr Lavrov, and the even more radical revolutionary populist and critic Pyotr Tkachov.

It was the next generation of émigrés—Pyotr Kropotkin, Georgy Plekhanov, Vladimir Lenin, Lev Trotsky, Aleksandr Bogdanov, Anatoly Lunacharsky—who eventually returned to Russia to establish the Soviet state. And, of course, not a few of those who returned were to perish in the purges.

Russian émigrés of the Soviet period are traditionally divided into three groups: the First Wave—those who left during or just after the Russian civil war; the Second Wave—those who fled during World War II; and the Third Wave—those who emigrated in 1970 or later.

The First Wave

Following on the heels of World War I, the Russian civil war scattered a large exodus of highly educated émigrés throughout Europe and China.

The evacuation of some 150,000 people from the Crimea to

Turkey, in a short-lived attempt to keep the army together to continue the war, produced a helter-skelter of magazines with titles such as *Razvei gore v chistom pole* (Scatter Your Troubles in an Empty Field), *Shakal* (The Jackal), and *Eshafot* (The Scaffold).

Before the Russian revolution Germany had been a strong magnet for ethnic Russians, Russian Jews, and Russified German Balts. After the revolution, even larger numbers of Russian emigrants flocked across the German borders, where by 1920 some 560,000 of them had received assistance from the American Red Cross. When runaway inflation began after World War I, the German mark was so devalued (2.7 million marks for one dollar by August 16, 1923!) that in Berlin books could be published at a considerably lower cost than elsewhere. Berlin became an important center for Russian book production.

Among those who read their work in Berlin cafés were Ilya Ehrenburg, Pavel Muratov, Vladislav Khodasevich, Viktor Shklovsky, Vladimir Lidin, Andrei Bely, Boris Zaitsev, and Nina Berberova. No fewer than forty Russian publishing houses were founded in Berlin, as well as several newspapers. *Golos Rossii* (The Voice of Russia) was a daily publication with a rather vague political orientation. Eventually purchased by the Social Revolutionaries, it was renamed *Dni* (Days). A second daily newspaper, *Rul'* (The Rudder), numbered Vladimir Nabokov's father among its editors. Published between November 16, 1920, and October 12, 1931, it reached a circulation of 20,000 in the early 1920s. A weekly publication, *Vremya* (Time), was published by G. N. Breitman. There was even a communist Russian-language newspaper, *Novy mir* (The New World), supposedly financed by the Soviet government and intended to cover politics, literature, and economics. The monarchists published *Gryadushchaya Rossiya* (Russia of the Future). The Smena vekh (Change of Landmarks) publications *Nakanune* (On the Eve) and *Rodina* (The Fatherland) were published weekly, the latter in Russian and German. *Spolokhi* (Northern Lights) came out every month.

As the political climate changed in Germany, Russian writers began to leave Berlin for Paris (see the Goul interview for an instance), which became the unquestioned focal point of Russian literature abroad. Many writers such as Ivan Bunin, Aleksandr Kuprin, Boris Zaitsev, Ivan Shmelyov, Aleksei Remizov, Dmitry Merezhkovsky, Mikhail Iliin (Mikhail Osorgin), and Mark Aldanov (Mark Landau) made their home in Paris, as did the poets Konstantin Balmont, Zinaida Gippius, Georgy Ivanov, Georgy Adamovich, Dovid Knut, and Boris Poplavsky. After 1925 Marina Tsvetaeva joined them from Prague, where she had spent the previous three years.

Paris boasted more than thirty Russian Orthodox churches and seven institutions of higher learning. The most important of all the émigré newspapers, *Poslednie novosti* (The Latest News), as well as the more conservative *Vozrozhdenie* (Renaissance), were published in the French capital. In addition, throughout the 1920s Russian émigré painters, in particular Marc Chagall, Vasily Kandinsky, Aleksandr Benois, Mikhail Larionov, and Ivan Bilibin played a significant role in the artistic life of Montparnasse, Montmartre, and Saint Germain des Près.

Russian writers were likewise scattered throughout Eastern Europe. Riga was a center of Russian cultural life. One of the largest émigré newspapers of the period, *Segodnya* (Today), appeared there, as did *Slovo* (The Word). Riga had a Russian theater, and the Latvian University offered a number of Russian-language courses. Igor Chinnov, who appears in this book, is from Riga. After the annexation of Eastern territories, the Russian-speaking population in Poland numbered 5,250,000 (1921), out of a total population of some 27,000,000. The bulk of the Russian community in Yugoslavia was a product of the Crimean emigration, which funneled people there through Turkey. Some 73,000 Russian refugees reached Yugoslavia, but by the 1930s their numbers had been reduced to 35,000. In Bulgaria the Russian colony has been roughly estimated at 34,000. Since this was a largely military group, most were men. Among them was Pyotr Bitsilli, the brilliant Russian historian and literary scholar. In Tallinn there were over 90,000 Russians who in 1923 amounted to some 8 percent of the total population. Among Tallinn's poets were Yelena Bazilevskaya and Maria Karamzina. Boris Pravdin, a professor at the university, gathered around him a group of younger poets, including Dmitry Maslov, Elizaveta Ross, Boris Novosadov, and Boris Nartsissov; the group called itself Tsekh poètov (The Poets' Guild). Less than 3 percent of Lithuania's population were Russians, and cultural activity in that country must have been relatively modest. Russians living in Finland formed a group called Sodruzhestvo poètov (Commonwealth of Poets) which was active in Viipuri. It included Ivan Savin and Vera Bulich.

China in the early postrevolutionary period was home to an émigré community numbering approximately a quarter of a million. In the twenties and thirties half of this group left China for the United States, Canada, Australia, and South America. The rest settled in Harbin, Manchuria, a city of approximately half a million in the mid-twenties, of whom roughly 150,000 were Russians. In the Russian part of the city even the street signs were in Russian. Newspapers published in Harbin included *Zarya* (The Dawn), *Kharbinskoe vremya* (The Harbin Times), *Luch Azii* (The Ray of Asia), *Rupor* (The Megaphone), and *Russkoe slovo* (The Russian Word). Among its magazines were *Rubezh* (The Border), *Vestnik Manchzhurii* (The Manchuria Messenger), and *Nash put'* (Our Path—a fascist publication). The pro-Soviet newspapers were *Molva* (The Rumor) and *Tribuna* (The Tribune). Of the Harbin poets, Aleksei Achair appears to have been among the most popular. Petrov-Skitalets and Sergei Gusev-Orenburgsky (1867–1963) had been known as prose writers before they arrived in Harbin in 1921 from the "Far Eastern Republic." Gusev-Orenburgsky soon left by way of Japan and died in New York; Petrov-Skitalets returned to Russia in 1934. After the Japanese occupied Harbin in 1932 and bought the railroad in 1935, Harbin began to lose some of its Russian population to Shanghai. Here, in this far larger and more cosmopolitan environment, the Russian community lost much of its strength and impact.

The political involvement of the interwar émigré community was intense. Although anti-Soviet feelings ran high, the group's ideological spectrum was quite broad. Emotions occasionally exploded in violent incidents, such as the 1932 assassination of the French President Paul Doumer by Pavel Gorgulov, a Russian émigré physician and poet.

One of the groups which viewed Lenin's New Economic Policy (NEP) as a harbinger of Russia's normalization was the Change of Landmarks faction, which founded the newspa-

pers *Novaya mysl'* (New Thought) and *Nakanune* (On The Eve).
The magazine *Novaya russkaya kniga* (The New Russian Book),
headed by Aleksandr Yashchenko, promoted the theory that
Moscow would inevitably be forced to return to a more traditional form of government and that the émigré community
should renounce the extreme hostility which it had heretofore
displayed toward the Soviet Union. Roman Goul—Yashchenko's assistant at the time—supported the movement, although
later he renounced it.

Another movement which professed to find positive elements in the Soviet state was Eurasianism, founded by Nikolai
Trubetskoi, Georgy Florovsky, Pyotr Savitsky, and Pyotr Suvchinsky with the publication in Sofia in 1929 of a collection of
essays entitled *Iskhod k vostoku* (Exodus to the East). This group
was supported by some very prominent thinkers, including
Pyotr Bitsilli, Dmitry Sviatopolk-Mirsky, Georgy Vernadsky,
and Lev Karsavin. The "Eurasians," who drew some of their
inspiration from fascism and who believed in the need for
an authoritarian social structure based on religion, combined
nineteenth-century Slavophile ideals with a belief in a new
culture which would unify Europe and Asia. As the movement
became more and more pro-Soviet, both Trubetskoi and Florovsky disassociated themselves from it. The literary historian
Sviatopolk-Mirsky, however, returned to the Soviet Union but
was later—to use a Soviet phrase—"repressed."

The Mladoross (Young Russia) League, whose goal was the
creation of a "new totalitarian corporate state" for the *narod-
bogonosets* (the God-bearing people), was founded in Munich in
1923. In both ideology and behavior, the union emulated the
Nazis, its members even shouting *Glava! Glava!* (Führer) when
their leader Kazem-Bek appeared on stage. Their slogan was
"The Tsar and the Soviets!"

A similar group that was formed in July 1930 was called the
National Union of Russian Youth. Later, transformed into the
National Labor Union of the New Generation, it became the
party of the Solidarist movement. In 1940, when Pétain came to
power in France, the Solidarist K. Vergun wrote that democracy
as a world view was fading from the scene of history.

One of the most bizarre Fascist organizations was headed by "Count" Anastase Vonsyatsky, a dancer who had married a wealthy American heiress. Vonsyatsky played at soldiering, issuing instructions from his wife's Connecticut estate to his largely fictitious minions and calling for assassinations and terrorism on Soviet soil. Although he explicitly rejected anti-Semitism, he blissfully borrowed such Nazi rituals as the swastika, the Nazi salute (accompanied by the shout *Slava Rossii!* [Glory to Russia!]), and the title *Shturmovik smerti* (Storm Trooper of Death).

The less comical Konstantin Rodzaevsky, führer of the Manchurian-based Russian Fascist party, did not limit himself to the type of fantasy practiced by Vonsyatsky, but became actively involved in a number of serious operations. Some of these involved sending agents into Soviet territory. He attempted to finance his political projects by criminal means, such as kidnapping the son of a wealthy Jewish businessman. When the father refused to pay the ransom, the son's ears were cut off. Later, the young man was murdered.

Impoverished, hopeful that the political situation within the Soviet Union would return to normal, nostalgic for friends, family, and country, and afraid of being forgotten professionally, a number of writers returned to Russia in the 1920s and 1930s. Among these were the talented novelist Aleksei Tolstoy (who, not unexpectedly, made a brilliant and remunerative literary career for himself in the USSR), the Formalist critic Viktor Shklovsky, the "father of Socialist Realism" Maksim Gorky, Aleksandr Kuprin, Aleksandr Drozdov, the Prague poet Aleksei Èisner, the poet Vladimir Pozner (former member of the "Serapion Brothers"), Ivan Sokolov-Mikitov, and Nikolai Ustryalov (of the Change of Landmarks group).

The activities of Marina Tsvetaeva's husband, Sergei Efron, had the effect of compromising her totally. An active member of a movement to repatriate émigrés to the Soviet Union, Efron was later found to have been an agent of the Soviet secret police (the GPU) and to have helped track down the defected Soviet agent Yevgeny Reis, as well as Trotsky's son Andrei Sedov, and to have directed the assassination of both from Paris. When

Efron fled to Spain to escape arrest, Tsvetaeva was ostracized
by the émigré community. In spite of numerous vows never to
return, she did in fact follow her husband back to the Soviet
Union in 1939, just as she had followed him out of Russia in
1922. Impoverished and desperate, Tsvetaeva committed suicide; Efron was "liquidated."

Writers with reputations established before the Revolution
came to be referred to as the older generation—even though
some of them were still relatively young. Again, regardless of
age, those who did not make a name for themselves until after
they emigrated were lumped together as the younger generation. Some of the many émigré writers who had been well
known before the Revolution were Arkady Averchenko, Konstantin Balmont, Ivan Bunin, Zinaida Gippius, Aleksandr Kuprin, Sergei Makovsky, Dmitry Merezhkovsky, Igor Severianin,
Ivan Shmelyov, Aleksei Tolstoy, Nadezhda Tèffi, and Sasha
Chorny.

In a classic "fathers and sons" conflict of views, the younger
writers often failed to see any relevance for themselves in the
work of established writers. It was this lonely, alienated tradition that gave birth to Nabokov's *Invitation to a Beheading*. As can
be seen from the writers interviewed for this volume, a similar
split was later to occur between the Third-Wave writers and
their predecessors in exile.

The literary salon is an old tradition in Russian letters. In
the nineteenth century Zinaida Volkonskaya (1792–1862) established one at her villa in Rome, and it was there that Gogol
wrote much of his *Dead Souls*. In Paris Zinaida Gippius and
Dmitry Merezhkovsky maintained the tradition with their
Green Lamp Society. Before emigrating the poet Viacheslav
Ivanov (1866–1949) established a literary salon entitled The
Tower (Bashnya) in Petersburg in 1905–1907. After leaving Russia, however, Ivanov not only failed to reestablish his salon, but
generally avoided his fellow émigrés.

Russian émigré writers received government support from
their Slavic hosts, and Czechoslovakia attracted a sizable group
of Russian cultural figures. In the period 1919–1928 some
eighty periodicals and forty-five newspapers were published in

Prague. Thus, Prague's Russian salon tradition rested on a firm basis. Skit poètov (The Hermitage of Poets), established in 1922, included prose writers as well as poets. The group conducted weekly meetings and was directed by Alfred Bem, who was troubled by what he saw as an inability on the part of traditional, realistic émigré writers to find appropriate themes. Although the Hermitage held to no literary platform, one faction was drawn to acmeism, which had established itself in Russia in the poetry of Osip Mandelstam, Anna Akhmatova, and Nikolai Gumilyov. Acmeism was a reaction against the vagueness and otherworldliness of symbolism, which enjoyed its heyday in Russia roughly in the period 1890–1910. Other Hermitage poets favored Mayakovsky as a model. Bem tended to deprecate the so-called Parisian Note propagated by Georgy Adamovich.

Founded in 1924 by Vladimir Amfiteatrov-Kadyshev, Pyotr Kozhevnikov, Dmitry Krachkovsky (pseudonym: Dmitry Klenovsky), and Sergei Makovsky, all of whom lived in Prague at the time, the literary circle Daliborka was named after the coffeehouse where the group originally gathered. In addition to holding public lectures, they took a particular interest in young writers and a recommendation from Daliborka was often sufficient to allow a beginner to break into print. Also of interest were the "Literary Tuesdays" of the journal *Volya Rossii*, held in the Prague building where Mozart once lived, and the literary evenings of the Union of Russian Writers and Journalists in the Czechoslovak Republic, founded in 1922.

Among the Warsaw poets (who were considered to be closer to the Prague school than to the Parisian Note) were Lev Gomolitsky and S. Bart. One small group called itself Taverna poètov (The Poets' Tavern).

In Berlin The House of the Arts maintained close relations with the Petersburg House of the Arts. The Writers' Club included Andrei Bely and Viktor Shklovsky, both of whom eventually returned to Russia, as well as Ilya Ehrenburg, whose relations with the émigré community were themselves an interesting element of the cultural scene.

In Yugoslavia the Russian-Serbian Club, the Union of Russian Writers and Journalists (established in 1925, expired before

World War II), the Library of the Union of Russian Writers and Journalists, and the Zemgor Library all sponsored literary events.

In Vyborg the group Sodruzhestvo poètov (Commonwealth of Poets) was active, including Ivan Savin and Vera Bulich.

Émigré poets of the interwar period can be broken down into four basic groups: (1) late Symbolists, (2) followers of the Parisian Note, (3) poets who tried to emulate the formal experiments of Tsvetaeva, Mayakovsky, the pre-1940 Pasternak, dadaism, surrealism, Apollinaire, Rimbaud, and (4) those who followed Khodasevich's advice simply to write good poetry without trying to fit into any specific mold, although perhaps, as in Georgy Ivanov's case, leaning toward acmeism.

Symbolism had been the dominant poetic school in Russia from approximately 1890 to 1910. As in Western Europe, this was fundamentally an art-for-art's-sake movement. Underlying the philosophy of symbolism were the neoplatonic idea of a "higher reality" and Schopenhauer's concept of an ideal inaccessible to the rational faculty. Creativity was viewed as a spiritual act which did not so much communicate as suggest. A line of the nineteenth-century poet Tyutchev—"A thought expressed is a lie"—became an important slogan for the Russian symbolists. The mysterious and the exotic became almost prescriptive elements in poetry, and social-mindedness was generally rejected in favor of a highly personal, individualistic view. Synesthesia in art caught the imagination of many, and there were numerous attempts to duplicate the effects of music in poetry.

The Russian version of symbolism was linked to a generally eschatological mood and a sense of art as a mystical experience leading to a spiritual rebirth. Decadence played a strong role in the early development of Russian symbolism, while dark, prophetic notes marked the movement's later stages.

The chief émigré holdovers from symbolism were Konstantin Balmont, Viacheslav Ivanov, Zinaida Gippius, Dmitry Merezhkovsky, and even Andrei Bely, although he would have to be categorized somewhat differently from the others.

It was acmeism, and to a degree the poetry of Innokenty Annensky, which formed the basis for the Parisian Note, which actually came into its own in the second half of the 1920s and had a considerable resonance throughout the interwar period. The roots of the Parisian Note were more in a philosophy of life than an interest in poetic form (a feature which led to a cleft between its chief prophet, Georgy Adamovich, and Khodasevich, who stressed first and foremost the technique of prosody). The belief was that the poet should avoid radical experimentation, strive toward simplicity, and work with the so-called eternal themes of life, God, love, and death. This was combined with a consciousness of accomplished catastrophe, of the collapse of culture.

Among the adherents of the Parisian Note were Georgy Adamovich, Lidia Chervinskaya, Georgy Ivanov, Antonin Ladinsky, Irina Odoevtseva, Nikolai Otsup, Boris Poplavsky (who supposedly invented the term), and Anatoly Steiger. In my interview with him, Igor Chinnov lays out the philosophical bases for the movement.

Marina Tsvetaeva was a magnificent poet who clearly stood out among her émigré colleagues. She has been compared with Pasternak in her ecstatic identification with the forces of life, while the powerful, driving rhythm of her lines frequently recalls Mayakovsky; in addition, much of her output draws on the tradition of folk poetry, but she was quite unique in the comprehensiveness and intensity of her themes and manner. Highly individualistic, unique in the comprehensiveness and intensity of her themes and manner, Tsvetaeva did not fit at all into the Parisian Note. Georgy Adamovich conceded that some of her verse was "incomparable," but he saw no way that other poets could profit from her example. Gorky went even further, claiming she was "hysterical" and "controlled by the word rather than controlling it." He even faulted her for a weak command of Russian.

Other poets of an experimental bent were Aleksandr Ginger, Anna Prismanova, Viktor Mamchenko, and Yury Odarchenko.

The Second Wave

World War II swept aside the literary life of the First Wave. The newspapers *Poslednie novosti* and *Vozrozhdenie* closed when the Germans occupied Paris in 1940. That year also marked the end of *Sovremennye zapiski* (Contemporary Notes), the leading "thick" journal of the Russian emigration. The Turgenev library in Paris disappeared, possibly ending up in Minsk.

Some writers had already escaped to America, among them Vladimir Nabokov, Mark Aldanov, and Mikhail Tsetlin. Others, such as Ivan Shmelyov, Aleksei Remizov, and Mikhail Osorgin, found themselves in occupied France. Yet others returned to the occupied zone even before the Germans took over the whole of France. Among these were Dmitry Merezhkovsky, Zinaida Gippius, Nadezhda Tèffi, and Nikolai Berdiaev. There were those, too, who died at the hands of the Germans: Yury Felzen, Yury Mandelstam, Igor Voinov, the nun and poet Mother Maria (Elena Skobtsova), Ilya Fondaminsky, Vladimir Korvin-Piotrovsky, Mikhail Gorlin, and Raisa Blokh.

At the same time, there was considerable support among the Russian émigrés for the Germans, who employed such slogans as "A crusade against Bolshevism," "We are not fighting against the Russian people, but against the Soviet government," and "We wish to see as our neighbor a free and friendly Russia." In Paris a young Russian by the name of Yury Zherebkov was appointed Führer aux affaires russes.

By the fall of 1941 large numbers of Russian émigrés had gathered in Berlin to join in the fight against the Bolsheviks. Among them was the novelist Nikolai Breshko-Breshkovsky, who died in 1943 during a bombing raid on Berlin.

In Yugoslavia, General M. F. Skorodumov was appointed by the Germans to take charge of the affairs of the Russian émigré contingent. As a convincing demonstration of his loyalty, Skorodumov immediately staged a public book burning.

By 1943 the number of Russian volunteers in the German army reportedly reached two million, although they were scattered in small units over a large area. Within the German command, Borman, Rosenberg, and Himmler were opposed to the creation of a Russian army, as were Germany's Japanese allies. But by the middle of 1944, when Germany was obviously losing the war, the "Russian Army of Liberation" (ROA—Russkaya osvoboditel'naya armiya) was formed.

On the other side of the front, Russian patriotism led some

writers to adopt pro-Soviet positions and even to return home. The popular singer and poet Aleksandr Vertinsky went back to Russia from Shanghai in 1943. Dismissing a quarter century of emigration as a "misunderstanding," he married, had two daughters, and found a vast audience of listeners who still adored him. Another émigré to return was the poet Antonin Ladinsky. Some writers preferred to remain in Western Europe but accepted Soviet citizenship. These included Aleksandr Ginger and his wife Anna Prismanova, Aleksei Remizov, Viacheslav Ivanov, and Nadezhda Tèffi.

On October 4, 1944, the Soviet of People's Commissars resolved that Soviet citizens should be repatriated to the Soviet Union upon the conclusion of the war, and on February 11, 1945, the Allies signed an agreement to that effect.

As can readily be imagined, this process did not involve much "maternal mercy" for those who had fought against the Soviets. The former White General and popular novelist Pyotr Krasnov had been active in Rightist circles and had helped form Cossack units to fight against the Soviets during World War II. Captured by the Soviets, he was taken back to Moscow and executed. Other members of Vlasov's army either shared Krasnov's fate or were sentenced to forced-labor camps. In the Far East Rodzaevsky was executed by the Soviets. (Vonsyatsky was imprisoned only briefly in the United States.) Boris Khariton, an editor of the evening newspaper *Segodnya vecherom* (This Evening) was in Riga when the Soviets occupied the city. He at once disappeared into the maw of Siberia.

There was considerable resistance to repatriation, and many émigrés attempted to conceal their identities. As early as December 1946, Andrei Gromyko complained at the United Nations that the resettlement of refugees and displaced persons was being conducted in such a fashion that "war criminals, quislings, and traitors" were escaping punishment. The demographer Jacques Vernant quotes the Chief of the Soviet Repatriation Mission as having claimed in 1945 that five million Soviet citizens—prisoners of war and civilians—had been repatriated to the USSR.

Most Russians in Yugoslavia had supported the Germans, and by the end of the war many had fled the country. Of the former 35,000 only an estimated 8,000 to 12,000 were left in the country, but the Yugoslav authorities still viewed them as a sort of fifth column. Some departed the country clandestinely, while others were arrested as German collaborators. When Soviet troops occupied Manchuria in 1945, they arranged a "literary evening" in Harbin, sending personal invitations to local writers and journalists. Achair, Nesmelov, and Shmeisser were arrested, and they disappeared. Many of the journalists suffered the same fate. The books of two libraries were burned publicly.

Despite all this, a wave of patriotic pride swept over much of the Russian community. Pro-Soviet feelings were so strong that at a Shanghai writers' meeting a number of writers publicly supported Andrei Zhdanov's attacks on Anna Akhmatova. Although many local Russians had been born and educated in China, a significant number of them (including some of the writers) left for the Soviet Union, where they encountered a very mixed reception.

In 1948, when it became apparent that the Chinese Nationalist government could not win its war with the Communists, Russian émigrés were evacuated from other Chinese towns to Shanghai. But it soon became clear that Shanghai could not hold out for long either, and in 1949 most of the émigrés took refuge on the island of Tubabao, in the Philippine Archipelago. Literally bare-handed, they built a city of tents for the 5,500 residents, naming streets after such beloved Moscow and Petersburg thoroughfares as Nevsky Prospekt, Admiralteisky Prospekt, and Tverskaya. From Tubabao they dispersed to Argentina, Australia, Brazil, Paraguay, the Dominican Republic, and the United States.

In Europe the émigré community found itself deeply divided on the subject of the Soviet state. The Association of Russian Writers and Poets in Paris voted to expel members who had accepted Soviet citizenship, and a number of members immediately withdrew in protest, among them Georgy Adamovich, Vera Bunina, Gaito Gazdanov, Vladimir Varshavsky, and Leonid Zurov. Two weeks later Bunin himself withdrew from the association.

The late 1940s and early 1950s marked the height of the Cold

War, and an undetermined amount of money (most of it American) went into an effort to create a center for the struggle against communism. It was to have been focused to a large degree around Melgunov's League for the Struggle for the Freedom of Russia and the NTS (National Labor Union of the New Generation) and Radio Liberation (later renamed Radio Liberty), together with the Institute for the Study of the USSR, both of which had their headquarters in Munich.

In response, the Soviets launched a major espionage campaign against such émigré organizations and even instituted Komitet za vozvrashchenie na rodinu (The Committee for Return to the Homeland) in East Berlin in 1955, with its own radio broadcasts and newspaper *Za vozvrashchenie na rodinu* (For a Return to the Homeland).

The journal *Grani* (Facets) was founded in 1946 in Frankfurt-am-Main by Russian First- and Second-Wave emigrants. At the time the latter were still living in barracks for "displaced persons." The journal soon established ties with the First Wave, but ultimately became a forum for the publication of Soviet underground writing.

Emigration to the United States reached a peak in the period 1950–1952, with the result that New York became a major center of Russian-language publication abroad. *Novy zhurnal* (The New Review) was founded in 1942 by Mikhail Tsetlin, Mark Aldanov, and Mikhail Karpovich—all First-Wave figures who had moved from Europe to the New World.

While the Second Wave contained a number of intellectuals, it did not—as a group—possess the critical mass essential to maintain a cultural tradition abroad. The writings of First-Wave figures still tended to predominate in publications of the 1950s and the early 1960s. Since, at the end of the war, so many of the new émigrés found themselves in Germany, in the immediate postwar years that country saw a spate of émigré writings. In 1948 some eighty Russian serial publications appeared in Germany; by 1970, however, their number had dwindled to two.

For Russian literature the 1940s were, fundamentally, a period of disruption—first by the war and then by the movement of First-Wave writers to the United States. But in 1949 Sergei Maksimov (1917–1967) published *Denis Bushuev,* the most popular novel of the Second Wave. Even earlier, in 1948, Anatoly Darov (b. 1920) published in mimeographed form *The Block-ade*—about the siege of Leningrad.

In 1958 an anthology of prose and verse entitled *Literaturnoe zarubezh'e* (Literature Abroad) was published in Munich by a group of Second-Wave émigré writers—Olga Anstei, Ivan Elagin, Sergei Maksimov, Dmitry Klenovsky, Nikolai Morshen, Leonid Rzhevsky, and Aleksandr Kashin. The volume was intended to demonstrate that the Second Wave constituted a literary entity separate from the First Wave.

"Modern Russian literature," as defined by Yury Bolshukhin in the afterword to the volume, consisted of Second-Wave émigré and Soviet writings and was basically "moral" in thrust. Bolshukhin felt that the division between the two groups was artificial. His contention was that, having been formed by their experience in the USSR, Second-Wave writers saw themselves fundamentally as Soviet writers (or, rather, anti-Soviet writers) sent abroad by historical chance. Most First-Wave writers would have concurred in this evaluation.

Bolshukhin wrote that the bulk of First-Wave writers were inclined toward realism and that they seemed old fashioned when compared to Nabokov, Yanovsky, and "even" Varshavsky (although all three of these writers were First-Wave products). Bolshukhin conceded that the accomplishments of the Second Wave were still modest, but he pointed out that the group was small in number.

The verse that appears in *Literature Abroad* is often lofty in manner, with very traditional themes. Basically, the poets represented in the volume sought to transmit their impressions and musings in rhyme and meter. Bolshukhin's perception of a new modernism (although he did not use that word) now seems difficult to justify.

Perhaps one of the major achievements of the Second Wave was in the genre of memoirs and fictionalized descriptions. The tragedy of the age had not been reflected objectively in Soviet literature, and before the war it had been extremely difficult to smuggle manuscripts out of the Soviet Union. Deserving of mention in this genre are Gennady Andreev's *Solovetskie ostrova* (Solovetsk Islands, 1950), Boris Shiryaev's *Neugasimaya lampada*

(The Inextinguishable Lamp, 1954), the novel *Vrag naroda* (Enemy of the People, 1952, later republished in 1972 under the title *Parallax*) by Vladimir Yurasov (pseudonym of Vladimir Zhabinsky), Leonid Rzhevsky's *Mezhdu dvukh zvyozd* (Between Two Stars, 1953), and Yury Elagin's *Ukroshchenie iskusstvom* (The Taming of Art, 1952) and his *Tyomny geny* (Dark Genius, 1955).

Tatyana Fesenko in her 1963 memoir *Povest' krivykh let* (The Tale of Ragged Years) described her youth in Kiev, the German occupation, the time spent in Germany as an *Ostarbeiterin* (guest worker), her resolve to commit suicide if forced to return to the Soviet Union, the German landlord who threatened to hand her and her husband over to the Soviet authorities after the war, the poetry-writing of Ivan Elagin in a displaced persons' camp, the rescue by American soldiers of a Soviet repatriation officer from an enraged group of displaced persons, and Fesenko's own preparations to leave for the United States. It is an intense, deeply personal tale of one woman, but it was typical of the Second Wave as a whole.

A novel about the purges of 1937 was published by Nikolai Narokov (pseudonym of Nikolai Marchenko, 1887–1969) in New York in 1952 with the title *Mnimye velichiny* (Imaginary Numbers). Written in imitation of Dostoevsky's novels, it is intended to convey a moral message within a sensationalistic plot.

O nas (About Us), a 1972 work published by Irina Saburova in Munich in 1972, is a melodramatic novel with a very loose plot line about the immediate postwar years in Germany. The characters are overwhelmed by the struggle to survive—to eat, clothe themselves, and avoid forced repatriation to the USSR. They gradually rebuild their lives and even arrange poetry readings in those difficult times. At one point mention is made of *Gone With the Wind* and Saburova obviously felt a similarity of experience with that evoked in Margaret Mitchell's novel where it deals with the chaos, hope, and despair of the American South after the Civil War.

Both *Imaginary Numbers* and *About Us* are traditional realistic works displaying little artistic innovation, but they deal with the events that so wrenched the lives of the Second Wave and, as such, were found to be particularly meaningful to their readers.

The time span separating the First and Second Wave was appreciable—a quarter century—but nothing like that separating the First Wave from the Third. When the First-Wave critic Yury Terapiano in late 1959 summed up the tradition of Russian émigré poetry since 1920, he sensed an essential commonality of approach and world view in the "two generations." While observing that the former intentional sparseness of the Parisian Note was gone, Terapiano felt that an essential unity of manner had been achieved by the beginning of the 1950s. As examples of the common approach in the two groups he cites (a) a rejection of so-called "leftist" tendencies, or of what Khodasevich called "chaos"; (b) a rejection of symbolist "vagueness"; (c) an adherence to the traditions of the acmeists (Gumilyov, Akhmatova, early Mandelstam, Georgy Ivanov); (d) despite the proclaimed dismissal of symbolism, the influence of Blok and (partially) Tsvetaeva; (e) the influence of nineteenth-century Russian poets (Pushkin, Lermontov, Tyutchev, Baratynsky); (f) a less than expected influence of Pasternak, Khlebnikov, Mayakovsky, Esenin, Zabolotsky, Kirsanov, and Bagritsky.

Clearly, Terapiano's perceptions were influenced by his own personal tastes (he shakes his head over the way recent arrivals ignored the verse of Innokenty Annensky, for instance), but these are the perceptions of a sensitive contemporary critic and, as such, are not to be ignored.

Igor Chinnov, for lack of a better pigeon hole, is generally considered to be a member of the Second Wave, although he began as an imitator of the First Wave's Parisian Note. His verse is characterized by an economy of means (what is now referred to as "minimalism"), a sense of restraint, and a strong underlying aestheticism:

A black bird on a black and snowy branch—
A hieroglyph of sorrow.
A black burdock in the snow—
An ideogram of winter.

Shadows, mine and yours, on the white snowdrift—
Graffiti of silence.

The quivering of black branches and trees.
How restless

The Chinese calligraphy of the winter garden,
How fleshless
These abstractions of light and snow.

Chinnov's later work, while using the same system of formal devices, is more ironical, with elements of surrealism and the grotesque. His literary roots are actually quite cosmopolitan, and his general mood reflects the underlying pessimism of the exile experience.

While Chinnov is aesthetically an appendage to the First Wave, Ivan Elagin as a poet was truly a product of the new society. Instead of the idyllic landscapes so often encountered in the verse of First-Wave poets, Elagin often tended toward hyperbole and political verse:

The man is still alive
Who shot my father
In Kiev in the Summer of '38.

Probably, he's pensioned now,
Lives quietly
And has given up his old job.

And if he has died,
Probably the man is still alive
Who just before the shooting
Bound his arms
Behind his back
With a stout wire.

Probably, he too is pensioned off.

And if he is dead,
Then probably
The one who questioned him still lives.
And he, no doubt,
Has an extra good pension.

Perhaps the guard
Who took my father to be shot
Is still alive.

If I wanted,
I could now return home.
For I have been told

That all these people
have actually pardoned me.

Nikolai Morshen (pseudonym of Nikolai Marchenko, b.
1917) is from the Ukraine, which contributed disproportion-
ately to the Second Wave. Fraught with a sense of time, his
verse reflects the life and movement of an age in which the
individual is swept along by events:

In superstitious panic
I stared at walls surrounding me:
What space encloses me—
Four dimensional or four-walled?

I opened the door. It was twilight.
Objects gradually disappeared behind each other
And the air rustled lightly like foam—
Palpable, yet elusive.

The tide of dark air
rose to my knees, to my chest
And I had only to cross the threshold
To swim and swim, choking on stars.

Like Chinnov, Yury Ivask had his roots in the Baltics and
began writing poetry in a rather conservative fashion—somewhat in the manner of the Parisian Note. Later, he abandoned
this acmeistic simplicity and clarity in favor of a more intimate,
personal, associative verse and phonic experimentation. As a
young man, he conducted an interesting correspondence with
Marina Tsvetaeva, and in his later years he took a strong interest in Third-Wave poets. A First-Wave figure, he developed his
poetic manner quite late—after the arrival of the Second and
even the Third Wave.

Ivask taught Russian literature at the University of Massachusetts and became enamored of the image of a neighbor in
spirit and space, if not in time—Emily Dickinson:

The mad old maid of Amherst—
a face like the moon, eyes on fire,
her quill pen scraping.
                              On the left
a window. Another on the right.

And from beyond the wild roses,
the hawthorn and the maple (the glistening
garden—flowers for Thee, bright Absentee . . .

The Third Wave

The Soviets fought a bitter battle against the emigration movement, issuing numerous articles which paint a bleak picture of
émigré life. Here are just a few of their titles: *The Bitter Bread
of Alien Soil, Here They Are Crippled by Their Fates, In Penance,
Confession of an Emigrant, Escape from "Paradise", The Tragedy of
the Deceived, The Odyssey of a Renegade, There Is No Life Without the
Fatherland, Ten Years in a New York Dead-End, Invitation to a Quag-
mire, Lost Years,* and *I Kiss My Native Soil.*
As recently as 1985 the Soviet position on exiled Russian
writers was summed up by A. L. Afanasiev:

> The pack of Fascist sycophants and criminals whom we did
> not manage to finish off is now being augmented by disgusting
> little people who grab for their own servile piece of meat. These
> individuals—Voinovich, Brodsky, Gladilin, Aksyonov—only
> recently declared their devotion to the ideals of pure art and
> creative freedom and loftily held forth on their love of the Fa-
> therland. The opuses being penned about these "most recent"
> emigrés (with titles such as "Pushkin and Brodsky") engender
> nothing but revulsion. He who is capable of betrayal, betrays.

In keeping with this hard-line approach to emigration, the
Soviets resorted to a tactic last directed against Trotsky—the
deprivation of citizenship. Valery Tarsis, deported to the West
in 1966, was the first writer to be stripped of his citizenship.
Later came Aleksandr Solzhenitsyn, Vladimir Maksimov, Aleksandr Zinoviev, Vasily Aksyonov, Georgy Vladimov, Vladimir
Voinovich, and Edward Kuznetsov.
The history of Russian emigration is inexorably tied up with
Russia's Jews. These made up the majority of economic mi-
grants during the Tsarist period, and there was also a large
contingent of Jews among those obliged to leave Russia for
political reasons. Jews were very active in politics between

World Wars I and II, while Jewish writers and publishers played a significant role in literature of the First Wave. Later, the Third Wave was a largely Jewish phenomenon. As age takes its toll, the Russian émigré community is becoming more and more a community of Russian Jews.

The 1970s was a period of Jewish emigration from the USSR. While in 1970 only a little more than 1,000 Jews emigrated to the United States, by 1979 their numbers had peaked at 51,000. By 1983 emigration levels to the United States were back down to the 1970 level. The second half of the 1980s and especially the 1990s have seen hundreds of thousands of people emigrate every year. It appears entirely possible that the great historical movement of Russian Jewry out of the Russian Empire, begun in the late 1870s, will eventually be culminated. And many of the new arrivals will eventually make their way to American shores, for this is the historical direction in which the tide has flowed. For the time being, however, Israel is also home to a sizable contingent of Russian émigré writers.

Not only did the Soviet government cut off emigration by the end of the 1970s but it also initiated a program of anti-Semitism, a program more than matched by at least one émigré publisher. *Russky klich* (The Russian War-Cry), run by N. Tetyonov in New York State, is entirely devoted to promoting anti-Semitism by republishing the Russian editions of such works as *Mein Kampf*, speeches of Hitler and Goebbels, *The Protocols of the Elders of Zion*, Henry Ford's *The International Jew*, etc.

The ideology of dissent, which in many ways was developed first among the émigrés and then within the Soviet empire itself, is substantially to the right of Western European political thought. The cover of the Munich-based magazine *Veche*, for example, is printed in the three colors of the Russian flag. The journal is presented as a publication of the Russian "nationalist, Orthodox" movement and is diametrically opposed to such "democratic" publications as Siniavsky's and Rozanova's *Sintaksis* (see the Siniavsky-Rozanova interview).

In the early 1970s, when the Third Wave began to arrive in the West, the new writers soon found themselves at loggerheads with the older émigré editors of such publications as *Novoe russkoe slovo* in New York and *Russkaya mysl'* in Paris. The

totally different experience and world views of the older generation and the new arrivals ensured that these two groups
would, at the outset, find little common ground (although ultimately these difficulties were somewhat overcome). The readership of the already existing publications had been disas-
trously eroded by that time and more recent émigrés were
needed if Russian-language newspapers and journals were to
survive. A number of the newer arrivals, such as Aleksandr
Solzhenitsyn and Vladimir Maksimov, essentially closed ranks
with the older generation. However, the response of those
Third-Wave figures who found themselves shut out was to
complain bitterly of "censorship" and to found their own magazines and publishing houses.

The intense demands made upon literature in the Soviet
period caused many writers to react in their writings against the
inclusion of any political message. The hotly debated topic of
political involvement and disengagement appears repeatedly in
the interviews. In March 1987 a letter questioning the true significance of *glasnost* and signed by ten émigrés was published
in a number of major Western newspapers. To the amazement
of the signatories (four of whom are interviewed here), the
letter appeared in the Moscow newspaper *Moskovskie novosti*
and initiated a long awaited dialogue between Soviet and émigré writers.

In 1987 émigré writings began to appear in large numbers in
the Soviet Union. During the next two years Soviet magazines
and publishing houses brought out a flood of émigré novels,
stories, memoirs, and poems. Émigré writers visited the Soviet
Union, gave readings to large audiences, and found themselves
lionized. In 1990 the Soviet government reinstated the citizenship of a number of émigrés. By the end of 1991 the citizenship
of a number of writers had been restored; Vladimir Voinovich
and Vasily Aksyonov were even presented with apartments in
Moscow. The writings of all three waves appeared—some in
editions large even by Soviet standards. A four-volume collection of Dmitry Merezhkovsky, for example, appeared in an
edition of 1,700,000 copies. The Soviet Writers' Union, which
had formerly played a leading role in expelling writers, established an institute for the study of the émigrés' work. The same

Afanasiev who had attacked the exiles as "Fascist sycophants and criminals" is currently bringing out a collection of émigré writings which will contain at least six volumes. Afanasiev's introductory essay is entitled "Unrequited Love." 1991 was marked by a "Congress of Countrymen" (the beginning of which, ironically, coincided with the abortive coup). So many émigré books have appeared in Russia that there is even talk of a "glut on the market." At the same time, delighted as they may be to see their works appear while they themselves are lionized by Russian readers, none of the writers has chosen to return home on a permanent basis.

The Third Wave is wholly a product of Soviet society and, as such, was formed by aesthetic processes that developed in relative (but certainly not total) isolation from the Western literary world. Championed as the creation of an earlier Russian émigré, Maksim Gorky, Socialist Realism was force fed to the Russian literary public for decades. As a result, most émigré writers reacted by rejecting either the political aspects of this doctrine, or the artistic, or both. By 1981, during a conference held on Russian émigré literature in Los Angeles, none of the many writers present even bothered to criticize Socialist Realism, so irrelevant had it become for them.

Edward Limonov took literary vengeance by employing realism to depict a world of sexual perversion. His works are an intentional act of blasphemy against both past and present oppressors.

Vladimir Maksimov and Aleksandr Solzhenitsyn, on the other hand, have held to the grand tradition of nineteenth-century realism. They make no apologies for their refusal to accept twentieth-century trends. Solzhenitsyn, after arriving in the West and receiving the Nobel Prize, has chosen a posture of extreme isolation on his Vermont estate, devoting himself to a multivolume historical novel set at the time of the Russian civil war. The "knots" (his terms for the individual volumes) have thus far not achieved great success among Western readers, but in the Soviet Union his popularity is enormous, although far from universal.

While he lived in the Soviet Union, Vasily Aksyonov was one of its most popular writers, particularly among young people.

His *Island of Crimea* is an escapist fantasy whose Soviet upper-crust heroes drive fast cars, sport Saint-Germain cashmere coats, wash down their lobsters with champagne, light their Marlboro and Winston cigarettes with Ronson lighters, surround themselves with scantily clad California-style girls, and fairly wallow in slang.

In *Moscow 2042*, his major work thus far in exile, Vladimir Voinovich has also tried his hand at satirical fantasy. Using science fiction's most classic device, a time machine, as his artistic vehicle, the main character travels to Moscow, where he discovers that society has fallen apart and is in the throes of being taken over by Solzhenitsyn, who has had himself frozen so as to wake up in the future and return on a white stallion to conquer Russia. Proclaimed "Tsar Serafim," Solzhenitsyn has the entire population converted to Russian Orthodoxy, replaces machines with draught animals, requires men over forty to wear beards, and forbids women to ride bicycles.

The novel is sheer Swiftian satire. And like almost all of the works written by the émigrés, it is about Russia. Such an obsession with things Russian is not new in Russian émigré letters; even the cosmopolitan Nabokov noted the total fixation with Russia among his contemporaries in the First Wave.

Aleksandr Zinoviev is another adherent of political satire couched in fantasy. His best-known work, *The Yawning Heights*, is a sort of Russian *Animal Farm*, whose multiple allegorical voices are also intended as an attack on the author's oppressors. And, like Voinovich, Zinoviev has difficulty deciding which is the greater evil—the Soviet government or that uncrowned tsar of Russian émigré thought, Aleksandr Solzhenitsyn. Zinoviev's fundamental message is that of protest. He sees literature as a vehicle whose purpose is to serve a political end.

While still in the Soviet Union, Andrei Siniavsky composed one of the major attacks on the theory of Socialist Realism and then set about creating works of fantasy to back up his pronouncements. Here in the West, Siniavsky wrote a tongue-in-cheek autobiography, *Good Night*, written in a modernist, self-conscious manner.

One reaction against realism was fantasy, and another was what Russians now call "modernism" or "avant-gardism." The

émigré avant-garde sees Russian literature and art, both in
Russia and in the émigré community, as dominated by a layer
of official Soviet culture that has attempted to suppress the unofficial culture of the intelligentsia. The latter established its
own literary "establishment"—Pasternak, Akhmatova, Mandelstam, and others in the USSR and such figures as Brodsky
and Solzhenitsyn, and even Dmitry Bobyshev, Lev Losev, and
Yury Kublanovsky in the émigré community (although the last
three would probably be astounded to see themselves included
in such an "Establishment"). While the Russian intelligentsia
likewise rejects official Soviet culture, it sees itself as the bearer
of the standard of classic Russian culture—just as did adherents
of the Parisian Note in their day.

The avant-garde, on the other hand, rejects both official
Russian culture and the icons of the so-called intellectual establishment. In the words of Henri Volokhonsky, "we didn't like
Pasternak because they shoved him down our throats." Aleksei
Khvostenko, Viktor Tupitsyn, Genrikh Khudyakov, and Konstantin Kuzminsky maintain their watch over the grail of Russia's avant-garde.

In poetry Naum Korzhavin and Natalya Gorbanevskaya are
fundamentally involved with traditional genres and devices.
Gorbanevskaya's verse, which is often intense and reflects her
political activity, can also be lyrical. Korzhavin, a firm believer in
the moral message of art, rejects out of hand any modernist
experimentation. Artistically as well as politically, both poets
are in the same camp as Maksimov.

Perhaps the most gloomy of all Russian writers, Fridrikh
Gorenstein is above all a writer with a moral message. His
major work, *Psalm*, is constructed in the form of a series of
parables and describes a Ukraine punished by God with famine, the sword, lust, and disease. Each of the five "parables" is
prefaced by philosophical musings on man's violation of the
wisdom of his Creator. Although the roots of the work are
strictly biblical, Gorenstein views this orientation as an artifact
of this particular work and not as a method he necessarily
intends to follow in future writings. Like almost all of Gorenstein's work, *Psalm* is concerned with Jewish topics.

Perhaps the most observant and witty of all the masters of

the humorous short story in emigration was Sergei Dovlatov, who found his niche in the small, ironic details of émigré life. And although many of his themes are Jewish, he was a confirmed citizen-of-the-world, as well as an opponent of the subjugation of art to politics.

This latter point accounts for one of the biggest artistic disagreements in émigré letters. The art-for-art's sake camp and the political-moralist writers have split into two uncompromising factions.

Joseph Brodsky, a stubbornly independent man who even as a fifteen-year-old dropped out of school to devise his own education, who at twenty-three responded to the Soviet judge about to sentence him for "parasitism" that his poetic gift was "from God," and who has maintained a love-disdain (actually, more disdain than love) relationship with his fellow Russian émigré writers, "did it his way." In his 1987 Nobel speech he defined the function of poetry in precisely these terms—as uniqueness, as a refusal to shape either himself or his art according to anyone else's pattern. When the Czech émigré Milan Kundera mourned the "end of the West," Brodsky responded that such statements sounded grand and tragic, but were all histrionics: "Culture dies only for those who fail to master it, the way morality dies for a lecher."

Boris Khazanov, a lyrical prose writer and an eloquent essayist, is a man in the art-for-art's sake camp who is torn by a triple feeling of belonging—to Russian, Jewish, and world culture. Khazanov's novel *Anti-Time* begins as a nostalgic romantic autobiography of a young Jew who learns that he is adopted. His real father, who had been a loyal revolutionary, decides, when released from prison, to emigrate. But he feels he has no moral right to leave his son behind. Russia, he says, is a land without hope, without a future, and its people are as incurable as the country itself. Like many Jews, he had believed in the revolution, fought for it, but now he realizes that the time has come to leave.

His son refuses to go with him and returns home to discover an ugly scene in which the apartment of his adoptive parents, who are Russian, has been searched by the authorities. In a concluding scene of futile rage and love, the stepfather, to protect his son, threatens the secret police agents with a gun and is led away to prison. The Russian who raised a Jewish son and sacrificed himself for him thus represents the same Russia as the police henchmen.

Another of the "younger" writers is Sasha Sokolov, a master of parody and satire. His novel *Palisandria* has been, appropriately, discussed by the American Slavist D. Barton Johnson as one of the first Russian contributions to international magical realism, alongside Grass's *Tin Drum* and Marquez's *One Hundred Years of Solitude*. Sokolov's works are masterpieces of style, but their very stylistic intricacy stands in the way of his gaining any popularity outside the Russian language.

John Glad

The Older Generation

1

Igor Chinnov

Poet and essayist (b. 1909). Chinnov was born in Riga, Latvia, where he was trained as a lawyer. In 1944 he fled to Germany. He moved to Paris in 1947, returned in 1953 to Germany, and eventually moved to the United States in 1962. There he was a professor of Russian literature at the University of Kansas and Vanderbilt University. In 1989 a selection of his verse was published in the chief Soviet literary journal *Novy mir* (The New World), no. 9.

Verse collections: *Monolog* (Monologue) (Paris, 1950); *Linii* (Lines) (Paris, 1960); *Metafory* (Metaphors) (New York, 1968); *Partitura* (New York, 1970); *Kompozitsia* (Compositions) (Paris, 1972); *Pastorali* (Pastorales) (Paris, 1976); *Antiteza*

(Antithesis) (College Park, Md., 1979); and *Avtograf* (Autograph) (Holyoke, Mass., 1984).

English translations: Three poems, trans. Theodore Weiss and L. P. Izborsky, *TriQuarterly*, no. 28 (1973): 433–434; R. H. Morrison, ed. and trans., *America's Russian Poets* (Ann Arbor: Ardis, 1975); five poems in *Russian Poetry: The Modern Period*, ed. John Glad and Daniel Weissbort (Iowa City: University of Iowa Press, 1978).

College Park, Maryland, 1978

JG   Igor Vladimirovich, when did you begin writing poetry?

IC   I began writing poetry while still a law student. After I graduated I took up Slavic literatures and languages in Paris. But my first collection wasn't published until 1950, by Rifma Publishers, which was run by Sergei Makovsky. In former days Makovsky had edited the famous St. Petersburg literary review *Apollon*. When my first collection came out—it was called *Monologue*—the Paris Federation of Russian Writers and Poets set up a discussion panel on the book. There were numerous speakers, including Georgy Adamovich, a friend and follower of Gumilyov and a member of the Poets' Guild, as well as Georgy Ivanov. Sergei Konstantinovich Makovsky himself was there, and after the conference he published a report on it in the premiere issue of his New York review *Opyty* (Experiments). The journal no longer exists. But I do remember a Pushkin anniversary dinner one evening in Paris, where I read a poem on Pushkin composed just for the occasion. The speakers there were Ivan Alekseevich Bunin, Aleksei Mikhailovich Remizov, and Boris Konstantinovich Zaitsev, who would later host another dinner, this one in my honor upon my arrival in Paris eighteen years later.

My dinner was in 1970. Gregory Adamovich and Vladimir Veidle came and gave talks on my poetry. Veidle was another Silver Age man, and I imagine that there are still people around in Leningrad who remember him. Irina Odoevtseva, Gumilyov's disciple and a member of the Poets' Guild, and Yury Konstantinovich Terapiano, who always reviewed my books in *Russkaya mysl'* in Paris, were also there. Those are the two evenings I remember. A year later, in 1971, after my return to Paris, I learned, to my sadness, that both Adamovich and Zaitsev had passed on. I lived in Paris for about ten years. I also lived in Germany. But Paris is still like a hometown to me.

JG Then you would say you're a postwar poet.

IC Yes, my prewar poetry is of hardly any significance. I published a few things in a Paris-based avant-garde review called *Chisla* (Numbers). What happened was this. While I was living in Riga, I was discovered by Georgy Ivanov, who took a liking to my poetry and to an article I had written. He had it all published in *Chisla*. But it was only with the publication of my first book *Monologue* that the real Chinnov appeared. At that time I wrote in the style of the Parisian Note, a movement headed by Adamovich himself. Its hallmark was simplicity— a limited vocabulary, pared down to only the most essential words. We were so eager to replace the specific with the generalized that sea gulls, larks, and nightingales were all reduced to "birds," while birches, oaks, and weeping willows became "trees." We all believed that we should write as if there would be no more poetry after us, that what we wrote in exile would be the last Russian poetry, and that we should add no ornamentation, nothing superfluous. We strove for the most Spartan word stock, without ornamentation and without frills. Our vocabulary included only what was rudimentary and indispensable.

JG You say that you are a representative of the Parisian Note, and yet you began writing poetry only after World War II. One usually thinks of the Parisian Note as a prewar phenomenon.

IC Absolutely. I am something of a hanger-on.

The Parisian Note took acmeism and developed it further. As Vladimir Veidle once wrote, I probably went farther than anyone else. He was convinced that I had reached the limits of that style, that the simplest of the simple poetry had now been written, and that nothing was left but repetition. He claimed that I'd come to a dead end and that I was heading off in a new direction.

The poetry in my first book *Monologue* as well as in *Lines* is unembellished. There is no ornamentation. But in my seventh book, *Antithesis*, I began writing free verse. Some of the poems, while neither iambic nor trochaic, are quite rhythmical. I have always striven for musicality and wanted my poetry to be pleasant to the ear. Not everybody agreed with this. The poetry of Anatoly Steiger—also of the Parisian Note and a fine poet—has a drier sound to it than mine. He used musical orchestration and ornamentation, but his poems are more bitter than mine, with the exception of one of my later books, *Partitura,* which includes some very sad pieces as well as poems in the grotesque.

In my first three books, I do not use elements of the grotesque. These books contain some free verse and a certain amount of vocabulary enrichment. In other words, I have strayed from the notion that we must limit ourselves to the most basic, indispensable language, and I have begun to write more freely, if you will. It's something I had to do. I could no longer restrict myself; I could not remain static. *Metaphors,* my third book, contains some enrichment of language. However, I am not that fond of those first three books of mine. I like the others better, *Partitura* in particular. That book has a great deal of the grotesque in it.

JG Do you consider yourself a cosmopolitan writer?

IC I most certainly do. The Russian titles of all my books are single words with Latin or Greek roots—*Monologue, Partitura, Kompozistia.* My intention here was to emphasize the importance of cultural tradition, particularly the Greco-Roman European tradition. I attach a great deal of meaning to that. I am a Russian poet, and I love Russia, but I also love our European civilization and culture as a whole.

JG Much of what you're saying reminds me of Mandelstam's manifesto, *The Dawn of Acmeism,* which contains those very thoughts. Of course, as you say, acmeism is considered to be the precursor to the Parisian Note.

IC Even though I have turned away now from the style of the Parisian Note, I am practically its last living representative. The most typical was Steiger. There were several others, including Yury Terapiano, a good but underrated poet. But I am the only remaining one in America. I gave up that style because one can't go on repeating oneself. I decided to expand the vocabulary I used. Now I no longer strive for lexical simplicity and poverty, but rather for its opposite. I try to include words which have never been used in poetry before. My seventh book is called *Antithesis*, as you know, since you were the publisher. It serves as a counterpoint to the book preceding it, *Pastorales*. There is none of the grotesque in *Pastorales*. There is only the beauty of the world coupled with a bitter sense of doom and the brevity of our life on earth. There is nothing to suggest what is to follow in *Composition* or *Antithesis*, both of which abound with foreign words, and feature a return to a grotesque, satirical, and even sardonic style. That is absent from *Pastorales*.

I am to a certain extent an imagist. I use a great many images and figures. Mine is a very tangible poetry. For instance, we always think of the minotaur as having the head of a bull. In *Pastorales*, however, I rework the image into one of a cow with the head of a minotaur. Or another example from the same poem: everyone knows that fossilized beetles were sacred to the ancient Egyptians. These were real live azure-colored scarabs. The Egyptians considered them sacred. So I have the scarab's "malachite brother buzzing about in the grass, reflecting its sky blue."

The critics were absolutely correct in noting the vivid color of my poetry and its abundant images. But I have other poems which are practically devoid of images. My first book *Monologue* is written in the style of the Parisian Note—where I kept the number of words to a minimum: sky, snow, wind, light, dark, ray, sunset, maybe sea or tree (without saying whether it was an oak or a birch or something else).

Then, gradually, I added individual features—as opposed to general ones. I abandoned the general for the specific.

JG Which non-Russian poets have influenced you?

IC I'm not sure that anyone has influenced me, but I do favor certain less well-loved poets. Of my favorite poets I would mention the later work of Gottfried Benn, also Rainer Maria Rilke, Eduard Mörike, to name a Romanticist, even Karl Krolow. I'm not very fond of the German modernists because their poetry is unmusical and rather unpleasant sounding. Of the French I very much like Jules Laforgue with all his poems on stars and moonlight. In some ways he resembles Guillaume Apollinaire. Apollinaire and Jules Laforgue are among my favorites. Of the modern poets I like Jules Supervielle and a few others.

I never felt much for the surrealists, not because of their

strange imagery; no, I like that immensely. But because of a certain amount of disorder, sound disorder. They seem to forget that each poem is also a structure of sound.

JG Of the poets living in Russia today, whom do you find particularly noteworthy, and who in your opinion is undeserving of his reputation?

IC To get a book from Russia is a major event for me. There are a number of very talented poets there. I like Novella Matveeva. I like Bella Akhmadulina, of course. I find Leonid Martynov interesting. He doesn't write in my style, but he's so inventive, particularly in sound, and his imagery is so rich. I'd also mention Yevgeny Vinokurov. One of his poems, by the way, was clearly influenced by Georgy Adamovich and another by Anatoly Steiger. In other words, you can see the influence of the Parisian Note in both cases.

JG Does he make mention of them?

IC No, but it's clear that he's read them. Russian poetry is fettered by its lack of contact with foreign poetry. This phenomenon has occurred before. Russian poets of the 1970s, for example, sat stewing in their own soup. And I fear that poets in Russia now not only have no access to émigré poetry, but they're cut off from world poetry as well.

Yevgeny Yevtushenko is a very good poet, but he writes quickly and carelessly. Poems such as "Babi Yar," "Stalin's Heirs," and before that "Winter Station" helped in gaining fame for him, but they bear no relation to true poetic quality.

Andrei Voznesensky also did himself some good by writing his collection of poems *They Use Formalism to Frighten Me*. He justified his innovations by citing Lenin's revolutionary style, although Lenin would, of course, have indignantly rejected Voznesensky as a poet. That's obvious on the face of it. Voznesensky borrowed a lot from Marina Tsvetaeva and was right to do so. Even Pushkin said: "I take whatever I find." That's how Andrei Voznesensky came by his fame. I'm not so sure that the quality of his poetry justifies his fame and glory. There are other minions of fortune, but I do not envy them. I realize that my life has been totally different from theirs. Furthermore, I am not a popular stage performer (*estradnik*).

JG Whom of the émigré poets would you mention?

IC I have always, always loved Georgy Ivanov, even his early Petersburg poetry from the days of the Poets' Guild and the *Apollon* literary review. It was aesthetic poetry. Georgy Ivanov was a snob and an aesthete, and I see nothing wrong in that. There is intelligent snobbery and imbecilic snobbery. Georgy Ivanov's writing was not what you would call effeminate, but it was never very masculine either. His were marvelous poems, not truly decadent and without anything like the homosexual you find in some of Mikhail Kuzmin's poetry. Ivanov's poetry is very moving, very elegant. You could feel that the poet had made up his mind to write beautiful poetry.

There's nothing bad about that. Today, of course, the word "beauty" has been compromised and is avoided. Everyone tries to sidestep it by continually redefining its essence. In reality beauty is that which we always think about when writing poetry or which inspires us in one way or another. Georgy Ivanov was one of my favorite poets and remains so to this day.

When I first met him, I gave him some poems and the articles I had written. He read the articles and said, "This is mush, but it's creative mush." He then arranged for their publication in *Chisla*, which was run by Nikolai Otsup, a follower of Gumilyov's and also a member of the Poets' Guild. That was the beginning of my creative existence.

JG You're are not a young man, but your manner continues to develop. What do you think of the criticism written about your verse?

IC I'm very happy to have been written about as much as I have, but it would seem that many critics have failed to take note of the most important thing, that is, my attempts to find intonation which is musical but at the same time not out of the ordinary.

JG Russian émigré poets don't generally have a lot of readers. How do you feel about that?

IC I could answer your question like this. I wrote a poem about my trip to Colombia, to Bogota and Cartagena. The Gold Museum in Bogota is a wondrous collection of native Mexican pre-Columbian art. In the poem I talk about how the masters who produced those marvelous Mexican figurines of pure gold remain anonymous. That is followed by these lines:

> You also are a goldsmith, a master of feelings and rhymes,
> Of sounds and images.
> And though we have writing . . .

I go on to say that either there was no native Mexican writing system or if there was, it was inadequate, and so

> And though we have writing,
> Our country does not know our names.

The last lines go:

> We do not compete with idols in eternity
> But indulge ourselves in Russian poems.

What are we without an audience in our homeland? We write poetry in Russian in the hope that it will reach Russia. There is nothing anticommunist in my poetry, nothing so terribly decadent. In fact, my poetry could be allowed, and so I hope for some amount of liberalization, for the realization that émigré poetry is a part of Russian poetry and that we should not—and in fact cannot—be summarily excluded from Russian poetry. I feel that I speak for an eternal Russia, even if I am deprived of any influence over her.

Yury Ivask

Poet, scholar, essayist (1907–86). Ivask was born in Moscow, but his family moved to Estonia in 1920, where he graduated from law school at Tartu University. In 1944 he fled to Germany and studied Slavistics in Hamburg after the war. In 1949 he moved to the United States, received his doctorate in Slavistics from Harvard University, and was appointed professor of Russian literature at the University of Massachusetts.

Verse collections: *Severny bereg* (Northern Shore) (Warsaw, 1938); *Tsarskaya osen'* (Imperial Autumn) (Paris, 1953); *Khvala* (Praise) (Washington, 1967); and *Zolushka* (Cinderella) (New York, 1970).

English translations: R. H. Morrison,

ed. and trans., *America's Russian Poets* (Ann Arbor: Ardis, 1975), pp. 45–
51; selection of poems in *Russian Poetry: The Modern Period*, ed. John
Glad and Daniel Weissbort (Iowa City: University of Iowa Press, 1978),
pp. 286–88.

Amherst, Massachusetts, March 13, 1986

Just two weeks before I was scheduled to interview him and
give a lecture on Russian émigré literature at the University of
Massachusetts at Amherst, where he was professor emeritus,
Yury Ivask suffered a heart attack and died. Following are excerpts from a letter written to me by Professor Ivask at the
beginning of March. The headings are my own.—Ed.

Family Background

My great-grandfather on my father's side was an Estonian miller. My grandfather, an agronomist, married a German woman,
and we spoke German at home. While still a young man, my
father left Estonia to settle in Moscow and consequently became
totally Russified. My mother's maiden name was Frolov. She
was the daughter of a Moscow jeweler who was a member of
the respected Zhivago merchants, the real Zhivagos, that is.

Our family would never have left Russia had it not been for
the famine, cold, and terror. I was thirteen when we moved
back to Estonia, where I spent over twenty years.

Cultural Belonging

A thirteen-year-old boy is a tabula rasa. But even as a youth I
knew that I was Russian, and Russian alone. I had almost no
contact with Estonians. And while I may never set foot on Russian soil again, I feel her soil in her language. The Russian language, Russian culture, and Russian Orthodoxy are ingrained
in my soul.

At the same time I feel an inseparable bond with Western

Europe. I have dedicated poems to all the nations of Europe. At one time I fell madly in love with Portugal, of which Russians know very little. But my greatest love is Italy. On October 1, 1980, I was fortunate enough to be presented to the pope in St. Peter's Square. I gave him the Russian poems I had dedicated to him. Although I remain Russian Orthodox, I nevertheless love Catholicism.

Emigration to the United States

I emigrated to the United States together with my wife, now deceased, in the fall of 1949, and we were naturalized five or six years later. I am grateful to America, for only here was I able to devote myself to that which I love most—Russian poetry.

On the whole America does not figure in my verse. The only exceptions are my poems dedicated to Emily Dickinson, in my opinion a brilliant poet. This American poet was paradoxically antidemocratic. She spent something like twenty years locked up in her house, refusing to see anyone. It was a stroke of good fortune that brought me to the town of Amherst, where Emily lived. I think the best line I've ever written is "It was still her July" (*Eshche ee iyul'*). It captures the hiatus of vowels and glides which poets find so elusive. I am often unsatisfied with my verse, but I take great pride in those three words.

Emily is still very much alive for me. At times I stroll with her in verse:

I see the crisp autumn lines
Of your star-crossed palm in mine
And flee with you,
Emily . . . my sister.

Mexico

I adore Mexico. I have been there seven times and am indebted to that country for a deeper understanding of the meaning of life, if you'll pardon the cliché. In the little town of San Miguel de Allende I came across a slightly open gate that led into a courtyard. Working up the courage to walk in, I was struck by two distinctive smells. One nostril caught the scent of a rose, the other the stench of baby diapers. It was then that I realized that I had always perceived the world in terms of contrasts, and that realization inspired the following line about Mexico: "Oxymoron. The smell of roses, urine, and eternity." Yes, at that instant I was beyond time, suspended in a kind of eternity. It was the most extraordinarily existential moment of my entire life.

I also wrote a cycle of poems called "The Conquest of Mexico." The cycle was written in the folk verse style that Pushkin used for his satirical but somewhat ribald tale of the Priest and his helper Balda. In "The Conquest of Mexico" three fantasized Russians, all Khlysts (members of a Russian sect of flagellants), fall from the sky and land in Mexico. As the anarchists of Christianity, the Khlysts have always held great interest for me. These three then take over Mexico in a bloodless conquest. Only recently did I realize what led me to write this poem. As a youth I shared Dostoevsky's dream that Russia would be the world's savior. Now I no longer believe in that. I am repulsed by the communist messianism emanating from Moscow. Here I was projecting my former idealistic messianic desires onto Mexico. The rhythm of the poem is light, something akin to rhymed prose, but it has its serious side too.

Religion

The one thing I revere more than Russia is God. For me the church, Orthodox in the East, Catholic in the West, is one.

To use English terminology, as a poet I see myself as belonging to the metaphysics. I barely mention Christ in my poetry. Christ is the highest sacrament, the metrics of life. All history, both in Europe and America, is the history of Christianity punctuated by the major heresies. The first of these were Aryanism and Monophysitism. A later heresy, which still exists, although it is beginning to weaken, is Protestantism. The most recent and the most dangerous is communism. But I have not lost hope: even this heresy will be overcome.

I have done things for which I should repent, but I am not good at the poetry of repentance. My Christianity is one of happiness and light, rooted in life here on earth, but with the hope that life will continue in some other form where there are roses and, yes, thorns too, even sharks (vegetarian sharks). There is no need for definitive harmony. All is in flux, Heraclitus said. I would hope that all will remain in flux, forever in motion. At times the concept of Nirvana repels me: communism crushes the individual; Buddhism denies his existence altogether.

I've often written that man's chief task is to work in harmony with the Creator. Berdiaev was not the first to say that. The Apostle Paul said the same thing in his Epistle to the Romans. We are God's children, said Paul, His heirs. And His creatures hopefully await the revelation of His children, His people. That means that we must help and bring joy to God.

A belief which comes through in much of my poetry can be summed up in two lines from the poet-wanderer Aleksandr Dobrolyubov, which I used as the epigraph to my poem "Man at Play":

There never was and never will be a sky
Until the world ascends into it whole.

The Creator grants man a patch of land to be turned into an earthly Heaven, with roses and weeds, sweet aromas and foul stench.

Poetic Traditions, Influences, On His Own Verse

My poetic language includes many archaisms, the loftiest Church Slavonicisms and the lowest vernacular, but it also has its place in metaphysics. My line: "Come to me, child" harks back to the prayer-poem of the English metaphysic Lord George Herbert:

*

I heard a calling: Child,
And I replied: My Lord.

In my work I have, with good reason, drawn on the Greek
Hesiodic tradition. The Russian Hellenist Zelinsky and the poet
Viacheslav Ivanov both called classical mythology a second Old
Testament that leads to the New Testament of Christ the Savior.

While I was greatly influenced by the English metaphysical
poets, there were others too whom I admired—mostly Russian
writers and poets. If I were to name a single writer, it would not
be Tolstoy or Chekhov, but Dostoevsky. Konstantin Leontiev,
with his lean and hungry look, also influenced me. I devoted a
lengthy monograph to that long-forgotten thinker.

Even more important to me was Vasily Rozanov. I edited a
volume of his selected works, for which I wrote a long preface.
It was published by Chekhov Publishers in New York. Ten
years ago one of my secret friends in Moscow read both the
preface and the collection. He was dumbfounded. Rozanov is
not one of life's great teachers, but he had an amazing ability to
find an inner truth in what would seem to be contradictory
ideas. He was both a reactionary and a revolutionary, a Christian and a critic of Christianity. His Russian was inimitable,
something akin to Avvakum's ranting. I see Rozanov as a pas-
sionate apologist for life, with an extraordinary eye for the here
and now. I'll quote one line as an example: "Happiness is a half-
salted pickle after a swim." Rozanov was the last Russian genius, with the possible exception of Ivan Bunin.

I remember reading Derzhavin's "Ode on the Birth of the
Royal Heir" one day at our dacha, when I was about nine. I
reveled in the poem's booming tones, as well as its vagaries,
obscured by the unusual syntax. But oh, that sound! I walked
among the trees, chanting the poem. Everyone in my family
teased me about my fondness for Derzhavin's antiquated language.

Later, in the 1920s, like many other young people, I was
spellbound by Blok. I declaimed Blok's verse as I had Derzhavin's. By this time we had moved to Estonia, and the white
nights there were identical to those of Blok's Petersburg. But I
can see now that my fascination with Blok was superficial.

In the 1930s I fell in love with the poetry of Marina Tsvetaeva. We corresponded, and later her letters to me were published. I met her in Paris in December 1938. Although I could
see that she was physically unattractive, I felt as though I had
met a goddess. Only a goddess, a muse, could tap her finger on
the marble table in that Paris café and say: "I have never had any
interest what-so-ev-er except poetry."

Tsvetaeva's poetry led me back to my childhood adoration
of Derzhavin. They both thundered. But Gavrila Derzhavin
growled as well. Their baroque style was an inspiration. Their
often archaic language was mixed with peasant speech, and
this blend influenced my own poetry. Derzhavin's roar, the
baroque poetry of the English metaphysics, and the dynamic of
the Baroque itself—each possessed tremendous power and
style. It is that style which I find in the poetry of my children's
generation: Dmitry Bobyshev, for example, is a product of Petersburg (he grew up in Leningrad and later emigrated to America). His dynamic, bold poetry also harks back to Derzhavin.

Recently I read the poetry of Irina Ratushinskaya for the first
time. She was sentenced to seven years in a *gulag* in Mordovia.
A disgrace! I am sorry for her, but it is not out of pity that I find
her poems enchanting.

I have always maintained that Russia has had only three
great poets: Derzhavin, a Tatar; Pushkin, a mulatto; and Mandelstam, a Jew. But they are all Russians first. The following
verse of Mandelstam's could be applied to the poet himself:

Tongue-tied, he brought with him
our torment, our riches,
the rustle of verse, the bell of brotherhood,
and a harmonic downpour of tears.

While my poetry may be bookish and intellectual, I agree
with Mallarmé that poetry is not thought alone. Thought must
be turned into emotion, and only then can it be turned into
poetry. Of course, I find it difficult to judge my own poetry.

"Poetry comes suddenly," Marina Tsvetaeva once told me,
"you never know from where." Other poets have said the same
thing, and my own experience confirms this. I planned out my
Mexican cycle as well as "Man at Play." Nevertheless, nearly

every line came in a flash. I've always sought out spontaneity, but not always with success. Still, all intellectual poets, myself included, find themselves paying homage to language over logic.

Russia

The most Orthodox Russian poetry was written by Osip Mandelstam, a Jew. I believe that Mandelstam's only equals in Russian poetry were Derzhavin and Pushkin. My venerable friend and teacher, Father Aleksandr Shmeman, marveled at Mandelstam's profound and incisive understanding of the Russian Orthodox liturgy.

Three years ago I managed to visit the USSR. In Moscow, near the Tretiakov Art Gallery, I had a meeting with someone who is both a remarkable scholar and a truly wise man. And there, together, we recited Mandelstam's verse:

> The Eucharist's eternal dawn lingers,
> Over communion, games, and song.
> The divine vessel before us
> Pours forth eternal joy.

I dare not reveal my friend's name.

Among the images I use to portray Russia is that of the Russian Cinderella—Zolushka—an unkempt laundry maid, a peasant who is, at the same time, a princess, a double for Elizabeth I, who misspelled her own name on official documents. The fast rhythm for this poem was suggested by the accented verse of Mikhail Kuzmin's cycle "The Trout Breaks through the Ice." Later Akhmatova used the same rhythm in her "Poem Without a Hero," which gave me hope for Russia's future:

> In Russia's pagan springtime
> Jeremiah falls silent
> Beside his fateful River.
> An etherial troika rushes past.
> Uncover your face, my beauty,
> Let the fools be awed.

I, too, envisioned a new, free, God-fearing Russia in "Man at
Play." In this poem I hear the voice of the Tempter: "and what if
Russia is reduced to straw and she does not dwell in the house of
the Lord?" And what if only a void remains in her place? But I answer the Tempter: "Get thee from me, Satan! Slave, free thyself!"

I have another vision of a Russia renewed: Russia of the
common man. I believe in Philistinism, the kind that is compat-
ible with faith and spirituality. My latest collection of poems, "I
Am a Philistine," is now at the printer's. Pushkin's line "I am a
Philistine" was written in jest. I am serious.

A Philistine is not necessarily a boor. He is a petty bourgeois—the bulwark of modern society. I, too, am a petty bourgeois. I have my own little house in Amherst: *Klein aber mein*, I
always say. I once saw some graffiti in Hamburg: "Philistines
have spiritual needs too."

The Parisian Note

It was actually Georgy Adamovich's "Note." It was he who said
that we are the children of emigration, who still have hazy
memories of Russia, but now live without her. We have mas-
tered her language, but we know few words. Therefore we
should write simply, without experimentation. Write only about
what's important, he said, about love, about sorrow, about
death. Anatoly Steiger was one of best poets of the Parisian
Note. Chinnov is another, although he has long since left the
movement. I felt that Adamovich was right in what he said, but I
could never make myself respond to the gloominess of Montparnasse. That poetry seemed bland and eclectic. I much preferred Marina Tsvetaeva.

Visits to Russia

I have been to Russia twice since our family left Moscow. I was
in Pskov when, along with Estonia, it was under German occupation. It was a sad time.

Then in the summer of 1983 I spent two weeks in Leningrad

and Moscow with a French tour group. I was amazed by what is left in Leningrad of St. Petersburg. I spent an unforgettable morning on Vasiliev Island, gazing at the Neva, which is monstrously wide and hostile and yet dazzling. I also went across the river to the Winter Palace, Rastrelli's brilliant marvel of Baroque architecture. I am from Moscow, and I remember people saying: "Petrograd is not Russian. People there don't speak good Russian. They stress all the wrong syllables." But ever since early adulthood I have been disloyal in my thoughts to Moscow, for love of Petersburg. I've even dreamed of Petersburg at night, always to wake up soon afterward and find the vision gone.

I stood at the tip of Vasiliev Island and whispered Pushkin's verse: "I love you, Creation of Peter."

And from Mandelstam:

And above the Neva—embassies of half a world,
The Admiralty, the sun, and silence.

I thought I'd die of happiness!

Previously I had looked at Petersburg through the eyes of Gogol, Dostoevsky, and Blok, as well as Andrei Bely: constant fog and foul weather. They slandered Petersburg, although I admit that theirs was a slander of genius. Every day I was there the sun shined. It was as if Pushkin and Mandelstam had put a halt to the bad weather created by the first three.

I've written many poems about that city, the creation of the brilliant architect Bartholomeo Rastrelli. My "Ode to the Outcast" is dedicated to St. Ksenia of Petersburg, and to the exile, the outcast, and the émigré.

In it St. Ksenia saves Peter's City, which the Tsarina had cursed: "May Petersburg wither!" Ksenia, who lived in the mid-eighteenth century, is buried in Smolny Cemetery, where I went to pray. My friends in the Soviet Union were happy to learn that she had been canonized in the Russian Church Abroad. The walls of the chapel near her grave site were covered with graffiti, such as "Save my son in Afghanistan."

Ksenia often went to the sites of buildings under construction. She would carry bricks and mortar with her. She was an amazing woman. I am sure that it is she who saved Petersburg.

In one line I sic Russia upon her [Russia's] enemies, particularly writers from the Third Wave, some of whom see Russia as a toad, a shrew.

Samizdat

At home I have a thick volume of typewritten pages: my poems published in samizdat. I sometimes joke that I am now, at least unofficially, a Soviet writer.

On the Comments of Literary Critics

Georgy Adamovich wrote sympathetically about me, even though he was no fan of my poetry. It was a gesture of friendship. He often said that friendship was above literature. Vladimir Veidle wrote approvingly of my work, although I doubt that my dissonant baroque style ever really appealed to him. I am most proud of the comment of one Moscow reader (printed in the Parisian *Vestnik RSKhD* [Herald of the Russian Student Christian Movement]) to describe my cycle "Man at Play." He was well acquainted with "Man at Play," and the subtitle of his review read: "A Game of the Pen and a Victory of Inspiration." A thorough article on my poetry was written by my colleague Professor Laszlo Dienes. Aside from yourself, Temira Pachmuss has written about me in the English-language academic press.

A Last Wish

I would like to see "Man at Play" republished. I would also like to republish some of my articles in a collection to be entitled *In Praise of Russian Poetry.* As of now, my verse is scattered through various journals. I have my own approach to literature. It is partly formalistic and partly stylistic. It can be summed up as an attempt to mythologize the writer, the poet.

Roman Goul

Novelist, historian, and editor (1896–
1986). Goul fought in the Civil War on
the side of the Whites and was evacuated to Germany in 1918. In 1933 he emigrated to Paris, after a brief arrest by
the Nazis. In 1950 he emigrated to the
United States, where he edited *Novy
zhurnal* (The New Review) in New York.
Novy zhurnal, despite Goul's prediction
for it in this interview, is still appearing.

Books published abroad: *Ledyanoi
pokhod* (Icy Campaign) (Berlin, 1921); *V
rasseyanii sushchie* (Those in Diaspora),
(Berlin, 1923); *General Bo* (Berlin, 1929);
Skif (Scythian) (Berlin, 1931); *Tukhachev-
sky, krasny marshal* (Tukhachevsky, Red
Marshal) (Berlin, 1932); *Krasnye marshaly*
(Red marshals) (Berlin, 1933); *Dzerzhin-*

sky (Paris, 1936); *Oranienburg: Chto ya videl v gitlerovskom kontsentratsion-
nom lagere* (Oranienburg: What I Saw in One of Hitler's Concentration
Camps) (Paris, 1937); *Kon' ryzhy* (Red Horse) (New York, 1952); *Azef*
(New York, 1959); *Chitaya "Avgusta Chetyrnadtsatogo" A. I. Solzhenitsyna*
(Reading A. I. Solzhenitsyn's *August 14*) (New York, 1971); *K voprosu ob
"avtokefalii"* (On the Question of Autocephaly) (New York, 1972); *Od-
vukon'* (Astride Two Horses) (New York, 1973); *Ya unyos Rossiyu: Apolo-
giya emigratsii, Rossiya v Germanii* (I Took Russia With Me: In Defense of
the Emigration, Russia in Germany), vol. 1 (New York, 1981); *Rossiya vo
Frantsii* (Russia in France), vol. 2 (New York, 1981); and *Rossiya v
Amerike* (Russia in America), vol. 3 (New York, 1989).

Translations: *Azef*, trans. by Mirra Ginsburg (Garden City, N.Y.:
Doubleday, 1962); *Comrade Ivan: A Play in Three Acts* (written together
with Victor Trivas), translated by Elizabeth Reynolds Hapgood (New
York: MOST, 1969). A number of Goul's books have also been translated into German, French, and Spanish.

College Park, Maryland, November 17, 1982

JG Roman Borisovich, in the 1920s you worked in various
magazines and newspapers.

RG Yes, I was the secretary of the biographical journal *Novaya russkaya kniga* (The New Russian Book), edited by Professor Yashchenko. As I recall, the journal lasted for two or
three years. Before that I worked for *Zhizn'* (Life); that was
earlier, 1921–22, I think. *Zhizn'* was edited by Vladimir Stanke-
vich, a former commissar in the headquarters of the provisional
government. After that I worked for *Golos Rossii* (The Voice of
Russia), edited first by Shklyaver and then by Krymov. But I
didn't work long for newspapers or write much for them. At
one time I worked for the tabloid *Vremya*, which was headed by
the well-known Grigory Naumovich Breitman, who I believe
had been the editor of the Kiev newspaper *Poslednie novosti* before the Revolution. *Vremya* was a weekly, very bourgeois paper, but you could always pick up a few marks there. Breitman
and I had a good relationship, and we of the younger set—Ofro-
simov, Korvin-Piotrovsky, Ivanov—used to drop in on him
fairly frequently with articles of various sorts. Still later I worked
in *Nakanune* (On the Eve) as the editor of the literary supple-

ment. That was in 1923–24, but then it went out of business. Before me the literary editor was Aleksei Tolstoy, and I held the position for about a year, after he returned to Soviet Russia.

Still later I worked in the German publishing house *Taurus*, which published Russian books. After that I devoted my time to writing Russian books, since they were selling fairly well in various translations. *Azef*, for example, which was originally called *General Bo*, was translated into nine or ten languages, and all the publishers paid—especially the German, so that I managed to make ends meet. *Tukhachevsky, the Red Marshal* was translated into the Scandinavian languages, French, German, English, etc.

JG How big were the print runs in Russian in the 1920s and 1930s?

RG The size of an edition was always a secret of the publisher. One of my publishers was Abram Saulovich Kagan, who now lives somewhere in New York. Another was Yakov Noich Blokh, who ran the publishing house Petropolis. At one time they had a publishing house in Peter (Petersburg-Leningrad) and put out some wonderful books—the Russian poets Gumilyov, Akhmatova, Georgy Ivanov, Mandelstam. They were lovely people, but I never could learn how many copies had been printed. You had to get an advance, since anything after that was very tenuous. The first edition of *Azef* sold out in six months, and they put out a second edition in one volume. Try as I might, however, I never did learn how many copies they printed, and I'll probably go to my grave without knowing.

JG In *I Took Russia with Me* you quote with approval the statement sometimes attributed to Zinaida Gippius: "We are not exiles; we are envoys." What do you take this to mean?

RG I think she was entirely correct. Russian culture in the Soviet Union was totally eradicated. All those who did not agree with Marx, Lenin, and Stalin were annihilated. Many books were banned from distribution in libraries by Krupskaya's famous decree. Thus the preservation of Russian culture in the rest of Europe, for the most part in Berlin and Paris, fell to the émigrés. This is the mission on which we were sent, the torch we had to pass on to future generations.

JG Several of your books were published in the Soviet Union in the 1920s. Was that hard to do?

RG No, they were pushed through by friends of mine, Soviet writers who had come to Berlin and with whom I had become friendly—mostly Ilya Gruzdev, whose relationship to Gorky was something like that of Eckermann to Goethe. Konstantin Fedin also helped. He was later to become the dreaded general secretary of the Writers' Union, but he was a perfectly decent human being and a good friend of mine. These men were able to clear my books through the publishing houses. Those were liberal times, and books like that could get through. But soon afterward those works ended up in the banned-book repositories. I recently learned from a certain bibliophile in the Third Wave that it's impossible to get hold of them in Russia today.

JG Even here they're hard to find.

RG Yes, it's impossible to find them here. My book *Icy Campaign* was banned even though at first it was treated as an exposé of White Army terror. This too was nonsense, of course. The book was an exposé, not of White Army terror, but of all the horrors of the Civil War. So in the end, realizing that *Icy Campaign* was not suitable material, they put that book too into the banned repositories. I was told this by a number of Soviet writers—Solzhenitsyn in particular, who said that after the success of his *Ivan Denisovich*, written during the Khrushchev era, he was given access to the repository. There he found everything he needed, all my books, even those which had been published abroad. *Icy Campaign* was there, although it was terribly counterrevolutionary. I was amazed. I asked him how he came to mention my book in *The Gulag Archipelago*, and he said, "I read it in the repository." I should add that *Icy Campaign* was initially quite popular in Russia. Gorky wrote about it, as did Èikhenbaum and a number of other writers of that time.

JG You have seen all three waves of Russian emigration. How would you characterize their relationships?

RG I think the relationship between the First and Second Waves is quite good. In fact we have merged into one. At first, however, things were very difficult. I belonged to a group of émigrés in Paris who helped destitute members of the second emigration. Our group was not very big. There were Melgunov, Kheraskov, and myself. Nikolaevsky and Zenzinov helped out by sending money and clothing from America. We set up a committee of sorts, and we were able to assist many new émigrés. In one case we helped someone to escape from Europe to South America, and we continued helping in terms of money, clothing, and getting him a job.

Perhaps I'm not typical of the first emigration, since I have always had a dislike for barriers between people. I welcomed émigrés from the Second Wave, and the Third Wave as well, with an open heart. People are people. Psychologically, however, there are differences between the first and second emigrations, and again between the first and third, in particular. That's only natural. The third emigration grew up in the Soviet Union, whereas we grew up under His Majesty the Tsar. Those are two entirely different conditions.

Naturally our relationship with the third emigration is much more complicated, since they are further removed from us. At the same time I'm on the best of terms with members of the third emigration. . . . I don't like barriers; you know that.

JG   But you've published very few Third-Wave people in *The New Review.*

RG   What do you mean? I once made up a list. We've published quite a few. I'd say the third emigration pretty much keeps to itself. They've started their own journals. But I've published quite a number of people, including Brodsky. I published Brodsky's poetry when he was still in the Soviet Union. We've published Yury Krotkov, if you want to include him in the third emigration, Anatoly Kuznetsov. . . . There are quite a few, I can't agree with you.

JG   You left Russia toward the end of the Civil War.

RG   I left Russia—rather I was taken out of Russia, a fact I'm still very happy about, on January 1, 1919. I was sent to Germany on orders from the Ukrainian directorate and the German High Command. I would have been shot otherwise. The Bolsheviks were attacking Kiev, and I was being held at the Pedagogical Museum, which had been turned into a prison for all the soldiers Petlyura had rounded up. I was there right up to the last minute with about five hundred others, when a general with a name something like Westphalen (but not *the* Westphalen, of course) realized that we would all be shot when the Bolsheviks entered the city. The Bolsheviks had brought along a contingent of the Cheka, headed up by Latsis and Portugeis, and they were going to show no mercy. So the Germans and the Ukrainians agreed to evacuate us.

JG As a man who left Russia so long ago, what do you think about the "Soviet Russian language"?

RG I think the same thing about Soviet Russian that Kornei Chukovsky did. Some of the new words are just fine and have become part of the living language. Take the word *perekur* (smoking break), for example. When I was in the army, we never had a word like that. Solzhenitsyn writes that someone gave the order for an eight-minute smoking break. That's an example of street talk. Then there is a single verb to express the idea "We'll break for a smoke and work this out" (*My eto perekurim*). I think that's fine. But there's a lot that grates on the ears of an old émigré like me. Soviet bureaucratese is just awful, and Kornei Chukovsky was absolutely right when he lambasted it mercilessly. But even so, nothing can be done about it now.

JG You write that the Russian intelligentsia no longer exists, that now there is only a semi-educated Soviet class.

RG Yes, I was repeating what Solzhenitsyn had said, and I think that that's the absolute truth. It's not 100 percent true, of course. Sakharov, it goes without saying, is a Russian intellectual of the highest order. And then there are Solzhenitsyn and Shafarevich, and many others as well. But by and large a wave of educated illiterates has overwhelmed the Russian intelligentsia. This was a product of Marxism-Leninism, and therefore, to be expected. The well-rounded world view that characterized the old intelligentsia simply no longer exists.

JG What sort of future do you see for Russian culture in general and for Russian literature in particular?

RG I'm very pessimistic, even apocalyptic. Without some sort of worldwide cataclysm, I don't see any future at all, because the Soviet Union is incapable of evolving. We've seen that over a period of more than sixty years, and all those alleged attempts at "evolution" were lies—nothing more than Lenin's military strategy. Take NEP (the New Economic Policy in the early 1920s). Many people "believed"—both in and outside the Soviet Union. Back then I was one of a group called the *Smeno-vekhovtsy;* we believed too. The land at that time was in the hands of the peasants, not the state. It was, I suppose, the only time throughout Russian history when the peasants were satisfied with their lot. The workers were not tied to their factories. Houses and small businesses were returned to their former owners. There was relative freedom for literature and the arts. At that time it was thought, and one could believe, that in a short while we would have a national government based on law. Now, after all the collectivizations and all that grandiose structuring and restructuring, I don't see how they could turn in a more liberal direction, even if they wanted to. But there are some optimists among my American friends.

JG To whom are you thinking of turning over *The New Review?* What plans do you have for the future?

RG I have very few plans, naturally. I'm approaching ninety. When the Third-Wave émigrés first began to arrive here, I very much wanted to pass *The New Review* on to one of them. I had talked to Vladimir Maksimov, but he declined. It turned out that he was already engaged at *Kontinent.* I talked to Viktor Nekrasov, but he declined also. Then I talked to some other people, and they backed off. So I had to keep running it myself. I see no chance of handing over control of the journal to anyone else because there are so few people of my calling and my culture, if I may say so. After all, the first emigration is dying off. I don't know who will take over *The New Review.* I believe it will die when I do.

JG You really think so?

RG I do.

JG Let's talk about submissions. When you select manuscripts for publication, do you try to create a certain profile for *The New Review?*

RG Why, yes. *The New Review* does have its own "profile." That, by the way, is a Soviet expression. We would never say that. But you could say, if you like, that *The New Review* does have its own "profile," its own personality. The concept behind it is that of the old Russian "thick" journal, a successor to the

Paris-based *Contemporary Notes.* And since this is the tradition we follow, everything we publish adheres to a high cultural level. There are, for instance, many things published in Third-Wave journals which I would simply never print. If I did, I would get hundreds of angry letters from my readers.

JG What would you *not* publish in *The New Review?*

RG Some of the things are just plain pornographic. Our readers are not accustomed to that sort of thing.

JG Are you referring to Limonov?

RG Limonov did ask me to publish something of his—but without success. I can understand the attempts of Limonov and Mamleev and others like them to fit a literary horse with a pornographic saddle. You can make quite a name for yourself, but that's not for *The New Review.* And what's more, it's not interesting.

JG The new émigrés are describing their own lives in the Soviet Union, which were radically different from your life in Russia. As you yourself said, you have little in common with them.

RG What do you mean by "little in common"? The last thing I published was a novella by Yury Krotkov. He was Soviet down to the bone. He had been an informer for twenty years. He himself wrote about this. He knew the whole loathsome business, inside and out. I published his story, leaving in a number of risqué passages. That, after all, is the style of the third emigration. And what do you think happened? In response to those sexual passages I immediately received a heap of letters: "How could *The New Review* permit such a thing!" But I've published a lot of things that depict life in the Soviet Union very clearly. For nearly ten years I published the stories of Varlam Shalamov.

JG It was thanks to *The New Review* that I first learned of Shalamov and began translating him.

RG And I think we managed to publish him without a lot of fuss. We did not make it into a special publication. But we *were* the first to publish him, because he was a marvelous writer. And I believe his work will endure, because he is historically an extremely important figure. He was able to depict the inhuman hell of Kolyma as no one had done before. Solzhenitsyn may have done the same in *Gulag Archipelago*, but from a different perspective. We've published a lot of Soviet material.

JG Of all your books I liked *Azef* best of all. What gave you the idea for it?

RG I got the idea for *Azef* when an acquaintance in Berlin mentioned to me that he had just read Savinkov's memoirs. Savinkov wrote a book called *Memories of a Terrorist*, which he had first published in the journal *Byloe* (Bygone Years) and later as a separate book. "Such incredible material!" my acquaintance said. As it just so happened, I had a copy of *Memories of a Terrorist*, but had never gotten around to reading it. When I did, I decided to write a novel with Azef as the main figure.

Now at that time I was very good friends with Boris Ivanovich Nikolaevsky. He was a famous man, a Menshevik, but he was known as a historian of the revolutionary movement. I asked him if there was any material on Azef, and he said there was. Nikolaevsky had been in touch with a cabaret singer called La Belle Heidi de Hero. Actually, she was German. Azef had lived with her in his last years. Nikolaevsky contacted her, and she gave him Azef's letters. Nikolaevsky himself wrote a short book about Azef. He showed me copies of the letters, and they intrigued me. I started working on the novel, which totally engrossed me.

The book was an instant success in Russian; it came out in nine or so languages in England, America, and Germany, and in France and Poland and Latvia . . . just about everywhere . . . in Spain. . . . The French writer Christian Maigret, when he wrote his French-language review, called me a forerunner of Camus and Malraux. Camus wrote a play about Russian terrorists based on the book. I don't remember the name, but it did get staged.

JG I believe you no longer have books translated into English still in print.

RG No, nothing still in print. *Azef* was not really a big smash in English. It sold quite modestly. Still, it was published three times in English, first in England with a foreword by Stephen Graham and then again in America in the same edition. Doubleday then published a translation by Mirra Ginsburg. But it didn't do that well, and I can understand why. Azef is not a subject for everybody. A lot of people couldn't care less about Azef.

JG You fought in the Civil War. What novel in your opinion best reflects that period?

RG I don't know that I could name a novel, except perhaps Sholokhov's *And Quiet Flows the Don.* It has since been said, of course, that Sholokhov probably plagiarized the whole thing from Fyodor Kriukov, the Cossack writer who died during the Civil War.

JG The question of whether or not Sholokhov wrote that book is still being debated. Professor Herman Ermolaev has written about it, and he believes that it's still unproved.

RG There is no way to prove it. Anyway, I would be hard pressed to name a work of fiction that truly reflects the Civil War. If we're talking about nonfiction, then Shukshin's *1920* would be of great interest.

JG Well, there's also Solzhenitsyn's *August 1914.*

RG *August 1914* doesn't cover the Civil War.

JG No, but it leads up to it.

RG Yes, it does, but as to what's available on the war itself, and what will become available, I really don't know. There are so many interesting memoirs that we may have no need for fiction.

JG What about *Doctor Zhivago?*

RG *Doctor Zhivago* is a good novel, but even though it deals with the Civil War in some places, it does so only spottily.

JG You have had some harsh words for Andrei Siniavsky.

RG I have no personal disagreement with him, since I have never met him. As far as his early writing goes, I reacted to it quite positively through *The New Review.* But when he wrote that obscene book, *Strolls with Pushkin,* I was shocked, as were many other people. I'm no prude; people can write about whatever they want, but *not* the way *he* writes: intentionally vulgar, intentionally coarse. For example, he says that the thing that troubled Pushkin the most at the time of his death was whether his wife was screwing around or not. That's gutter talk. He could have found another way to say the exact same thing. It's the vulgarity of it that so upset me.

So I decided to let him have it, and I believe I was quite

successful in my attempt. My article brought many favorable responses and letters thanking me. Siniavsky's a talented man but a little bit touched, and I'm not fond of some of these eccentricities.

JG   Tell me about Voloshin's letter to Yashchenko.

RG   Oh, that was an incredible letter. It was in January 1923. A young lady, a quite attractive one, showed up at the offices of *The New Russian Book*. I remember her to this day: she was extremely pleasant, clearly from an intellectual background, dressed very modestly, and quite reserved in her manner. She came in and asked to see Professor Yashchenko. No sooner had Yashchenko asked her in than she said to him, "I have a letter for you from Maksimilian Andreevich Voloshin." Yashchenko literally jumped to his feet. "You mean Max?" he said. He and Voloshin had been very close friends in Russia, and they had been together in Paris as well. After the woman left, Yashchenko read the letter to me. It was about forty-five pages long, and contained an incredible description of the terror in the Crimea after it was occupied by the Red Army. Bela Kun was the man responsible for the terror, and he was aided by Rosalia Zalkind, a flaming Bolshevik from the same area as he. Together they shot something like 100,000 or 150,000 White Russians.

In his letter Voloshin told about how Bela Kun once spent the night in his apartment. Now, Voloshin was an otherworldly sort of man, and he was able to enchant even a mass murderer like Bela Kun. They got to be on such good terms that Bela Kun even let Voloshin cross off every tenth name on one of the death lists. So Voloshin crossed off 10 percent of the names, although it tormented him to think that the other 90 percent would be barbarously murdered. Then he described how he prayed both for those who were to be killed, and also those who would be doing the killing. Well, Yashchenko made the mistake of showing a unique historical document like that letter to too many people. He carried it around with him wherever he went, and finally he lost it. It was stolen.

JG   Tell me about the history of *The New Review*. How was it founded, and how did control of it pass to you?

RG   The history of *The New Review* is a long story, but I'll try to

summarize it briefly. When Hitler marched into France, and
Sovremennye zapiski (Contemporary Notes) shut down, many
people on the staff went to America, including Mark Aleksandrovich Aldanov and Mikhail Osipovich Tsetlin. Tsetlin was
the journal's poetry editor. The two of them decided to go on
somehow putting out *Contemporary Notes,* that is, to continue
publishing a "thick" journal that would be a voice of freedom in
Russian.

JG Why didn't they keep the old name?

RG Maybe there was some reason they couldn't. Maybe they
didn't want to. I don't know. I hadn't reached America then.
Aldanov and Tsetlin didn't have any grants or subsidies. They
probably didn't go looking for any. I don't know: maybe they
did apply and simply didn't get any. Anyway, they raised the
money privately and decided to begin publishing. Aldanov
even wrote to Bunin in France so that they would get out at least
two issues.

They put out two issues. People subscribed, and things went
on from there. Of course, neither Tsetlin nor Aldanov could
have imagined that a small, privately funded journal like *The
New Review* would last so long. Tsetlin died after the eleventh
issue was published. After the fortieth issue Aldanov left his
editorial post and returned to Europe, and the journal fell to
Mikhail Mikhailovich Karpovich. He was a professor at Harvard, and when he became the sole editor, he invited me to
become his secretary, and in 1952 I began work there.

Karpovich was a very busy man. He taught two courses at
Harvard; he served as dean; he had problems at home; his wife
was ill. He was always tending to family matters. So I was in
charge of editing manuscripts and bringing them to him for his
approval or disapproval. And when he died in 1958, I became
the editor, and to this day I have been running the journal.

JG How many issues of *Contemporary Notes* were there?

RG 70, no, 71. And if I put out number 160, that will make
230 issues of a thick journal, which I think I can say, modesty
aside, is a major contribution to Russian culture.

JG Of all the writers published in *The New Review,* which do
you see as having been the greatest discoveries?

RG Shalamov was a discovery. It was in 1963, I think, when I received the manuscript—by accident. One day a professor of Slavics called me and said he'd been in Moscow and had brought back the manuscript of a Russian writer. The next day, or maybe the day after, he came in with a six-hundred-page manuscript. I was very happy to get it, although I was unfamiliar with Shalamov's writing. I had read some of his poetry, but I wasn't impressed. I published Shalamov's short stories over a ten-year period, and I consider him to be a true discovery. We've had a lot of serious writers, a lot of interesting writers. Let's see, we've had Miliukov, Berdiaev, Maklakov, Lossky, Shestov, Frank, Fedotov. . . .

JG Tell me about Mark Aldanov.

RG Aldanov I knew well. He published quite a bit in *The New Review,* nearly all of his later work. While you're publishing, you know, it doesn't seem to you that you're "discovering" any particular writer, but when you go back and pick up an issue and come across this manuscript or that article, you realize what valuable material you've got.

JG How many copies of *The New Review* do you print?

RG Not very many: 1,500 to 1,600 copies, but we distribute in thirty-six countries. That's something. All the major libraries, all the universities, they all subscribe. I have colleagues in Japan who subscribe. The Soviet Union subscribes through American agencies: the Lenin Library gets a copy; so does a library in Leningrad. Copies even go to Mongolia, to Ulan Bator—to a certain government agency, of course. There are probably people whose duty it is to read it. Fine, let them. We have a number of subscriptions like that: just a post-office box. And over the years we've gotten a lot of mail from the Soviet Union, including some marvelous letters.

JG Do you save them?

RG Yes, I do, and I've published many of them as well. For example, Solzhenitsyn once wrote us that *The New Review* is an extremely important journal and that it should go on publishing no matter what may happen. And Arkady Belinkov once wrote me: "We are all indebted to *The New Review.*" I've gotten all sorts of compliments like that.

JG Tell me about Aleksei Tolstoy. You and he were friends.

RG It's very hard to tell you about Aleksei Tolstoy in a sentence or two. He was an unusually talented person. He was gifted in everything he did. First of all, he was a physically imposing figure. Very elegant. He exuded talent in everything he did, whether he was writing a story or just telling you a joke. Bunin once wrote that Aleksei Tolstoy was talented even when he was turning out hack work.

But he was deaf to any moral criticism. Once he said rather foppishly to Yashchenko: "I prefer a life of ease and elegance." And he had plenty of occasions to prove that there were no limits to what he would do. The things he did when he went back to the Soviet Union! He rewrote all his books, like *Road to Calvary*, which had once been a good book, just to suit the censors. He turned out all sorts of trash, like *Bread* and *Engineer Garin*, and what have you.

He praised all the concentration camps. And on top of all that he collaborated with the Soviets when they tried to blame the Germans for the slaughter of Polish officers at Katyn. He was a member of the commission headed, I believe, by Burdenko, and he signed the document attesting to the claim that it was a German slaughter. His favorite expression was French (which he spoke poorly). He used to say: "Je m'en fous," which means "I don't give a damn"—only worse. I don't want to use the real word. If anyone touched on a sticky subject, he would just say "Je m'en fous" or "Pardi mon oncle." Another pidgin French expression he would come up with.

JG How about Konstantin Fedin?

RG He and I were close friends. He was a good man, but you couldn't compare him to Tolstoy. He didn't have Tolstoy's brilliance. Fedin was a talented writer of prose, and if only he had been able to write freely, I think he probably would have accomplished a good deal. For instance, his short story "The Garden" would have been all right or his novella *Anna Timofeevna*. But he was a very sick man. He had tuberculosis. Then as a writer he was very vain, and as soon as he began to feel that his illness was sapping his talent, he started turning out hack stuff.

Then he decided that in order to stay on top in the literary world it would be best to hold some sort of post, and that's what he did. First he became general secretary of the Soviet Writers' Union, then chairman of the Writers' Union, and finally a member of the Supreme Soviet—position after position after position. Ultimately he got the Stalin Prize for Literature. . . . It was one thing after another.

I liked him a lot, but to be honest, he did a lot of nasty things to Soviet literature. He did some mean things to Pasternak when Pasternak won the Nobel Prize for *Doctor Zhivago.* Fedin stopped publication of Solzhenitsyn's *Cancer Ward* but basked in bureaucratic glory. He had a dacha in Peredelkino, a spectacular set of mahogany furniture, and despite his illness he lived past eighty.

JG Nabokov.

RG Well, that's not my area of expertise. I know that Nabokov is always acclaimed, but I could never finish a book of his.

JG You knew him, didn't you?

RG I met him fleetingly, but I didn't really know him. Nabokov was a snob from head to toe, and I found that repellent. In the international snob world he was a treasure. And that blown-up, snobbish style helped make a big name for him, and so now he's well known and published and applauded. I sometimes pick up a book of his and start reading, but I've always found that his stuff was not for me.

JG Sasha Chorny.

RG Sasha Chorny was a charming man. I met him in the twenties, after he arrived in Berlin. He had been completely crushed by the Revolution. He couldn't write a thing. His earlier work was quite sharp, but after he emigrated, he started writing pretty badly. But he was a charming human being, pure as can be!

Chorny hated Bolshevism. I hate Bolshevism too, and so do a lot of other people I know, but I've never seen anyone hate like he did. Even more than Bunin in *Days of Damnation.* Chorny could not talk about Bolshevism and remain calm. I remember once we were in a student restaurant in Berlin, and he told me how when he was leaving Soviet Russia, a Cheka agent was examining his manuscripts. The agent ripped one of them up; he threw another one all over the place and handed over a third to someone else, all for no reason whatsoever. "If I had had the strength," Sasha told me, "I would have bitten his head off." He didn't stay in Berlin very long. He moved to Italy and then to France, where he died.

JG   Boris Pilnyak.

RG   Pilnyak was a marvelous writer. That I have to say. He was a writer I really loved. Extremely gifted. As with Aleksei Tolstoy, his talent was something you could just feel.

I knew him fairly well. In Berlin we would get together often, and we would go drinking and do all the things friends do together. He wrote an interesting work called *Mahogany.* It was never published in the Soviet Union. The censors cut it to shreds. But Petropolis did put out a lot of his stories. Pilnyak was not only a good writer; he had a strong character. He wrote something called "Story of the Unextinguished Moon," about how Stalin had General Frunze killed on the operating table. One had to have a great deal of artistic courage to do that. Fedin, for example, never wrote anything of that sort. It wasn't the kind of issue he could raise. And Pilnyak ended up paying for it, poor fellow.

JG   Our time is up, Roman Borisovich. Let me just say that I hope you won't let *The New Review* die.

RG   For your sake, I'll try not to.

Makers of Fantasy and Humor

2

Vasily Aksyonov

Prose writer (b. 1932). A physician by training, Aksyonov gave up the practice of medicine to become one of Russia's most popular writers. After participating in the editing of the unofficial almanac *Metropole*, he was forced to emigrate in 1980. He is now writer-in-residence at George Mason University in Fairfax, Virginia. His Soviet citizenship was restored in 1990.

Books published abroad in Russian: *Zatovarennaya bochkotara* (New York, 1980); *Ozhog* (Ann Arbor, 1980); *Zolotaya nasha zhelezka* (Ann Arbor, 1980); *Ostrov Krym* (Ann Arbor, 1981); *Aristofoniana s lyagushkami* (Ann Arbor, 1981); *Bumazhny peizhazh* (Ann Arbor, 1982); *Pravo na ostrov* (Ann Arbor, 1983); *Skazhi izyum*

(Ann Arbor, 1985); *Poiski zhanra* (Frankfurt-am-Main, 1986); and *V poiskakha grustnogo bebi* (New York, 1987).

English translations: *The Steel Bird and Other Stories* (Ann Arbor: Ardis, 1979); *The Island of Crimea* (New York: Random House, 1983); Ed., *Metropole* (New York: Norton, 1983); *The Burn* (New York: Random House-Vintage Books, 1983); *Surplussed Barrelware* (Ann Arbor: Ardis, 1985); *Quest for an Island* (New York: Performing Arts Journal Publications, 1987); *In Search of Melancholy Baby* (New York: Random House, 1987); *Our Golden Ironburg: A Novel with Formulas* (Ann Arbor: Ardis, 1989); and *Say Cheese* (New York: Random House, 1989).

College Park, Maryland, 1982 and 1983

JG Your fellow writer and émigré Sergei Yurenen writes that you are unquestionably the leader of the avant-garde movement in modern Russian prose. What does he mean by "avant-garde," and do you make a conscious attempt to write in that manner?

VA Who is avant-garde and who is "rear guard" is, in fact, all relative. In my case, however, there came a point when I decided which writers I take after. It was not a conscious choice, but something I became aware of as my writing developed. The tradition I find myself following goes back to the Russian avant-garde and from there back to Gogol rather than Dostoevsky. Soviet critics refer to it as the official mainstream tradition, but what I'm talking about is thought to be more a matter of style. In Russia the avant-garde is viewed as somehow borrowed from the West, if you follow me. My stylistic roots are thought to be newer than the mainstream. But in fact it's just the opposite.

The tradition I'm talking about is a very ancient one that has its roots in folklore. Folklore was not copied from anything. Folklore exaggerates: it plays with metaphors. The tradition which official criticism deals with, on the other hand, is indeed very young. It's the tradition of those boring Petersburg novels which so closely resemble translated nineteenth-century German novels. They are actually sociological tracts. As for the style, it also came from the French. So you see, in reality what is thought to be new is actually older than what is perceived as traditional.

JG Which Western writers do you feel are the closest to you?

VA I've gone through various periods of literary interest. When I began writing I was strongly influenced by twentieth-century American literature, what we call the "big five": Hemingway, Faulkner, Steinbeck, Fitzgerald, and Dos Passos. Of those, Dos Passos was the one with the most avant-garde composition and structure. And when my friends and I were just starting out, we spent a lot of time talking about him. Much of his work was translated into Russian before the war because at that time he was flirting with Communists and leftists and was even said to be a member of the party. For that reason he was translated as a "progressive writer." But Dos Passos' work was well outside the Soviet version of official literature; he was avant-garde. Later, in the 1950s, we dug out his books again, and they exercised a great influence on us. Only then did writers of our own heritage, writers who had been forgotten and cut off, start to turn up, like the Oberiuty (a 1920s literary circle whose Russian acronym stands for "Association for Real Art") or Isaak Babel or Mikhail Bulgakov or Andrei Bely.

JG Were the books of Bely and Bulgakov really as hard to lay hands on as the Oberiuty?

VA No, easier. The Oberiuty also became famous, but in a very funny way. People began talking about the Theater of the Absurd, but that was long, long ago, back in the late 1950s or the early 1960s. A number of excerpts appeared in some Soviet journals, including Ionesco, Camus, *Waiting for Godot*. . . .

JG *Waiting for Godot* was translated and published in Russian?

VA Yes, in *Inostrannaya literatura* (Foreign Literature). And then came Ionesco. Theater-of-the-Absurd writing was given fairly wide circulation, and there were many articles written on it. Then in 1965, a friend of mine said to me: "Did you know that the Theater of the Absurd got its start in Leningrad?" He then proceeded to pull out some sadly faded copies of the plays of Vvedensky and Kharms. That was a truly surprising discovery.

JG Vvedensky and Kharms are now published in the Soviet Union. True, Zabolotsky had a connection with the Oberiuty. . . .

VA He did. Vvedensky and Kharms both died in the

purges—unlike Bulgakov. He was just silenced as a writer, or he silenced himself. He never actually became a *persona non grata*. Or take Bely: you couldn't officially call Bely an "enemy of the people" either. He died peacefully enough, but most of his work was thrown out. And his very existence was virtually negated.

JG Tell me about 1963.

VA 1963 was critical for the younger generation of Soviet artists and writers. The party had mounted a massive attack on their work, an attack which began with the provocation of the avant-garde artists at the Manege exhibition. Nikita appeared with his camarilla, and they ranted and raved in a disgraceful way. "We're going to tear you people to pieces!" they said. Later they did the same to the writers. In 1963 Andrei Voznesensky and I were hauled up on the stage in the Kremlin's Sverdlov Hall. There, in front of the entire Politburo, Nikita waved his fists in the air, threatening us. . . . It was a bit like . . .

JG The Roman Coliseum?

VA Partly like that and partly like an avalanche. As when you're climbing a mountain and you feel the snow slipping from under you. It seems as though there's nothing to stop you from tumbling along with everything else. The whole business got to me, and I realized that we live in a totally absurd world. That reality is so absurd that a writer who makes use of the absurd or the surreal is not coloring his work. Rather he is trying to make some sort of harmony out of this reality, which falls down around him like garbage into a dump. That's when I started to write my first avant-garde pieces—plays actually. My first avant-garde piece was a play called *Always on Sale*, which was produced by the Sovremennik Theater. These days I have moved away from the avant-garde, but I do use it. I'm probably not as avant-garde, though, as I used to be.

JG You wrote that at the end of the 1960s you switched from writing about young people to total satire.

VA That's exactly what I was talking about, for example, in my play *Kiss, Orchestra, Fish, Sausage*. It's set ostensibly in an unnamed Latin American country ruled by a strange junta, but for the most part it reflects the atmosphere prevailing in Russia at the time—the attacks on the arts, the events, the discussions,

and the debates. Strangely enough, the play was nearly performed in Moscow at the Lenin Komsomol Theater. Of course,
it *wasn't* performed.

JG The heroes of your stories, or at least most of your stories, are always young people, and your readers tend to be
young. But you're almost fifty now. Some people say you're too
old now to be a writer for youth.

VA Yes, in my case "youth" has been dragged out to an
absurd degree. And it's not only me; all the writers of my
generation were officially considered "young writers" up till
they were forty-five. But my characters have aged, and my
readers have aged. In a recent work, *In Search of a Genre*, my
main character is the same age as I. The public—critics, too, and
my readers—makes no distinction between the author and the
main character of the book, as if we were one and the same
person. Nothing could be less true. I use my own experiences,
so there may be a lot of me in my characters, but they are still
fictional products of the imagination. I deal with the problems
of middle age. Any longing for the past, for instance, is something which my younger characters never experienced. Then
there is a certain feeling of anxiety—the kind of vegetative air
typical of middle age. But in another recent book I managed to
get away from the steady preplanned aging process, and I made
the hero younger than myself: thirty. The action starts out in
Moscow in 1973 and ends up in New York ten years later, but
the hero is a member of the younger generation. I made a point
of not writing about myself but concentrating, instead, on people of a different generation and background.

JG You don't plan to switch to non-Russian topics?

VA I'm thinking about it, but one way or another what I
write about will have something to do with Russia. I've now
finished the draft of another novel on a subject still closely
connected with Moscow, with my life over the last few years,
and with the group of people involved with the literary almanac
Metropole. I think that after that I'll write a book with an American setting. I may use my younger days in retrospect, that is,
the early 1950s, before the death of Stalin. Or the story may
involve a Russian living in America with a view of his distant
past. You could call it a map showing the starting point of the

journey which brought him to these shores. After all, it's not as if twenty or thirty thousand intellectuals, not to mention 300,000 other émigrés, just got together and decided to leave Russia. It didn't happen just like that. There are serious reasons behind the whole phenomenon of Russian emigration to the United States.

JG In the preface to *Surplussed Barrelware* you call the 1960s a "quixotic society." What did you mean by that?

VA In the 1960s society was prisoner to a number of illusions. In literature too it seemed then that we could throw off the murky past of Stalinism and move ahead toward some sort of liberalization. To put it quite simply, it seemed we could take a few steps toward a happier, freer life.

JG It was then that your mother wrote *Journey Into the Whirlwind*, wasn't it?

VA Yes, she wrote it in the early 1960s and submitted it to *Novy Mir*. *Novy Mir*, for all intents and purposes, agreed to accept it.

JG Was it Tvardovsky who made the decision?

VA No, Tvardovsky killed it. The entire editorial board had agreed, and Tvardovsky killed it. Some of his views were rather narrow, you know. His reaction seems to have been something like this: "These victims of Stalinist terror, the people she's writing about, were all from the privileged classes. That's no good. It's the peasants who really suffered, and she should write about them." As if the peasants were the chief victims of government measures! I'd say the intelligentsia was probably the very first to suffer.

JG Tell me about the criticism aimed at *Ticket to the Stars*, *Oranges from Morocco*, and *Surplussed Barrelware*.

VA You've lumped together some very diverse works. If you take, for instance, *Oranges from Morocco*, *Ticket to the Stars*, and *It's Time, My Friend, It's Time*, those three books deal with the problems of youth. In fact, several critics have gone so far as to say that they're all one and the same book—with the same character, plus a few changes. This was a more or less deliberate attack on the part of the Komsomol and party critics, who had begun to perceive an imminent threat in the new generation of fictional heroes.

Now as far as *Surplussed Barrelware* is concerned, that *is* surrealism, and they were pretty confused as to what it all meant. The criticism was simply moronic. They just couldn't figure out what I was getting into, what I was opposing. They knew I was against *something*, and they suspected I was up to no good. It's just that they hadn't the foggiest notion what it was.

Let me tell you a little story about *Surplussed Barrelware*. There was this critic. . . . He's a big shot in the Central Committee now—Aganyan. He wrote under the pseudonym Aganov, but his real name is Grisha Aganyan, a thoroughly disgusting character, I have to say. Anyway, he wrote a long, condemnatory article after *Surplussed Barrelware* came out. I read it. It had been published in *Komsomol'skaya Pravda,* and it was pretty much what I had expected; I knew it wasn't going to say anything good. But then a friend of mine came to me and said: "Look what he's trying to hang on you." I hadn't paid any attention, but then they showed me that he was accusing me of counterrevolution. Here's what happened. At the end of the book the heroes pull into Koryazhsk Station. The station has a tower next to it with a set of statues of Soviet heroes. There's a border guard, a miner, a milkmaid . . . things like that. Now, the tower has an electric clock showing 19:07. And what it says in the book is "The train was due in ten minutes, and it arrived ten minutes later on the dot, but no one got on, and the train left, dissolving into the landscape." Well, I couldn't see anything strange about that, and finally my friend said: "add 10 to 1907 and you get 1917. The train pulled out and no one got on. No one got on the train of the Revolution." That was it! And I hadn't seen that at all! It was Freudian. I hadn't been thinking in such primitive terms, but that's just how primitive Soviet logic can be.

JG Let's talk about form. I want to come back to Yurenen. He writes that *The Burn* is a fairly optimistic novel, and that the reaction on the part of the authorities was due more to dissatisfaction with the form than with the content.

VA Well, not entirely, although in the final few years form had been the major source of hassle from the authorities, since the school of "rural prose" had become the standard. Even though it was officially foisted upon us, it actually turned out to be just a low-grade folk style. So the publication of *In Search of a Genre* created something of a sensation, and a lot of young writers from the provinces sent me letters saying that they now realized that they didn't necessarily have to write like Abramov or Astafiev. Before we had always been told that anything else was simply not allowed, it was not for us. So there were always problems with form. They wouldn't allow even my plays. They were heavily enough encoded so that they could have been produced one way or another, but the form was unacceptable—un-Soviet, un-folk, if you know what I mean. What happened with *The Burn* was really something else. It's a very modernistic work, very surrealistic, but it earned me an official warning from the KGB, and not about form, but about content.

JG Some of the "Rural Prose" writers, Vladimir Soloukhin for one, take offense at the term.

VA I don't think he's part of that group.

JG All right then; let's take Fyodor Abramov or Valentin Rasputin. What do you think of them?

VA I think that theirs is a very tragic story. I'd insist on putting it that strongly: it was tragic. These were not untalented people, and they started out very well. Some of them stood out—Vasily Belov and Boris Mozhaev, for example. You could feel in their work a cry of protest, artistic as well as social, against this stagnation. But then the ideological machine did something very clever. It didn't give them a chance to become dissidents, although they were headed in that direction much more so than I or other writers like myself with our little for-malistic tricks. I suppose that this is just how my life has shaped my view of things, but I really can't get all that excited about how the season's planting is going to turn out; if butter should appear on the shelves of my hometown of Kazan for the first time in twenty years—that would be a lot more important. But the party machine really put those writers to good use. They started to promote them, forcing them into the worst sort of Russophilism.

JG Yes, but that wasn't exactly alien to them.

VA No, it wasn't, but there are Russophiles and there are Russophiles. There are the enlightened ones, the type you're likely to see at a local party meeting, right?

JG Whom exactly do you have in mind?

VA Fyodor Abramov, for instance. Even Viktor Astafiev. And Astafiev is a lovely person. I know him personally. I was shocked to read that he was one of the leaders of the campaign being conducted against young rock groups in the Soviet Union. These were groups which had dared to write and perform their own material—material that did not exactly conform to accepted standards. Almost all of these people involved in "rural literature" reaped their rewards; they've all been named laureates of various state prizes. And why? What's the point? Why is the machine using them? Some of their writing can be pretty strong. But with time it starts losing its efficacy. Secondly, I think that the main point in putting these people on a leash was to once again create a culture isolated from Western culture, to cut the few weak links that had been reestablished between Russian culture and Western culture. And you could hear people saying: "Hey, look at us good party members! We care *so* much about what the grain looks like, about feeling those little grains in the palms of their hands."

JG After the publication of *Oranges from Morocco* you officially repented on the pages of *Pravda* in April 3, 1963.

VA It actually had nothing to do with *Oranges from Morocco*, but rather with Khrushchev's attack on the arts. He was screaming: "We're going to tear you people to pieces. You're either for us or against us! You're getting in the way of our Polish friends in their efforts to build socialism, and we're not going to let you make this into another Hungary," and so on and so forth.

JG Once you repented, did things calm down?

VA Yes, and I'd like to tell you why. I never had any intention of repenting. But then there was a semi-underground emergency meeting of the editors of the magazine *Yunost'* (Youth), and they all came to me, including my writer friends, and asked me to write an article or do something to save their journal. Those were their words: "to save the journal." And so I did it. I wrote a piece saying that I had written poorly, but from now on I would write well. And that was all there was to it. And you know what? It ended up not doing me the least bit of good; they still wouldn't publish my work.

JG Tell me about *Metropole*.

VA That is a very long and involved story, and there's a lot that is still unclear. It was completely a spur-of-the-moment thing. Some people believe that the whole idea was a provocation carried out by some of our own friends, but I'd be hard pressed to believe that.

A friend of mine, a younger writer named Viktor Yerofeev, and I began talking about how there was simply no outlet whatsoever for the younger generation. And so we wondered if we shouldn't try to get something going here to bring things out of the underground. Who first said "Let's put out a journal," I don't remember now. In any case, we had discussed it among ourselves. And after that things got rolling, with more new people getting involved.

If it was supposed to be some sort of provocation on the part of some "comrades," they didn't get any mileage out of it. We spent an entire year working on *Metropole*. It wasn't a secret. It was all over Moscow. I don't know how the Writer's Union could have failed to know about it, and the KGB certainly knew. They were keeping an eye on us, and I was very closely followed. Maybe they *were* trying to keep it going, to come up with something they could use for whatever motives they may have had. But who besides Russian literature in general had anything to gain from that? Literature gained, only literature. The authorities lost out. *Metropole* was completed and was a literary event that brought to the fore some extremely interesting younger authors, as well as some older ones who could have otherwise never appeared. It made an impact throughout the world.

JG What if the authorities had gone ahead and permitted the almanac to be published? After all, it didn't contain anything really political.

VA No, there was nothing political there. We were specifically trying to be very reasonable. We didn't want it to turn into a bullfight. So we turned down all of the strong stuff in what was supposed to be a positive move. We were reaching out to them (the authorities), giving Soviet literature one more chance, as if to say, "Let's try and open up some windows and get rid of this awful stench you've got here." Well, their response was to say "to hell with you" and to caulk up all the openings.

JG Did you submit the manuscript for *Metropole* anywhere?

VA No, we were thinking of having an opening—some sort of social event, maybe with saxophones and women modeling clothes, you know, to break up all the monotony and boredom. Then we would be able to submit it to the State Publishing Committee. But they didn't even let us get that far. The hysteria began before we could start. They banned the champagne brunch, closed down the café where it was to be held, and started a witch-hunt.

JG When exactly did they start removing your books from the libraries?

VA After the *Metropole* blowup, early in 1979. That's when the official order came down.

JG Do you view yourself as having been forced to leave?

VA Yes, for all intents and purposes I was forced out. Otherwise why would they have stripped me of my citizenship after only three months? How else can that be explained? I was warned that if I went ahead and published *The Burn* I would have to say good-bye. They were quite direct about it. I felt surrounded, and I saw no way out. It was—knuckle under and turn into a reptile, give up writing what I wanted to write, and become a literary technician and kiss ass.

JG Well, now you are here in the West, and the question arises: the world which you describe differs so radically from the Western world that the Western reader finds it not only quite distant, but incomprehensible as well. What are the chances for you as a Russian writer of acquiring an American following? Is that possible? Is that something you strive for?

VA Yes, of course, but that's not my main goal. I will continue writing for the same readers I've always had, some of whom live outside the Soviet Union. But that doesn't mean that I don't want American readers. I think Americans would be interested in reading about this unknown world. After all, they read science fiction.

Perhaps in time I'll begin to enter the mainstream of American life, but that doesn't mean that I'll leave my past behind me.

There's enough in my past I could write about to last me the rest of my life, however long that may be. When you leave the country at forty-eight, that gives you enough to write about. But this new American experience I find fascinating.

Take for example my novel *Paper Landscape*, the first twelve chapters are about Russia. The last one takes place ten years later when all the characters are in New York. Even a police major ends up working as a bodyguard. And I took a great deal of interest, not only in the formal side of their development, but also in how their language changes, their way of speaking: it changes so gradually that they don't even notice it. Someone says: "She was standing beside her car, which had a left front *flat*," and I use the English word. It's a sort of game. But that's the way people here speak.

JG   As a Soviet writer you used a lot of slang, a lot of in-talk. Don't you think that now you'll have to struggle to preserve your language, and that for that reason alone you'll want to avoid using slang?

VA   Of course, it's impossible from such a distance to keep abreast of everyday changes in the language. But up till now anyway I haven't experienced any loss, and I don't expect to, at least for the foreseeable future. It's not that big a problem anyway. I'm not a scholar of slang.

JG   Does it depress you to think of the tiny editions of your books here, as opposed to there?

VA   Well, the number of copies that the Russian émigré publishers turn out is virtually nothing. But I try and console myself. I even wrote a humorous piece on the matter. Let's say Ardis publishes 2,000 copies, which is nothing for a novel published in the Soviet Union. The entire printing will sell, mostly to recent émigrés, of whom there are about 300,000 or so in the world today. So proportionally if the book were to sell out in the Soviet Union, it would sell two million copies. That's some consolation.

Or another example: I have a collection of plays which "appeared" in 1978 in samizdat—four copies. Over here—as an émigré—I'll have a thousand copies, a fantastic increase in volume!

JG How do you view the current state of Russian prose? There are those who believe that Russian prose as well as poetry is in a state of decline compared to literature in the West. Do you agree?

VA Absolutely not. I more or less keep up with writing in the West, and I wouldn't say that it's that far ahead of contemporary Russian prose, if it's ahead at all. Maybe the average level of writing is better here, but literature in the West fortunately, or maybe unfortunately, never had to go through the kind of earthshaking events that affected the very existence of literature. And this struggle for survival, this sickliness, this depression, these attempts to free itself from slavery permeate the very best of contemporary Russian literature and lend it a tremendous artistic strength.

JG Which writers do you have in mind?

VA A lot of people, Aleksandr Solzhenitsyn, a master. Or, say, the all-encompassing satire of someone like Aleksandr Zinoviev, who may not appeal to me personally; there's a lot there I don't see eye to eye with him on, and even artistically we're pretty far apart, but still his work is extremely serious and also new. Or if you look at some of the younger people, there's Sasha Sokolov, who is developing into a very interesting writer. Edward Limonov is back again, shrill, outrageous, dirty, vexing, and dissonant, but mix all those things together, and you end up with a pretty good bouquet.

JG All right, but those are all émigrés. What about Soviet writers?

VA Soviet literature . . . the people still there . . . you see, it's all part of the same literature. The border doesn't run along the edge of the Soviet Union or the camp of peace and socialism, as they call it; it's a border dividing literature and para-literature, fake literature. It's a border that runs through Soviet literature and, interestingly enough, very often through an individual book. Take Kataev, a brilliant writer. He has a book where you can see that border weaving in and out like an Amazon on horseback. "Rural Prose" writers have the same border running through their books.

As for the top people—there's Andrei Bitov, a marvelous

writer, simply marvelous. And Fazil Iskander. I'd say that contemporary Russian literature has a dozen first-rate people, and that's enough.

JG To what degree is *The Island of Crimea* escapism: a piece of free Russia, a life of extravagance . . . ?

VA Well, it was all a game from the very start, but a game which, given the fact that it's a serious work of fiction, became something of a model of Western society. That is, the island serves as a model of Western society. So on the one hand it *is* a game, a make-believe: what Russia would be if it weren't for. . . . But on the other hand, I tried to make it sound very realistic. The idea is fantasy: there is no such island; the Crimea is a peninsula, and there is no such country. Call it surrealism, or what you will. That was why I decided to keep the style very strictly realistic, conservative, and traditional throughout the entire book. And because I did, what you get is a reflection of the modern Western world face to face with total aggression, a kind of mechanical consumption.

Washington, D.C., August 15, 1990

JG Vasily, what's changed for you since I first interviewed you?

VA A lot has changed. For one thing, I've become an American citizen, a resident of Washington, D.C. I've been living in America for ten years now, and I've grown accustomed to her.

JG And Russia?

VA For a long time Russia served me as a source of literary material. The living link grew weaker and weaker. All these years I've had a sense of a rapid disengagement from current Russian life. Strangely enough, at the same time there was a rapprochement with her culture, which became more and more precious to me. But now that we are being engulfed by an onslaught of Soviet visitors—friends and enemies, and just ordinary people,—I am considering dividing my time in equal parts between America and Russia. I find myself drawn closer and closer to Russia, and I dwell in her problems.

This morning the news arrived by telephone that Gorbachev

has issued a proclamation returning Soviet citizenship to those who had previously been deprived of it. If that news is confirmed, the situation will be altered. It'll mean I'm no longer an enemy of the state.

JG Just yesterday you told me that exile was not yet over. Is it over today?

VA I'll feel a lot freer, I'll travel, maybe buy myself a dacha in the Crimea. . . . America is my home, but I have never felt myself to be an American and never will. But these years of exile have formed me into a sort of cosmopolitan renegade.

JG Tell me about your trip to Russia. After all, you're a star over there.

VA I was surrounded by television cameras from the hour I arrived to the hour I left. My former popularity is returning. *Our Golden Ironburg* and *The Island of Crimea* were printed in the magazine *Yunost'* (Youth). *The Burn* will come out in a separate edition of 500,000 copies. I have proposals for plays, films, etc. This fall alone four or five of my books will appear. The censors have cut out some of the erotic scenes and strong language, but those spots are indicated by ellipses; that's progress. There are no political limitations whatsoever; in that sense freedom is total. In our wildest dreams we cultural figures never imagined things would go so far. Russia is experiencing an amazing period. Sometimes it seems to me that I am living in the provinces, in a backwater; the main events of the period are going on there.

JG So America is a dacha for you, even in the sense that you can't get any writing done in Russia.

VA You're absolutely right, John. You can't write there. Maybe that's why Soviet writers have rushed headlong abroad, but you can't write abroad either. Everyone seems to be in a fever of activity.

JG Are there any hostilities between those writers who emigrated and those who stayed behind?

VA *Glasnost* is revealing a lot—all sorts of petty betrayals, but I hope to God we don't begin settling scores. Certain circumstances are better forgotten than clarified.

JG So all is forgiven Voznesensky and Yevtushenko?

VA That's too painful a topic. I don't know what I have to forgive Voznesensky. He just tried to stay on top, under all circumstances. He might not have done anyone any good, but he didn't harm anyone either. Yevtushenko, on the other hand, wrote that some ran away to *Radio Liberty*, while others fought on the barricades. I'd like to know what sort of barricades come with state prizes, complete collected works, and round-the-world trips! But then there are many émigrés who say: "you conformist bastards were busy kissing the government's ass while we were being thrown out of the country by the KGB."

I don't deny the service rendered by certain liberal circles of society who were active during the so-called period of "stagnation." They accomplished a lot—particularly some party members. They accommodated themselves to the status quo, wrote speeches for Andropov, Podgorny, Brezhnev, but there were liberals among them who worked behind the scenes for reform. And there are a lot of writers about whom I cannot say that.

JG Give me some names.

VA I can't say that representatives of so-called "Rural Prose," such as Belov and Rasputin, laid the ground for *perestroika*. They had the chance and let it pass. The bait cast out by the Central Committee proved too tempting, and they quickly were co-opted by the establishment, publishing their works in enormous editions and raking in prizes—all the while weeping crocodile tears over poor old Aunty Matryona (peasant figure in Solzhenitsyn story). No wonder so many of them were drawn into the camp of the black hundreds.

JG A last question: what should the task of literature be now?

VA Literature will be dissipated, squandered, if it is not ripped free from the whirlpool of everyday life. We must get away from subjects that are "topical." It is true that Russian writers have always been involved in politics and have been viewed as philosophers and political-opinion makers, but now that is no longer necessary, thank God! Let the politicians occupy themselves with politics, that's their job. Release literature from this burden.

Vladimir Voinovich

Prose writer (b. 1932). Voinovich became well known in the USSR in the early 1960s. After protesting the arrests of Andrei Siniavsky, Yuly Daniel, and Aleksandr Solzhenitsyn, he came under severe pressure from the government and was expelled from the Writers' Union in 1974 and emigrated to West Germany in 1980. He is best known for his satirical novel *The Life and Adventures of Private Ivan Chonkin*. After emigrating he wrote *Moscow 2042*, a novel satirizing Soviet life and Solzhenitsyn. In 1990 his Soviet citizenship was restored to him.

Books: *Zhizn' i neobychainye priklyucheniya soldata Ivana Chonkina* (Paris, 1976); *Ivan'kiada, ili Rasskaz o vselenii pisatelya Voinovicha v novuyu kvartiru*

(Ann Arbor, 1976); *Putem vzaimnoi perepiski* (Paris, 1979); *Tribunal: Su-debnaya komediya v trekh deistviyakh* (London, 1985); *Antisovetsky Sovetsky Soyuz* (Ann Arbor, 1985); *Moskva 2042* (1987); *Shapka* (London, 1988); and *Khochu byt' chestnym* (Moscow, 1989).

English translations: *The Ivankiad; or The Tale of the Writer Voinovich's Installation in His New Apartment*, trans. D. Lapeza (Ann Arbor: Ardis, 1976); *The Life and Extraordinary Adventures of Private Ivan Chonkin*, trans. Richard Lourie (New York: Penguin, 1978); *In Plain Russian: Stories*, trans. Richard Lourie (New York: Farrar, Straus & Giroux, 1979); *Pretender to the Throne: The Further Adventures of Private Ivan Chonkin*, trans. Richard Lourie (New York: Farrar, Straus & Giroux, 1981); *The Anti-Soviet Soviet Union*, trans. Richard Lourie (New York: Harcourt Brace Jovanovich, 1986); *Moscow 2042*, trans. Richard Lourie (New York: Harcourt Brace Jovanovich, 1988); *The Fur Hat* (New York: Harcourt Brace Jovanovich, 1989).

College Park, Maryland, April 1981

JG You were made famous when Khrushchev sang a song of yours from atop the Lenin mausoleum:

> We will leave our mark
> On dusty pathways
> Of distant planets.

VV Yes, you see, I began by writing poetry. I had always dreamed of writing prose, but it seemed I just wasn't meant to be a prose writer. Or a poet either, at first. I was able to get my poems into print only once in a great while, and even then the best ones never appeared. But in 1960 I got a job in radio. One day at the end of a program, the editor decided that she urgently needed a song about cosmonauts. There weren't any cosmonauts yet then. It was a year before Yury Gagarin's flight.

JG But they were already planning for it.

VV They were obviously planning something, but the fact is that this was 1960, and Gagarin didn't go up into space until 1961. My editor needed a poet and a composer, and so she called up all the leading songwriters: Isakovsky, Matusovsky, Dolmatovsky, Oshanin. Each one asked how long he had, and she would tell him a week. They were all famous songwriters, and so they were offended. Song, they said, is a lofty art form. How could she expect a song to be produced in a week? A song requires thought and feeling; it has to come from inside you. A song, they said, would take at least a month. This editor did not know me at that time, as I had only been working there for about two or three days.

I went to her and asked if I could give it a try. She was surprised, especially when I promised that I'd have it by the next day. But she had nothing to lose; she knew no one else was going to get her song done in time. So she said okay, and I went home. There's a line in the song that goes: "We still have fourteen minutes left." That's exactly how long it took me to write the words: fourteen minutes. Well, she was amazed the next morning when I showed up with the song. She liked the words, and she called a composer. He wrote the music at once, and that very day we recorded it, and it was broadcast. The song achieved instant fame. Everybody in the Soviet Union knew it.

Not everybody knows it now because they play it without the words. An entire generation has grown up without hearing the words. Later, after cosmonauts Nikolaev and Popovich returned to earth (and they had sung the song in space), they were given a big parade in Red Square. They were among the first cosmonauts in space. Khrushchev appeared atop the mausoleum and sang, or rather howled, a few of the words from that song, and so it became even more famous.

JG Being of "proletarian origin" is often a plus in the Soviet political system.

VV My own background is proletarian, although my origins are less so. My father was a journalist, my mother a schoolteacher. And while she had trouble in college and graduated late, my family nevertheless had an intellectual bent. But my background is proletarian through and through. I started work at eleven years of age, as a shepherd on a collective farm. Later I did just about everything there was to be done on a collective farm. Then I moved to the city, where I worked as a metal worker and a carpenter. In the army I was an airplane mechanic. So I had an ideal proletarian background until I became a writer.

JG In other words, you never received any formal literary training?

VV No, I didn't. I never formally studied literature, and I'm glad I didn't. I was twice rejected by a literary institute. There was a time when I tried to get in. But I think they did the right thing, and I'm grateful to them.

JG Where did you get the idea for *Chonkin?*

VV In Moscow in 1957. It was the first idea that I ever had for something to write about. I was standing on a street corner drinking a cup of soda water. The lady selling the water was telling another woman about how hard her life was, how she had a delinquent son who was impossible to manage. And oh, if only her husband were alive! But he was an army colonel who was killed in the war.

I had seen women like this before, and I thought to myself: "You made it all up! You were never married. Or if you were, he was no colonel!" So I tried to picture what must have really happened. She must have met some soldier on the eve of the war. He was called up as soon as the war began, and all contact with him was cut off. And she forgot him. And then she had a son, and since she didn't remember who the father was, she made up the rest. I then wrote a story like that. It was not very good, but it had an interesting plot. There was no hero, just that woman.

Then I wrote some other stories. I wrote a novella called *We Live Here.* But I kept on going back to that first idea. Who was the man whom that woman imagined? What really had happened to him? I gave it some thought, and I started to work out in my mind what sort of soldier he might have been. Then suddenly I recalled an incident which happened when I myself was in the army in Poland. I was walking around our base one day when I saw a strange sight—a horse pulling a cart, but no rider. I looked under the cart and saw a soldier lying between the wheels. He had gotten his leg caught in the reins, and the horse was slowly dragging him along. He was making no effort at all to extricate himself from the situation. Later I saw the same soldier again with his head all bandaged up, and I asked someone who he was. "You don't know who that is?" they answered. "That's Chonkin." And that was it. I never found out any more about him. He died in some accident, and the picture I had of him remained exactly as it was. I didn't know who he was or who his mother was, or his grandmother or his grandfather, just that image.

Toward the end of *Chonkin*, when the war is almost over, he's all bandaged up, and everyone thinks it's because he was wounded. In fact, the same sort of accident happened to him. Anyway, that's how I got the idea for Chonkin.

The book is treated by the critics as satire. But I did not write it as such. What I wrote was the story of the relationship between Chonkin and his girlfriend Niura, the weaving together of their fortunes and so on. The satirical elements appeared only as the result of circumstances forced upon me by the Writers' Union and the KGB and various other Soviet organizations, all of which exerted a strong influence on the plot.

JG Do you plan to continue *Chonkin?*

VV Aside from the sequel, *Pretender to the Throne?* Yes I do. But it will be the last one on Chonkin because the original idea has branched out so much that it would take more than a lifetime to turn it all into a book. For that reason, when I write the third volume, I'll have to be careful not to include all the possible plot developments.

JG You don't write about war in the gloomy, tragic key common to Soviet literature. Why not?

VV That is my inner reaction against the seriousness which is part and parcel of Soviet literature. Soviet literature has a lot of sacred cows. Everything is off limits, everything is holy. When I wrote the first volume of *Chonkin*, for instance, a lot of people—not only people in positions of power—but just ordinary old people told me that I shouldn't make fun of a war in which so many people died. I had trouble convincing them that I wasn't making fun of anybody who had died, but of some of the idiots still alive; the idiocies of life itself. Eventually people got used to the idea. Nowadays I never meet people in the Soviet Union who would say that.

But when I presented the first part to *Novy mir*, it didn't get published. One of the editor-in-chief's assistants read it and said, "Back in 1930, I was on a steamer, where I met some Czech schoolteachers. When they asked me what I knew about Czech literature, and what my favorite book was, I answered *Good Soldier Schweik*. They got very upset and said that *Schweik* was an insult to the Czech people." He added that he was probably going through the same reaction those teachers had felt. Now, however, most people have gotten over those feelings. Even big party officials read it and laugh.

JG How did you find the atmosphere among other writers in Moscow? How were you treated by other writers who had become famous and were publishing in the Soviet Union? Did they condemn your books, or did you have good relations with them?

VV It depends on whom you're talking about. Many people looked upon me with scorn and indignation, although I had done nothing to deserve it. I realized that my part in the Writers' Union and in official Soviet literature in general had come to an end. The time had come when both literary and moral survival meant having to adapt to oneself too drastically. I had to define certain artistic boundaries and stay inside them. For instance, I couldn't even begin to think of publishing *Chonkin*.

JG So you had lost all hope. . . .

VV No, at first I had a glimmer of hope. I never harbored illusions, but I had not planned *Chonkin* to be so biting. But a book never comes out the way the author plans. I had intended it to be more of a lyrical type of book—but when I saw the way the book was turning out, I realized that I couldn't publish it. And *Chonkin* was my best book. I could survive in Soviet literature only if I were to publish the kind of thing I didn't want to write. Since I always feel a need to communicate, not with myself, but with the reader, this meant I wouldn't even be able to write. It's important for me to publish and to get feedback from the reader, and that was why I reached the point where I felt that I had exhausted every possibility in the Soviet literary scene.

There are others who perceived the position I was in as a challenge to them, as if I were setting myself up as all good, while they were all bad.

I know they say that one should speak well of the dead or not speak at all, but I have to say that while Trifonov was a good writer, he was one of those who came to resent me most strongly, even though earlier he had at least respected me as a writer.

JG What had your relations overall been like with the Soviet Writers' Union? You were expelled in 1974, I believe.

VV Yes.

JG What were they like before that?

VV In 1962, right after Khrushchev sang, or howled, that song, I was accepted into the Writers' Union with much pomp and circumstance. One novella of mine had appeared in a magazine, but I had not yet had a book published. Usually you need at least one, if not several, books published to get in to the Writers' Union. Up until 1968 I was even elected to a number of posts in the Union. Then my relations with that organization took a sharp turn for the worse. After that it was all downhill. As early as 1968, and then again in 1970, they tried to expel me. In 1968 I was severely reprimanded. Then in 1970 I received another severe reprimand along with a final warning. When in 1974 the Writer's Union again met to expel me, I got a call from the secretary, a KGB general named Iliin, who said, "We don't want to have to expel you. Come on down, and we'll talk it over."

"No," I said, "I have no desire to stay."

"Look, come on down. We'll talk."

"No, you can't do anything anyway. You've tried all the regular measures—one severe reprimand, then another severe reprimand, then a severe reprimand with a final warning. All you can do now is expel me."

"Don't worry, we'll just issue another severe reprimand."

"No," I said, "I've had enough. I'm the one who'll do the reprimanding now: I don't want to have to talk to you people again."

And that was that. Our conversation ended, and I was expelled.

JG Did you get notice of your expulsion in writing?

VV No, not a thing. It was a very cowardly way of kicking me out. I was the one who wrote to them.

JG There were no speeches?

VV Well, there probably were. But then I made a speech here in which I called the Writer's Union an underground organization. After all, they meet only behind closed doors, and everything is in safes under lock and key. I don't know who said what, but I'm sure that there were speeches. Everything is done in secret. That's the real derivation of the word "secretariat."

JG On August 21, 1980, both your wife's parents died, and on the same day you suffered a serious heart attack. Tell me what led to that.

VV When we decided to emigrate, our whole family faced an almost insurmountable problem. Totally insurmountable, as events were later to demonstrate.

My wife's parents were elderly, conservative people who could not imagine leaving the country. It was out of the question. Nor could they imagine giving up their only daughter and their only granddaughter. There seemed to be no solution. As a result of all this my mother-in-law fell ill and was put in the hospital, where she died suddenly. If we had had a phone, they would have called us, and then we would have been able to prepare my father-in-law. As it was, the hospital called him directly and told him that she had died. He ran out the door to tell us, but dropped dead of a heart attack. He died an hour after his wife. My own series of heart attacks had begun much earlier, on August 5. I was still sick in bed when the news struck, and I suffered yet another attack.

JG Former Defense Minister Marshal Malinovsky once called a poem of yours a stab in the back of the Soviet Army.

VV He did better than that. He said that the poem had shot the Soviet Army in the back.

JG A more modern image.

VV Yes, you see, I had already become fairly well known as a prose writer, and my songs were quite famous, even though I wrote them only as a sideline. But there were also poems that I wrote from the heart, poems which I could never have gotten published anywhere because they didn't conform to the accepted manner. After Khrushchev sang that song, I was asked to submit some poems to a newspaper called *Moskovsky komsomolets*. I chose those poems which I had been unable to get published before the song appeared. There was one about some soldiers who go to a dance where the girls refuse to dance with them. The girls prefer to dance with the officers. The song ends with the soldiers going home. And that so enraged the military chiefs that Marshal Malinovsky attended a meeting of the Political Agency of the Revolutionary Military Council (PUR)—which, you realize, is a fairly important organization—just to discuss the poem. Instead of worrying about how many warheads he needed and where he was going to get them, this marshal wanted to discuss poetry.

Then the poem was mentioned briefly in *Krasnaya zvezda,* the main military newspaper, and the people responsible for having published it were called in and warned. Nevertheless, I went on reciting the poem to army audiences, although I realized that it would cause some consternation among the political officers. I always said at these recitals that I had better luck writing poetry than prose, since one of my poems had been recited by Khrushchev and another drew the attention of Marshal Malinovsky. I avoided saying what sort of attention. So the political cadres—who are always at these performances—just sat and fidgeted nervously. Except on one occasion, they always applauded.

JG On October 23, 1980, as you were getting ready to leave, you wrote a letter of protest. You said that you yourself had not wanted to have to write such a letter. Why not? And how do you view yourself in general, as a nonconformist, as a dissident? What is your position?

VV I've often said that I do not consider myself a dissident, although by all the formal indicators I was. I wouldn't say I acted to defend human rights as a whole since I limited myself to defending the rights of just a few individuals. Besides that, I was published abroad. Most important, whenever they threatened me, I would take up the challenge, and that was always a source of some pleasure.

In fact it was the authorities themselves who were to blame. I believe a citizen has a duty to be loyal, but the state has a duty to be loyal to its citizenry. I'm not for smashing the state. I know too well what would come of that. Everybody knows what happened in 1917. The collapse of this government would be a terrible tragedy for millions of people. For that reason I do not consider myself a dissident in the political sense. As for being a nonconformist, any writer is a nonconformist. If his thoughts

conform to everybody else's then why would anyone be interested in him? He's interesting only if he's original.

It was suggested to me that I leave the Soviet Union, and I
was prepared to do just that. I wanted to leave on good terms.
But those bastards had on a number of occasions provoked me
into doing things I had wanted to avoid. And I had not wanted
to write that letter, that declaration. But there I lay, sick and
helpless, and they decided that that was the time to start playing cat and mouse with me. The same people who had pleaded
with me to leave—they were practically ready to take my suit-
cases to the airport for me—now had intermediaries telling me
that the matter hadn't been settled yet, but that if I behaved, I
would be let out. My letter was a response to that provocation.

JG I believe that at first a certain Yury Idashkin, a member of
the Writers' Union, tried talking to you or threatening you.
What was the essence of your conversation with him?

VV I should not really mention his name. He's already gotten too much publicity from my talking about him so much.
What happened was this. Idashkin let me know indirectly that
he had heard some people at the top saying that they had run
out of patience, that it was time to get rid of Voinovich, and that
if he wouldn't leave on his own, he could expect big trouble.
When my friend asked Idashkin just what sort of trouble he had
in mind, he said, "Well, I'm sure you realize that just about
anything is possible. He drives a car; he could have an accident.
Or maybe he'll get into a fight and be put in jail." But that's not
what did it. In fact, they had been threatening me constantly
since 1968, and I had gotten tired of it. So I took advantage of
the situation and left.

JG Your book *The Ivankiad* is named after Sergei Ivanko, a
real person, whom you accused of bribe-taking. Later he was
seen giving out autographed copies of your book. Tell me how
that came about.

VV I was hoping that *The Ivankiad* would get Ivanko and
some of his followers into trouble. But then I saw that his career
hadn't suffered at all. Just the opposite. I had given him a lot of
good publicity. When the book came out in English, Ivanko was
in the Soviet mission to the United Nations. A number of Americans went to see him, and some of them even asked him to

autograph copies of my book. I heard of one case when he wrote "to so-and-so from the book's hero." The funny part is that he keeps getting promoted. The Ministry of Culture discovered that the person in charge of approving visa applications for performers was taking bribes. They fired him and put Ivanko in his place. I guess he'll be asking higher prices now.

Washington, D.C., August 19, 1990

JG Tell me about the difficulties you had with *Moscow 2042*.

VV What do you mean difficulties! Here in the West you can publish whatever you like. But I know what you have in mind. Everybody says that the novel is a parody on Solzhenitsyn. In point of fact, Solzhenitsyn does represent a phenomenon worthy of description, but I would never write about a single person. The image in that novel is a generalized one—of a Russian messiah.

JG But it includes Solzhenitsyn.

VV Yes, there are elements of parody on Solzhenitsyn. Most readers received the novel favorably, but there were some for whom Solzhenitsyn is a holy cow, and they see arrows everywhere aimed at Solzhenitsyn. The New York émigré newspaper published the novel and got a lot of nasty feedback from Solzhenitsyn's minions.

One Soviet writer even maintained that the time has not yet come to criticize Solzhenitsyn, and it will probably never come. This is a form of idolatry, a cult of personality.

When Solzhenitsyn was being attacked in the Soviet Union, I defended him, and at no small risk to myself.

But as early as the collection *From Under the Rubble*, he was searching for *russophobes*. Now he's become simply arrogant.

JG You have a lot of friends among the writers who did not emigrate, but not with all of them.

VV I don't believe the vision of the so-called "Rural Prose" writers extends beyond their villages. Some even write in a semiliterate style. Before *glasnost* they were unjustifiably lionized. The backbone of literature had been broken, some of the writers had been driven into exile, and others were frightened into silence. And during that period these rural writers were the only ones who could be published. For some reason they were even described as "the people's conscience." Valentin Rasputin even wrote that "we have apostles of conscience," having in mind himself and his clique. And now they yearn for the good old days of "stagnation." In an artistic sense, they stood out only because they had no competition.

JG The first two volumes of *Chonkin* were chiefly humor, while *Moscow 2042* is satire. What will volume three of *Chonkin* be like? You're once more a Soviet citizen, or at least you can become one again if you like, so the need to struggle is somewhat diminished.

VV Nothing of the sort! I haven't been struggling just for myself. Of course, satire can exist without humor, but more often than not the two are combined. In a strictly generic sense, *Chonkin* is satire. Any human society is deserving of satire. I don't like random, undirected humor.

JG How did you conceive *Chonkin* when you were writing it?

VV As a novel that would be at once lyrical and realistic.

JG You recently made a statement for the Soviet press in which you said you "would return." Now that your citizenship has been restored, what are you going to do?

VV The same as before: stay here, and say the same things. What does it mean to have citizenship restored? I need more than citizenship; I need normal civil rights. And what capacity would I return in? And where to? Exile wiped me out financially there, left me without even a roof over my head. Realistic conditions have to be created for me to return.

JG How did emigration influence you as a writer?

VV I can't agree with those people who maliciously assert that we émigré writers live miserable lives and that we're washed up as writers. There are even some émigrés who hold to that view and who have given up writing. The displacement to the West was truly a shock, but I don't consider that my writing has suffered for it.

JG You've traveled twice to the USSR.

VV The first trip, in the spring of 1989, was a very emotional event for me, although I can't say I was particularly surprised by anything I saw there. My readers were enthusiastic, and I had packed auditoriums whenever I gave readings. As for the political bosses, they disliked me then, and they dislike me now.

JG A last question: what do you have to say on the topic "Russian émigré literature"?

VV I don't know what that is. There is simply Russian literature. I do, however, recognize that within the émigré community there can be a difference between Russian literature and literature simply written in Russian. I don't say that in a pejorative sense.

I am a Russian writer. I write in Russian, on Russian topics, and in the Russian spirit. I have a Russian world view.

The Aesthetes

3

Joseph Brodsky

Poet, translator, essayist (b. 1940). In 1964 Brodsky was arrested and sentenced to five years internal exile for "parasitism," but was eventually permitted to return to Leningrad after foreign and Soviet writers came to his defense. In 1972 he emigrated to the United States. In 1987 he received the Nobel Prize for literature.

Books: *Stikhotvoreniya i poemy* (Washington-New York, 1965); *Ostanovka v pustyne: Stikhotvoreniya i poemy* (New York, 1970); *Chast' rechi* (Ann Arbor, 1977); *Konets prekrasnoi epokhi* (Ann Arbor, 1977); *Rimskie elegii* (New York, 1982); *Novye stansy k Avguste* (Ann Arbor, 1983); and *Mramor* (Ann Arbor, 1984).

English translations: *Elegy to John*

?r Poems, trans. Nicholas Bethell (London: Longmans,
?oems, trans. George I. Kline (New York: Harper, 1973);
1 (New York: Farrar, Straus & Giroux, 1980); *Less Than
One: Selected Essays* (New York: Farrar, Straus & Giroux, 1986); *To
Urania* (New York: Farrar, Straus & Giroux, 1988); see also *Russian
Poetry: The Modern Period,* ed. John Glad and Daniel Weissbort (Iowa
City: University of Iowa Press, 1978), pp. 323–328.

College Park, Maryland, April 28, 1979

JG Joseph, you've been interviewed so many times that I'm
afraid this will just be a rehash.

JB Don't worry.

JG On the other hand I wouldn't want to miss anything
important. My first question is this: You've said that the Russian
poet Yevgeny Rein once advised you to keep your adjectives to
a minimum and concentrate on nouns, even if the verbs suffer
as a result. Do you follow his advice?

JB Yes, more or less. I'd say that's one of the most valuable
pieces of advice I've received over the span of my literary career. If, for example, we were to wrap a poem in some sort
of magical cloth which automatically removed the adjectives
when you unwrapped the cloth, you should still have a lot of
print on the page—verbs all over the place—but the adjectives,
for the most part, should be as few in number as possible.

You know, he taught me everything I knew in my early
period. He exercised an extremely powerful influence on everything I wrote at that time. To be blunt, he's about the only
person in the world whose opinion I take into consideration
today, albeit indirectly.

JG In the foreword to Marina Tsvetaeva's prose works you
wrote that all writers think hierarchically.

JB I was talking about artistic value, although artistic value
wasn't the only thing I had in mind. The fact is that every
writer, myself included, I suppose, rates other writers the way
the Tsarist government ranked civil servants, and over the
course of his life a writer changes his mind about who's up and
who's down, who's better, who's worse, and so on and so forth.
And all of that changes from time to time.

JG Poets at the top, prose writers at the bottom?

JB Well, that goes without saying. But I was really thinking of those authors who are closest and dearest to you. It seems to me that a writer—I guess I should say "I," since the one person I can talk about here is myself—a writer sets up his scale along the following lines: an author or an idea becomes more important than another author or another idea when that author embodies earlier authors or that idea embodies previous ideas and also leads to new ideas.

Everyone's thought process is, to some extent, hierarchical, since we've all been raised in one ideology or another, whatever its underlying principles may be. You end up with a sort of ladder with something at the top, be it God, King, or Country or what have you. Just dealing with the world on a day-to-day basis, a person sets up a certain hierarchy with, say, his boss at the top. Or if not his boss, then an idea which acts as his boss.

JG Does that include themes as well?

JB Themes—no. No, not at all.

JG In that preface you also wrote: "In the final analysis, all writers have the same goal: to overtake time, past or passing, and stop it."

JB Well, more or less, yes.

JG Straight out of Proust.

JB Of course.

JG I don't know if that's true of all writers, but it certainly applies to you. How do you explain that?

JB What really intrigues me more than anything else in the world—and always has intrigued me—is time and its effect on people, what it does to them, how it changes them, how it forms them. I mean the practical aspect of time as it runs through a person's life. But that's only one way of looking at it, I suppose, since time in the life of a person, and what it does to him and how it transforms him, is just a metaphor for what time does to space and what time does to the world. But the concept of time is so all-encompassing that I think it's best to stay away from it, or else we'll find ourselves in a blind alley. Literature is supposed to be about life. Writers are supposed to write about other people and how they interact with each other, and so on and so on. But none of that's really true; literature is not about life, because *life* is not about life. Life to one degree or another is about two categories: time and space. Kafka, for instance, worked exclusively with space, claustrophobic space and its effects. And then you have Proust, for example, and his claustrophobic version of time, if I can call it that. For me, at any rate, time is a much more intriguing and exciting category than space.

JG   I'd like once more to quote from your preface to the Tsvetaeva edition: "She [Tsvetaeva] did not intend her own isolation; it was forced on her from without by the logic of her language, by historical circumstances, and by the kind of people who were her contemporaries." It would seem that you were writing about your own isolation.

JB   I don't think I was writing so much about my own isolation as about hers. But all writers experience some degree of isolation. So that to a certain extent I was, of course, writing about myself. In fact Tsvetaeva's background and mine share some elements.

JG   Which exactly?

JB   Both of us have spent many years outside our homeland. Tsvetaeva was the greatest phenomenon Russian poetry has ever known, in my view, and the fact that we have this one experience in common alone justifies my existence.

JG   Do you feel any sort of gap between yourself and your audience?

JB   On the whole there is no such thing as contact with the audience. Even when you have a live audience in front of you, what you perceive to be contact is something of a false perception, since no matter what you write, people will hear something else. Or they will read into your words something of their own. Each person perceives what he sees through his own unique prism.

But when we talk about contact, I think what we have in mind is something a bit less complex. We mean the reaction of the reading public, the reaction which the author himself notices and interprets and responds to. Of course, this kind of contact may not be there. To tell the truth, I was never really interested in it, because all creative processes take place in and of themselves. In other words, their purpose is not to reach an audience or produce an instant reaction or to establish contact with the public, but rather—especially in literature—to produce an artifact of language and of your own aesthetic categories, a creation of that which language has taught you.

It's always more pleasant, of course, when the audience reacts by applauding and not by booing. But I think that both the reactions are inadequate, and it doesn't make much sense to depend on the public's reaction or to grieve over the lack of it. Aleksandr Sergeevich [Pushkin] once wrote, "You are your own tsar; go live your life alone on the road to freedom or wherever your free mind leads you." All that romantic language surrounds the kernel of a colossal idea: the only tête-à-tête a writer, especially a poet, has is with his language, with how he hears that language. The phrase "dictates of the muses" doesn't mean that the muses are dictating to you; it's the language, which at a certain level exists apart from your own volition. It's as simple as that.

JG   And that applies to other writers as well as yourself?

JB   To some extent. Strange as it may seem, a writer doesn't write for the public. Even the most well known public writers, the issue-oriented writers, don't really write to express their opinions; that's just their excuse for writing. What survives in literature is not what brings about improvement in society at large, but in the language, and that's all there is to it.

JG   Richard Sylvester has written about you: "Unlike the poets of the older generation, who came of age when Russia's high poetic culture was in bloom, Brodsky, born in 1940, grew up in a period when Russian poetry was in a state of chronic decline, and consequently he was forced to make his own way." There are two claims here: first, that there was a period of chronic decline and, second, that you did make your own way; but doesn't every poet do this? How do you feel about both these assertions?

JB   As far as the decline is concerned, that is true to some degree. You can't really talk of brilliant poetry in the 1940s and 1950s. Of course, there were some people who continued to write poetry. There were some wonderful poets. Akhmatova was still alive. Pasternak was still alive. But younger people like me had no idea of that. I remember when Rein offered to introduce me to Akhmatova, I was stunned that she was still alive. When we went to meet her, I really didn't know where we were going; I hadn't seriously read her work.

As for Pasternak, his name was somehow in the air. But maybe I just wasn't up to the task at that time; I don't know. I was at least twenty-four before I first read Pasternak intelligently.

Aside from Pasternak and Akhmatova, there were some remarkable people, Semyon Lipkin, for instance. But no one knew anything about them. Even Lipkin's closest relatives, if he had any, were totally in the dark. People wrote only for "the desk drawer." Tarkovsky was writing, but no one could read any of it. He didn't come out into the open until the late 1960s, and Lipkin is even more recent.

People such as my friends and myself knew very little about what was going on in poetry in our native land; neither, for that matter, did the rest of the world. So that in one sense Sylvester was being quite fair. What was coming out in print was absolute trash, too shameful even to mention—the sort of stuff you'd want to forget altogether.

As for making my own way, well, yes, that road was truly my own, although it was not so much a road as just feeling my way around blindfolded, picking up some things by ear, others by intuition. It was not a literary process. What we were doing—Yevgeny Rein, Anatoly Naiman, Dmitry Bobyshev, as well as Gleb Gorbovsky and Aleksandr Kushner—we were discovering poetics for the first time. In a certain sense this was a curious process; that is, not curious, but totally fascinating. We were rediscovering poetry. We weren't some offshoot movement or some later development or one element in a cultural process, least of all a literary process. We all came to literature, God only knows how, for all intents and purposes from the fact of our very existence, from life itself. Not as illiterate workers or peasants. We were more distant. We came to literature from a cultural and intellectual void. And the value of our generation lies in the fact that we carved out that road, if you want to put it that way. The word "road" is a slight exaggeration, although you could say that we at least beat a path, and at considerable risk to ourselves. We acted not only at risk, but on pure intuition, and—amazingly—intuition produced results not far removed from the sort of thing produced by the previous culture—before those historical literary links had been broken. That without a doubt says something about the human spirit.

JG Perhaps that, in part, has something to do with your tending to your own education, quitting school after the eighth grade.

JB Yes. I can say that now, looking back. When I left school, when my friends quit work or college and started in on poetics, the people we read—and we read a lot—we chose by instinct, by intuition. We had no feeling that we were continuing any sort of tradition, or that we had any mentors or spiritual fathers, or anything like that. We were, if not the black sheep of the family, then orphans. And it is a marvelous thing when an orphan begins to sing in his father's voice. For our generation it was something fantastic.

It was very difficult to get hold of the books of, say, Mandelstam or Akhmatova or Tsvetaeva, if you could get them at all. Although I had begun to write poetry more or less seriously when I was eighteen, nineteen, or twenty, I didn't read Mandelstam until I was twenty-three. And if you discover someone like Mandelstam, Tsvetaeva, or Akhmatova at twenty-three or twenty-four, and you've already made a beginning yourself, you don't perceive them as an influence on your work, but more as a sort of archaeological record. And they make an even stronger impression on you because you had no suspicion as to their existence. It's one thing if you grow up knowing who Mandelstam was. You have a general idea of what to expect; you have some notion of what you're going to find in his work. Otherwise you're guessing. It is as if you were using radar. You send out signals, and sometimes you get an echo, but more often you don't.

JG What about today's young writers?

JB God only knows. It's hard to say anything definite. They are lucky in that they can get hold of just about anything they need or anything that interests them. I wouldn't lump them all together, of course, since circumstances vary from person to person, and they could wind up just as isolated from cultural influences as we were, although it's hard to imagine that happening today.

JG Shortly after your arrival in the West, you said, and I'm quoting from memory, that you don't plan to "tar the gates of your homeland."

JB Yes, more or less.

JG Obviously, you were hoping to return.

JB No.

JG No?

JB No.

JG Have you now lost that hope?

JB Well, I never had it to begin with. That is, I would like to go back, but there is no hope of that. I didn't say what you quote with the intention of guaranteeing my return home. I just don't like that sort of thing, and I don't think I should be involved in it.

JG You have no desire . . . ?

JB To tar my homeland?

JG No, to go back.

JB Oh, of course I have a desire to go back. Why should that desire cease to exist? Over the years it hasn't faded. It's grown stronger, if anything.

JG You're a Russian poet but an American essayist. Does that bring on any measure of split personality? Do you think you are becoming less and less Russian?

JB That's not for me to say. As far as I'm concerned, in my inner self, inside, it feels quite natural. I think being a Russian poet and an American essayist is an ideal situation. It's all a matter of whether you have (a) the heart and (b) the brains to be able to do both. Sometimes I think I do. Sometimes I think I don't. Sometimes I think that one interferes with the other. Often, when I'm working on a poem and looking for a rhyme, I end up with English instead of Russian. You always have a lot of culls in this sort of production. How I end up paying this price doesn't really bother me.

Maybe I will become less Russian, but if I do, then that means my Russianness doesn't run very deep. On the whole I don't think that will happen, although it could. I just don't know. I still have the urge to write Russian poetry. I like what I'm doing, or perhaps I should say I *often* like what I'm doing. It's the process, not the result, that I find the most interesting.

As to whether I'm becoming less Russian or not, that's not for me to judge. Any definition of "Russianness" involves a narrowing of the Russian national consciousness, a sort of stylization. Russianness is a broader phenomenon. I think that if my Russianness is changing in any way, and maybe I'm flattering myself—it's not being diminished, but expanded.

JG In his article "The English Brodsky," Aleksei Losev writes: "Writers can have only one native language, a circumstance which is determined purely by geography. Even if you've learned two or more languages to perfection from childhood, there's only one world that's yours, only one linguistic cultural set of facts completely under your control. Everything else is foreign. A lifetime of study is not enough to rid you of your blunders." Do you agree with that?

JB That's absurd. Well, not absurd, but extremely high-handed and, I think I can say, provincial. It's not easy to find an example in Russian literature of a writer who has bridged two cultures. But bilingualism is the norm. Take Pushkin. . . .

JG But Pushkin was not known as a French poet.

JB He was not known as a French poet. But as a writer of letters he was no worse than his French contemporaries. For Pushkin and Turgenev two languages were the norm. It's just that due to all sorts of circumstances (over which we had no control) Russian poets have found themselves in a situation where they have no other choice but to insist on their ethnic identity. But the idea that a writer must be monolingual is something of an insult to both the individual writer and, I would say, to the human mind.

Look at the Europeans—the Dutch, the Germans, the English. For them to know two or three languages is perfectly normal. I know a lot of people who can write in more than one language. Poetry may be harder. Take Beckett. Take Joyce. Why should the Russians be inferior? I began writing essays in English for purely practical reasons. It's quicker. A magazine asks you for an essay or an article or a review, and I could write it in Russian and then have it translated, but that takes a lot more time, and a magazine usually has a tight deadline. That is the reason I started writing in English. And the fact that I'm a Russian poet and an English essayist is completely natural for me now. It's just like having two typewriters.

JG Would you like to become a bilingual poet?

JB No. I have no such ambitions. Although I'm perfectly capable of writing decent, readable poetry in English, to me it is a bit like a game. Like playing chess or building with blocks. Now that I come to think about it, I would say that the psychological processes that I go through when I write in Russian are often emotionally and acoustically identical to writing poetry in English. But I have no ambition to become another Nabokov or another Joseph Conrad. I simply don't have the time or energy or the narcissism. But I could easily imagine someone else like me writing poetry in both languages, in both English and Russian. I think that something like that is bound to happen sometime in the future. It's very likely that twenty or thirty or forty years from now there will be people for whom writing bilingually will be perfectly natural. It's a matter of perception. I perceive poetry, not as a certain story-line sequence, but as a reawakening of harmonic prosody. Then it becomes somewhat more difficult to write in a foreign language, but still possible. I've done it on a number of occasions just to prove to myself that I can do it, so that I wouldn't be bothered by it later.

JG How do you evolve as a poet?

JB I don't know how I evolve. I think the only way you can follow a poet's evolution is by his prosody, by his meters. Meter is perhaps the vessel or the reflection of a certain state of mind. Looking back at the first ten or fifteen years of my career, I think it would be accurate to say that I used more precise meters, such as iambic pentameter. This suggests a certain amount of illusion on my part or maybe just a desire or ability to place certain constraints on my language. Today I use a greater percentage of tonic verse, a lot more intonational verse, which, I believe, makes the language a bit more neutral, a bit more subtle. So switching from one meter to another or changing metric quality may provide some evidence of poetic evolution.

I'd say that if I can see any evolution in my own work then it's been an evolution away from a desire to neutralize the lyric element, to bring it closer to the sound made by a pendulum, that is, to have more pendulum than music.

JG Do you think that this departure from traditional meter will one day be accepted by Russian poets?

JB That's a matter of guesswork, and I'm not willing to make guesses. I think that what I do reflects my own evolution—if that doesn't sound pompous. But after all, my poetry is my life, my writing, my gospel, as it were.

JG Tell me about Akhmatova.

JB That's a long story. There is a lot to tell. It needs hours and hours, or it's not worth doing. It's very hard for me to talk about her because I'm unable to view her objectively—as apart from myself. I can't just say: All right, now I'm going to tell you about Akhmatova. Maybe I'm exaggerating, but I'd say she's an integral part of my being. This may sound somewhat cruel, but you somehow absorb the people you come into contact with, that is, those who are important to you. They become *you*. So I would not be talking about Akhmatova; I would be talking about myself. Everything I write, everything I say and do—all of that is Akhmatova.

I met her when I was just a kid, twenty-two or so. I had never seen anyone like her before. She was in a different league from anyone I'd ever known. She was an extraordinarily appealing woman, very tall. I don't remember exactly how tall, but taller than me. When we went walking, I tried to appear taller in order to avoid getting an inferiority complex. Looking at her you could understand why—as one German writer said—Russia has been ruled by empresses from time to time. She had a kind of imperial grandeur. And she was incredibly sharp-witted.

I was a barbarian in every sense of the word, culturally and spiritually. Most of the elements of Christian philosophy I may have today are due to her and my talks with her about religion. Just the fact that she had forgiven her enemies was the best possible lesson on the true meaning of Christianity, especially for a young person like me. Because of her I no longer take seriously my detractors, my enemies, even my former country, if you will.

We very rarely talked about poetry per se. She was translating then, and she would show us everything she wrote. I wasn't the only person who knew her well. There were four of us: Rein, Naiman, Bobyshev, and I—whom she called "the Enchanted Cupola." The Enchanted Cupola has since broken up, but in those days she would always show us her poetry and her translations. And at that time we had no particular feeling of awe. We weren't like little puppies begging on hind legs, accepting whatever she handed out. If we found this or that expression lacking, we would suggest improvements, and she would take our suggestions or not. We had a perfectly normal, direct friendship with her. Obviously we knew whom we were dealing with, but in no way did this affect our relationship.

In general, a poet by his very nature has to be unassuming. He has to be like a bird who will start singing, no matter what branch he lands on. Hierarchies don't exist for poets. I am not contradicting what I said earlier; I'm saying that to a poet, hierarchies of *people* don't exist. And our relationship was . . . well, I don't know what to say about it. That's a long story.

JG   Let's talk about your trial then.

JB   There's nothing to talk about. It was a zoo.

JG   All right, let's try a third topic—the influence of John Donne.

JB   That's nonsense.

JG   But you've written about that yourself.

JB   I did write a poem, a long elegy on John Donne, and he. . . . I read him for the first time, or I began to read him, at twenty-four or twenty-five, and naturally he left a big impression on me, certainly no less than Mandelstam or Tsvetaeva. But to talk about his "influence" would be to denigrate it. He did influence me. Naturally he influenced me, but then who am I that John Donne should have influenced me? You can't see it in my poems. At least I don't *think* you can see it. The thing I learned from Donne, more than from anyone else, was strophics. Donne, like most of the English poets, especially the Elizabethans—or the Renaissance poets, as the Russians call them—was very inventive in strophics. When I started writing poetry, the concept of "strophe" didn't really exist, if for no other reason, because there had been no cultural continuity. And consequently I became interested in the topic. Donne's was a very formalistic sort of influence, one that has more to do with a poem's structure than its content.

Donne is much more profound than I am. Besides, I don't think I could ever have become a dean in a cathedral like St. Paul's. He was much more perceptive than I. I think that almost all the English poets I've read have had some influence. Almost *anything* you read has some influence on you, and many times it's not only the *great* poets, but even the ones who are quite mediocre as well, because they show you what not to do.

Boris Khazanov

Pseudonym of Gennady Faibusovich, writer and essayist (b. 1927). Khazanov was arrested in 1949 for "anti-Soviet propaganda" and sentenced to imprisonment in a "corrective-labor camp." He completed medical school after release and was published both in the official Soviet press and in samizdat. Under pressure from the authorities, he emigrated in 1982 and settled in Munich, where he was an editor for the magazine *Strana i mir.*

Books: *Zapakh zvezd* (The Aroma of Stars) (Israel, 1977); *Idushchy po vode* (He Who Walks on Water) (Munich, 1985); *Ya voskresenie i zhizn'* (I Am the Resurrection and the Life) (New York, 1985); *Mif Rossiya* (Russia the Myth) (New York, 1986).

Munich, October 1988

JG Tell me about yourself, your arrest, the camp, and emigration.

BK I remember when I thought that thirty was old and fifty incredibly ancient. Now I'm sixty, which is older than my mother was when she died and almost as old as my father was at the time of his death. I was born in Leningrad and grew up in Moscow. I was still quite young when I started work in the post office. Later, I attended the university, where I studied Classics. All this was to influence my life. In my final year at the university I was arrested and spent six months in Moscow jails, first in the Lubyanka Prison, then in Butyrka.

JG When was that?

BK That was in 1949 and early 1950.

JG What were the charges?

BK I was convicted in absentia by a Special Commission, which sentenced me to eight years of prison on the basis of paragraph one of article 58.10—"Anti-Soviet Agitation and Propaganda." I was sent to Unzhlag, one of the biggest camps in the European part of Russia. I was paroled a little before the end of my term in 1955, thanks to the wave of rehabilitations under Khrushchev. That did not mean that the charges against me were dropped or that the sentence was rescinded. I was simply released, although I was not allowed to return to Moscow.

JG What were the conditions like in the camp?

BK As I said, it was a large camp with about seventy or eighty thousand prisoners. Since the camp was located in swampy taiga, the work consisted mostly of chopping down trees. An enormous amount of woodland was destroyed, and valuable timber was exported abroad. I can't really complain about my lot. Many people suffered much more than I did. My difficulties had to do with the fact that I was still young and "green." Later, when I was released, I did get to see something of real life, especially during the war. Although I had grown up in a poor family and lived in constrained circumstances, at first I found myself a sheep among wolves in the camp. The more so because I was in a criminal environment where there were very few educated people like me. In the eyes of the common people in Russia, to be an intellectual is an unforgivable sin. So, to make a long story short, it took me quite a while to make friends and grow the kind of thick skin I would need to survive. But things did take a turn for the better. At first, I had to do the same hard labor as everyone else. But then, because I was educated and had good handwriting, I was given lighter work.

JG Did you practice medicine in the camp?

BK No, at that time I still hadn't become interested in the subject. However, my subsequent decision to study medicine was motivated not only by interest, but by the belief, shared by most of the prisoners who were released at the time, that we would not be free for long. I was convinced that the thaw would pass and that we would find ourselves back in the more accustomed environment in which we had grown up. I was almost sure that I would be arrested again. This time, however, I would be better equipped, because I would know not only Latin and Greek, but medicine as well. If I could study for just two or three years in medical school, I could become a paramedic. In the camps being a paramedic puts you in an incomparably better position than being an ordinary prisoner. But since my passport had a mark in it that indicated my political "unreliability," it was hard to get into medical school. To the untrained eye, my passport was no different from anyone else's. But anyone working in the passport division of the local police would see the mark and know at once what it meant. In the Soviet Union there is a highly developed system of encoded marks. It's even used on library cards. That mark meant that I had one foot outside the law. All the same, I managed, with a few incidents along the way, to pass the exams and get into medical school.

I graduated from the Kalinin Medical Institute and, while still a student, started work as a doctor. Later I worked in a small town. Then I began to work for a samizdat journal and compromised myself by friendships with so-called dissidents. I myself was not a real dissident, since I was concerned with things literary, rather than political. My first book, *The Smell of Stars*, was published without my knowledge in Israel. After two searches and several visits to the Prosecutor's Office and the

KGB, all of my manuscripts, including an entire novel which I would later rewrite, were seized. It was then suggested to me that I should either leave the country or prepare for the worst. I had been under investigation for several years, so my actual departure from the country was not difficult. By the time we left, my wife and son had warmed up to the idea of emigration and were very anxious to leave. The last member of the family to accept the decision turned out to be me.

JG Why did you choose Germany? After all, your Jewish background is important to you. Germany would seem to be the last place you would choose.

BK Like everyone else who was leaving the country at the time, I couldn't imagine what my future would be. I didn't even really know where I would go. The main thing was to leave. The rest was up to fate. I would have loved to go to ancient Greece. But, unfortunately, there were no tickets to be had. That left us with two choices—Israel or West Germany.

The arguments for Israel don't require an explanation, but the choice of Germany really does need explaining. I had had a great deal of exposure to German language, literature, and philosophy, not to mention music. As a child I had studied German, and I spoke the language fairly well. I subsequently forgot it, but when I was fourteen or fifteen, during the wartime evacuation, I began to study the language again. It may seem strange that I was interested in German, especially in those days, when everything the language evoked was regarded with hatred. But that is the way it was. I had always had German books, and I had grown accustomed to the rarefied atmosphere of German culture. It holds something special for me.

JG Only German culture?

BK Yes.

JG Not French or English?

BK There was a French phase, but strange as it may seem, ever since the war, Germany was my first love. That's not to say that I closed my eyes to the fact that Germany was tainted with fascism. In Moscow I read a great deal more about that than most of my friends.

It is hard to describe the feeling I had when I got off the plane in Vienna. This may sound strange, but it was seeing signs written in German that affected me the most. It was as if I had landed in ancient Rome and seen signs written in Latin and heard people speaking the language. It was like realizing that the language of the great books—of Socrates, poets, and wise men—was real after all. That this was not a make-believe country like Borges's civilization of Tlön. I should add that my feelings for Germany, the constant feeling—or should I say constant illusion—of déjà vu always came through the prism of literature, history, or philosophy. Most Germans, as it turns out, have no consciousness of what, to me, is an extremely important fact—that they are the descendants of the great, eternal German republic. I know that all of this irritates my comrades who have suffered the same fate as I. But, what can I do? I really do have an affinity for Germany.

JG So, yours is a case not of dual, but triple identity.

BK I have always identified with more than one culture and have become accustomed to this way of thinking. I can't understand the attitude that you must have only one affiliation, that you must be either a Russian or a Jew, for example. I'm a Jew, but I consider myself a Russian intellectual. And I couldn't care less how those who proclaim themselves to be true Russians feel about that. I'm no less a Russian than they are. We all live— at least should try to live—in the great European community, because Europe is our common motherland. And that motherland encompasses Russia, Germany, and Greece, as well as Judea.

JG And how do you feel in Germany now?

BK I emigrated when I was over fifty. At that age it's ridiculous to deceive yourself into thinking that you can become completely assimilated, enter into that life, and feel at home. I feel like an outsider, but I am not unhappy with that kind of life. It is very interesting. I have many German friends and acquaintances. I have to say that Germans, who at the time I didn't know very well, were very helpful to my wife, my son, and me. We have to be thankful for that. And we have to be thankful to a country that gave us refuge and the opportunity to lead at least some kind of life.

JG You write in one of your articles that the Third Wave left Russia with the ideals of the 1960s. But we are now approaching the 1990s. Has anything changed in the culture or literature since that time? Is the émigré community a time capsule in which everything remains as it was? Or will it remain a cultural colony of Russia, as the New York émigré critics Pyotr Vail and Aleksandr Genis have suggested?

BK I can't shake the belief that we have exhausted the supply of ideas brought here by my generation of émigrés—the Third Wave. Perhaps that simply goes hand in hand with the demise of that generation's potential as a whole. Their ideas now sound banal. That goes for both the political views of Third-Wave émigrés and even more so for their literary views, as reflected in the statements and work of various writers.

JG Could you talk about those ideas in more concrete terms?

BK I'd like to limit my answer to literature as the expression of that wave of emigration. The Third Wave is multifaceted, of course. But if we limit ourselves to literature, then from the very beginning we see a certain core element of writers who were well-known and popular while still in the Soviet Union. Most of them are former Soviet writers, in that they had been members of the Soviet Writers' Union.

JG Give me some names.

BK Solzhenitsyn, Voinovich, Vladimov, Gladilin, Korzhavin, Maksimov, and, to a certain degree, Siniavsky. They all began their literary careers during the thaw of the 1950s and early 1960s, and many of their names appeared for the first time in *Novy Mir* or *Yunost'*—the journals that in those days set the tone. Nowadays, even if they are very diverse, all of those writers belong to the same school. Of course, writers like Solzhenitsyn, Maksimov, and others differ significantly from one another. But they share certain elements of world view. Not concrete convictions, but the approach they take to any literary endeavor—in other words, their literary credo.

JG Can you be more specific?

BK I'll need to think up a term for it. I don't want to say "Socialist Realism," because that term has already lost its meaning. It would be worth discussing Socialist Realism seriously, not so much in the political, as in the aesthetic sense. But let's put Socialist Realism on the back burner for now, and call the writers we have been discussing "Soviet Critical Realists."

These writers, who consider themselves public figures, form a new school of realism. They view literature—prose or poetry—as an artistic investigation of reality, where reality encompasses both the life of a particular individual and the life of the entire community at a given moment. For that reason their writing is very social minded. It's no coincidence that, while still in the Soviet Union, the writers I've mentioned were critics of the Soviet system and way of life. They wrote for the common people, that is, they wanted their work to be meaningful to a large number of people, including those with no literary background. These writers think, not without reason, that their work expresses the aspirations, hopes, and moods of the masses. They are interested in the common people, the peasants and the workers, who represent Soviet society. As a rule, they try to avoid introspection. Their prose is concerned with the real world and is based on the assumption that there exists some kind of single, uniform version of reality that we all must accept. The goal of such writers is to examine this reality and find in it some undiscovered truth. To them reality is what it is and nothing more. You could say that these writers shun intellectualism and refinement. They don't want to be the literary aristocracy. All this leaves its mark on their language and style.

JG   In other words it's a kind of primitivism?

BK   No, it's not primitivism in the least. I wouldn't want you to think that I am belittling that school. I could name several books that I hope will go down in the history of our literature. But in my view the potential of that school has been exhausted. It's on the wane, and a completely new and different kind of writing will develop in its place. Already, that generation of writers has run out of things to say. But I must add that many of the writers of that generation are extremely talented, and we can be proud of them. I love the work of both Voinovich and Siniavsky, although the latter is on the sidelines of that school. That's a different issue. I respect and even like Solzhenitsyn's work a great deal. But all of this is from an entirely professional standpoint. As writers, Solzhenitsyn and the others belong to the past. Perhaps this is purely biological. That generation is getting old. Naturally, we can't expect a rich, new wave of literature from émigrés. At the same time, we can see a different phenomenon in the émigré community that contradicts the writing we've been discussing. Take writers such as Gorenstein or Brodsky, who cannot even be called an émigré poet in the true sense.

JG Then what is Brodsky?

BK Brodsky is perhaps the only one of our writers, not only here, but in the Soviet Union as well, whom you could call a modernist poet. The other writers we've been talking about are all premodernists.

JG From what you've said, although I know you didn't want to sound negative, the writers you talked about earlier are of a lower quality. As I see it, a person with your outlook would say that the cream of Russian literature was destroyed—and it really was destroyed—and that a new, anti-intellectual, proletarian culture and literature, which were not as refined as they might be, rose up in its place. And you can't blame the writers for that, because they were deprived of what they would have gotten naturally if things had been normal. That might explain the lower quality.

BK I don't agree.

JG I don't claim it's true. I just want to understand your thoughts on this. I realize that you all have to live together and see one another on a regular basis. You yourself complained that there are no serious émigré critics. But stand in their shoes for a minute: how can they say what they really think when they know they are going out tonight and will mingle with the usual group of writers?

BK Literary progress is merely the substitution of one literary paradigm for another, that is, the substitution of underlying belief systems.

JG I don't find that kind of relativism in what you said previously.

BK Hold on. I don't consider the writers we talked about as being, in any way, inferior. But who would dare consider himself so great a writer that his work will still be read in twenty or fifty years?

JG The overwhelming majority of writers think precisely that.

BK You have to believe it, of course. Writing is an impossible occupation. If a writer doesn't have faith in himself, then what's the point of writing? The only support writers have is the fanatical belief that they can express with the pen something that has never been expressed before. But let's get back to our topic. The work of the writers we have been discussing doesn't satisfy me personally. I find it dull. I find Solzhenitsyn, for example, dull. Even though he is respected and known throughout the world and will leave an indelible stamp on literature, his work still bores me. I think that he's banal. The kind of literature which he so clearly represents—let's call it "Socialist Realism" for now—is alien to me. I've already said that I use the term "Socialist Realism" in an aesthetic sense, not a political or social one. I assume that one can be a Social Realist and an enemy of the Soviet state at the same time. The one doesn't exclude the other. It's a style of writing whose day has passed. After all, if what you have written about can be better expressed by a different medium, then, in literary terms, it's a fiasco. When you read that kind of literature you feel you could do without all the literary machinations—the made-up heroes, the story line, the "he said" and "she said." It might be better to simply write a history of the revolution.

JG Let's be still more concrete. Which works of "Socialist Realism" do you have in mind?

BK Vladimov's last novel about war. Maksimov's books. I should tell you that I don't know any of these writers personally. I haven't ever even laid eyes on Maksimov. But his work bores me to tears.

JG You said earlier that he's different from Solzhenitsyn.

BK As far as I can tell his interests differ from Solzhenitsyn's. He's more of a pamphleteer, with a penchant for satirical articles. He hasn't attempted to write any sweeping epics, although his last book was an historical—or quasi-historical—novel. But the two have a lot in common. The way they put words together is really quite similar. They both have that nationalistic language characteristic of the Russian literary tradition. They can be included in the same literary school. I think that has to do with a similar literary upbringing.

JG Does Zinoviev also belong to that school?

BK When I listed the "stars" of our literary skyscape, I didn't

mention him because Zinoviev is not an artist, and we are talking about artistic writing. Zinoviev is diverse and extremely
gifted, but he doesn't have the self-discipline that art demands.
And—this may sound strange, but I'll explain later—he doesn't
have the requisite quality of irresponsibility. You see, among the
principles upon which literature as an artistic endeavor is based
are self-discipline and irresponsibility. Self-discipline is the trait
that allows the writer to master a style, or a style to master him.
It is the constant labor over the word, phrase, and paragraph.
It's our inheritance from Flaubert. In that sense the word, or
style, is an end in itself. It's impossible to write without self-discipline. Without self-discipline one can write letters perhaps or
the kinds of books Zinoviev writes. The second principle is irresponsibility. Let me explain. In literature all subject matter is
simply the writer's material. If that is not so, then literature be-
trays itself. For example, I consider Voinovich a true artist, because he has that quality of irresponsibility. Solzhenitsyn's work
has lost this quality, although it used to have it. Maksimov's
work, of course, lacks it. For the most part it is also absent in
Vladimov's work. Irresponsibility is an attitude that treats all
material, no matter what, simply as subject matter, and nothing
more. We grew up in the school of nineteenth-century Russian
literary criticism, and we believed Belinsky when he said that
science was thought in concepts, whereas artistic endeavor was
thought in images. We also believed that literature was written
for reasons greater than itself, that it consciously and actively
served the people. It should serve the people, but this should
not be the writer's intention. What does serving the people
mean, anyway? We have grown accustomed to seeing literature
as a means of evaluating reality, be it political, social, moral, or
religious reality. Whereas, in fact, all those things—scientific
ideas, the personal life of the writer and those close to him,
philosophical problems, religion, the existence of God, the horrors we saw in the Soviet Union—literally all of that is simply
material. It's material for something very difficult to define in
simple terms. Thought in concepts is not barred to writers. Take
Borges, for example. I consider him a very interesting writer.

JG I could have predicted that. But you have contradicted
yourself.

BK Okay, let me have it.

JG In your article "Exile and the Kingdom" you write: "we should call the disease of free literature by its real name. It is the disease of thoughtlessness." You go on to say, "it is not capable of creating an all-embracing myth." That doesn't fit with what you just said. If subject matter is nothing more than material, how can we talk about the creation of myth?

BK I think it does fit, and I'll try to defend what I've said. But I want to stress that a strictly noncontradictory world view, a kind of axiomatic system, is not appropriate to this discussion. But I don't think that I have contradicted myself. Literature is not an artistic investigation of reality. Such an investigation would presuppose that reality is predictable and uniform. Literature is the negation of that. But when I said that literature is not responsible for creating anything except itself, I did not mean that it should become self-oppressive or imitate the avant-garde drivel or aim at the destruction of form or go in for what was once called "spontaneous composition," Gertrude Stein's famous brainchild. The writer takes reality apart, or more precisely, creates a prose world. This world is similar to the one that presents itself to our ordinary consciousness. But it is not the only world there is. Writers interpret what I call "myth." They create their own reality, from which readers can draw what interests them and, perhaps, even something that will be of use to them. They may recognize in the author's characters people similar to those whom they have known or may accept the author's picture of reality as a snapshot of social reality or of their personal lives. But the important thing is that this reality, together with scientific ideas, philosophical constructs, religious teachings, and the rest, is material that the writer is free to manipulate. In the same way, writers are not responsible even to themselves. Their own lives are also part of their material. That is what enabled Flaubert to say: "Madame Bovary, c'est moi!" Without a twinge of conscience he used his own life or the dreams and romanticism of his youth, his longing to be someone else, as the material from which he created a fictitious world. I don't mean that this world stands in opposition to reality. I am not an advocate of entirely fictitious literature or unrestrained fancy.

JG Then what about Borges, whom you just mentioned?

BK Borges's work is very subtly, but strictly structured. I mentioned Borges because he epitomizes Flaubert's ideal of steadfastness and utmost discipline. One should take a lesson from him.

JG But where do you find reality in his work?

BK Everywhere, or at least recognizable pieces of it. But at the same time you find things never encountered in reality. Borges writes stories which are based on atypical models of thought. He writes a kind of philosophical fantasy based on themes borrowed from classical and Chinese thinkers, church fathers, mystics, gnostics. He makes reference to almost everyone except Russian writers. But in his work you observe the kind of free treatment of material we've been talking about. Borges's material is of the kind I just mentioned—Pascal's reasoning on the sphere or principle of literary translation, how to recreate the world view of Cervantes's hero, and anything else you can imagine. He manipulates all of this very freely. And he doesn't try to force anything on his readers. He is not a preacher or history teacher who drills into his readers—as Solzhenitsyn does—the truth about the Revolution, what led to Russia's downfall, and why the great Russian Empire became the spoils of communism. Borges regards these facts, this so-called "absolute truth" that the writer supposedly reveals, as no more than his material. In that sense his stories are completely fictitious. His work has little to do with the so-called philosophical search for truth. Truth is the Holy Grail of philosophy, and history is the belief that you can reestablish events as they were and the conviction that you have really done that. That is what I meant by the principle of artistic irresponsibility.

JG Limonov was not among the authors you mentioned in that somewhat disparaging list, but I imagine you probably don't see much discipline in his work either.

BK Limonov is a very different genre. He's a naturalist. . . . I'm not opposed to such exercises, but . . . so you want to bring him up again?

JG It's the first time.

BK Yes, I'm sorry. Limonov. . . . You understand, Limonov is not without talent . . . but I'm not comfortable with his work.

Not because of his use of unmentionable words nor because of his cynicism or honesty—which is not typical of Russian literature—but because that kind of writing is so easy. It's the easiest path to take. Because of its accessibility, naturalism is a disease many go through, especially the young. They have the feeling that while other writers are hypocritical and cover life's awful truth with fig leaves, they will undress man and show their readers the naked truth. But in undressing man, you lose a part of him. As soon as you take man's clothes off, you have taken away part of his being. Clothing is part of his personality. But you may want to go even further and remove his skin, which leaves only the bare anatomy. Then you can remove his muscles, and you're left with only his skeleton. And that is no longer man at all. It is the paradox of naturalism. In striving to strip reality to the bare bones, it undresses a woman to her underwear to see what is hidden there. Yet we all know that an undressed woman works on the imagination in an entirely different way from a clothed one. Doesn't the charm lie in dressing in such a way as to seem undressed? Limonov's books impressed Russian readers who had never seen obscenities, descriptions of different ways of making love, or sentimental sexual imbeciles spread across the pages of Russian literature. But the real nature of the human spirit, which is after all the domain of literature, disappears in that kind of writing.

JG Royalties being small, émigré writers are forced to write so much that they have little time to rest and recover from their latest endeavors. The result is, if not monotony, a sort of repetitiveness.

BK I don't know if emigration is the cause of that. In the end, repetition and self-reference are the fate of many writers. Even great writers have been known to develop the same theme over and over again, caught in a circle of favorite plots and characters. The same can be said of many artists, who kept drawing the same face. But, of course, you're right. Perhaps the difficulty of émigré life—the constant need to earn money—leads one into a state of permanent frenzy which doesn't allow time to stop and think, much less for the well of ideas to fill up again. Writing doesn't pay much, but it can keep your head above water. But if you stop for a moment, you'll begin to think that you can't write anymore. You have to prove to yourself constantly that you can produce new work. There are some very prolific émigré writers who publish one book after another. Unfortunately it's usually trash, because they repeat themselves. Having written one successful book, they duplicate it endlessly. But I really shouldn't make any generalizations. Isn't the rhythm of the creative process—like sex—different for everybody?

JG But it's a forced march if you aren't allowed to rest.

BK If you're talking about the creative rhythm, then I have to agree. For those who were official writers in the Soviet Union, the conditions of work and life were incomparably better there. If a book makes it past all the censors—which they say aren't as active now—it brings in a good income. It guarantees the writer a comfortable way of life by Soviet standards for at least a year. Soviet writers don't work as hard as those in the West.

JG You wrote both in the Soviet Union and in the West, though your fiction wasn't published in the Soviet Union. Putting censorship aside, what has changed for you?

BK For the most part nothing has changed, since in the literary sense I had nothing to lose. These days no one comes to my apartment and confiscates my manuscripts. No one drags me off for interrogation. That, of course, is a great improvement. As for my world view, my impulses, and the problems I try to solve, I have changed, just as everyone does. My earlier work doesn't satisfy me anymore. I hope that I will be able to create something new. But my basic approach to writing, which is a very personal thing, has remained the same. I was a loner there, and I remain a loner here. Essentially I work in a vacuum. I can't say that I have either gained or lost readers. Nothing like that has happened. Unlike writers who could have supported themselves with their work in the Soviet Union, I had nothing to lose.

JG In his book *The Unnoticed Generation* Vladimir Varshavsky wrote about the so-called younger generation of the First Wave which consisted of people who, unlike Bunin and Merezhkovsky, had not managed to make a name for themselves in Russia. Do you feel that you are in a similar position?

BK I remember those pages well, especially the part dedicated to Boris Poplavsky. I can't say that I ever applied them to myself. You see, I never really felt that I belonged to any particular literary generation. I never felt there was anyone who thought as I did. I did not fit into any group. So Varshavsky's book describes an entirely different situation from mine or Fridrikh Gorenstein's—another émigré writer I rate very highly. I don't compare myself with him. We are opposites in many ways. Our situations are similar, however, in that neither of us belongs to a group. I have published several books, and from time to time I also publish articles. But I have no idea who, if anyone, reads what I write. Strangely enough, the German translations of my books have received the greatest response. But that is not the readership to whom I address my work. As I see it, each of us has an image of the idealized reader, although none of us can say to what extent that image corresponds to reality.

JG   The First Wave was large enough that some writers could exist on their royalties, albeit poorly. The literature of the Third Wave, however, is subsidized by all sorts of organizations, both government and private. They cannot be self-supporting, since they have a smaller reading public—a circumstance which may accentuate their feeling of isolation. Adamovich, for example, called his collection of articles *Loneliness and Freedom.* Do you think that the Third Wave is in a different situation than the First or Second Wave?

BK   There is a huge difference. First of all, the postrevolutionary literary émigrés were highly cultured and educated people who felt quite at home in Europe. Most of them knew other languages. Whether they considered themselves Slavophiles, patriots, cosmopolitans, or Westernizers, they had all been raised in the school of Russian Europeanism. It did not matter whether they were reactionaries or conservatives, leftists or liberals. And they brought with them not only the culture of the early part of this century, but certain literary aspirations which allowed them to turn literature into a kind of public work. Finally, they felt they had brought their country with them. The one they had left behind—the Soviet Union—was a new and different country which was alien to them. They literally believed themselves to be the saviors of Russian civilization.

JG The saviors or the grave-diggers?

BK That's a difficult question. The émigrés of the Third Wave grew up in the Soviet Union and don't feel completely cut off from it. However, many First-Wave émigrés think that the country has been taken over by aliens. The country is there, while they—the mere remnants or sparks of that country—are here. Recent émigrés do not feel that they have been chosen to bear the great inheritance of the Russian spirit and culture. Whether that is good or bad is another question. Perhaps it is good. Whichever it is, Third-Wave émigrés feel differently about themselves. For the most part their cultural luggage is fairly limited. I don't want—and don't have the right—to point the finger at anyone in particular, but the Third Wave is like an isolated offshoot. It is a group of people for whom Western Europe is not a land of sacred wonders, as it used to be called in Russia, but literally a foreign land. To them it is merely a bunch of foreign people who speak foreign tongues. The words, objects, and sacred passwords of European culture, which permeated our earlier literature, are alien to the majority of Third-Wave émigrés. Those things don't speak to them at all. This is the result of living in a large country that considers itself the center of the universe, when in reality it is a backwater. That explains why so few in the Soviet Union are willing to find out anything about the world that surrounds them or about the languages spoken there. Many continue to live in emigration as if they were on an island, associating only with those like themselves.

JG Are you telling me the First Wave didn't do that?

BK Not to that extent.

JG Nabokov, for example, wrote about that.

BK Well, perhaps you are right. If you read the history of the German émigrés of the 1920s and 1930s, you find they have more in common with today's Russian émigrés than we do with the First Wave of Russian émigrés. In other words, you see the same thing in the German émigrés as you do in our generation of Russian émigrés. They were concerned, just as we are, with their isolation in the world.

JG But during that time—1934 through 1945—only about 150 German writers left.

BK Yes, but they were the cream of German literature.

JG Yes, but in terms of numbers and continuity. . . .

BK I realize that they are not exactly the same. But the German antifascist emigration was similar in many ways to the Russian anti-Soviet emigration. It's entirely proper to call our generation of émigrés the "Third Wave." It was motivated for the most part by political considerations. These were people unable to live in the conditions created by the Soviet government.

JG If they have so much in common, how does the German emigration also differ from the Soviet?

BK In the same way that Germany differs from Russia. An émigré community is like a small portrait of the mother country. Émigrés carry the soil of their homeland on the heels of their shoes. They speak the language of the motherland and share its ways of thinking. Even though it considered itself an Eastern country in the West, Germany was European. Russia, as someone once said, is merely Europe's eastern shore. Russian literature always had different intentions, breathed a different air. I think that's obvious. If we limit ourselves to language, we see in Russian a completely different cultural psychology. Compare the disciplined, serious, energetic weightiness of the German phrase—the manliness of its syntax—with the capricious, whimsical femininity of Russian syntax.

JG In Thomas Mann's *Magic Mountain* one of the characters says that to the German ear Russian is a spineless language.

BK That was Claudia Chauchat. There is something to that. It has to do with formal aspects of Russian—its fluid word order and hyperbole—which compare with Latin and other ancient, archaic languages. German syntax is very strict. In a way, its rules shape the way you think, forcing your thoughts into strictly structured patterns. The grammar precedes your thoughts, dictating them. German syntax disciplines thought. The strict sequence of verbal forms resembles a locomotive, one wagon obediently following another in the dependent clause while the engine—the subject of the sentence—rushes forward. Compare that with the whimsical anarchy of the Russian phrase. Turgenev compared Herzen's language with a living body. When I think about Russian, what comes to mind is a plant winding its way up a wall.

JG And German is like a barrel hoop?

BK German is both austere and somewhat clumsy, like a knight in armor. Finally, it has an energy that Russian will never have. German has certain linguistic devices, particles that express movement, which give it an unusual kind of energy. It's no coincidence that it's the language of the military.

JG Let's go back to what you were calling "irresponsibility." Do you think that Russian literature has more of it than German literature?

BK A writer's irresponsibility, as I described it, is different from the permissiveness of a particular language. Yes, Russian weakens the magnetism of the writer. Russian is prone to pleonasm. With very few exceptions the best Russian writers have been verbose. But while nineteenth-century writers could allow themselves that luxury, it's no longer acceptable in the twentieth century. That's why I talked about discipline. There are pleonasms everywhere, and we don't even notice them. When we say, for instance, "a small cottage," the result is a pleonasm. Russian writers have to be doubly on guard because of the great danger of diluting the language. To some extent that danger is part of the free, uncontrolled nature of our language. That freedom must have constant limitations put on it. Only then is it of real value. True freedom through discipline is a rule formulated by Goethe. As far as Western languages go, that rule is less visible in German than it is in French, which has become withered and more dense, like dried fruit. There is no danger of dilution. French literature has managed to become more cultivated. Young French writers inherit certain rules within which they must work. Russian writers, at least at the beginning of their careers, can throw all restraint to the wind and jabber on. And they are still called writers.

JG Let's talk about the politics of the émigré community. I quote you: "Total restoration, Eastern Orthodoxy, autocracy, nationalism, reactionary politics. . . ." To whom does that refer?

BK That article was somewhat polemic and written in irritation. It refers to the right wing of the Russian émigré community. Even the earlier generation of Russian émigrés had a right wing which, as far as we can tell, set the tone. If I understand you, you want to know how I feel about the nationalistic right wing of the current Russian émigré community, whose standard bearer until recently was Solzhenitsyn. Solzhenitsyn's is, of course, the most outstanding name associated with that crowd. But Solzhenitsyn often contradicts himself. And that does not mean that he is in any way irresponsible. Many writers contradict themselves. Take the long interview he gave to Augstein, the publisher of *Der Spiegel*. It came out in German, so many Russian readers don't know about it.

JG He didn't have much to say much about literature; Augstein even warned about that in the beginning of the interview.

BK Apart from that interview, Solzhenitsyn has not made many recent political statements like his earlier sermons. It seems he has decided to concentrate his energy entirely on his work. We can also assume that, on the eve of the publication of his works in the Soviet Union, he is examining what's happening in that country. That has probably put him under some obligation and made him more circumspect. I've already talked a little bit about his prose. As for his political views and his nationalism, we know a lot from his earlier appearances, his many interviews, articles, and statements on various topics. I have to admit from the outset that his views are completely alien to me. But there are people in the Russian émigré community who are greater royalists than the king himself, that is, more to the right than even Solzhenitsyn. There's a journal that comes out in Munich called *Veche*. A circumspect description of it might be a conservative-monarchist journal. If we are honest we should say it's monarchal-fascist. It is a product of the Russian émigré far right. The paradox is that it comes out in Germany, where nationalism, chauvinism, and fascism have been completely wiped out. The publishers of *Veche* are lucky that the Bavarian police are not interested in Russian literature and journalism, or else they would have been fined for a number of things. As one might expect, the cultural, linguistic, and literary level of *Veche* is quite low. The Russian is awful, as is often true of patriotically bellicose people. To be honest, I'd rather not talk about it any more.

JG *Golos zarubezhiya* (The Voice Abroad) is also published in Munich.

BK Yes, I know of it. Our editorial board subscribes to it. We even had the impression that to some extent it owes its come-back to us, since we are its constant target and source of nationalistic inspiration. But as far as I can tell, it has none of the anti-Semitism that is characteristic of Russian chauvinism and the Russian world view.

Anti-Semitism is the constant theme of *Veche.* It would be strange not to find anti-Semitism in *Veche.* I myself can't complain of being ignored by that part of the Russian émigré community. I'm not talking about my fiction, but about books like *Russia the Myth* or articles I've written on similar topics—my essay writing. Leaders of the Russian patriotic camp have written at length on some of my pieces. I have even earned myself the reputation of a Russophobe. I'm a Jew without a country, who doesn't understand the sources of Russian life and who has the audacity to chip away at all that is sacred to Russians. In other words, not only do I belong to neither the Russian ethnic nor literary tradition, but I hate everything Russian as well. It's hard to respond to that kind of criticism—if it can even be called criticism—because it's based on emotions. And to fight emotion with emotion is hopeless. All I can say is that I couldn't care less whether people like that—whose criticism is nothing more than abuse—consider me to be Russian or not. It doesn't make me change my mind. I've already said that I am both a Jew and a Russian intellectual. For me there is nothing contradictory in those two terms. Such a synthesis seems very natural to me. It's even fairly traditional.

JG You are one of the editors of the journal *Strana i mir* (The Country and the World), together with Kronid Lyubarsky. The journal seems to be distributed rather than bought and sold. For the most part this circulation takes place among Soviet readers, who can't respond . . .

BK . . . or pay for it.

JG Aren't you just casting into the ocean a bottle which will never come back?

BK Yes. The journal is distributed primarily in the Soviet Union, where we believe our main readership to be. We may be casting a bottle into the ocean, but we do get feedback, and fairly often. We even know who is getting our journal. We know that *Strana i mir* is kept in the special book repository of the Lenin Library, where it is read zealously by various people with access to that repository. We get letters as well as oral feedback. Our mailbox used to overflow with response. Now we receive even more material from the Soviet Union, as well as articles that have been written especially for our journal.

JG If the Soviet press is now full of what by Soviet standards are radical articles, why do people still read the émigré press?

BK We have asked ourselves that question. The émigré press is now faced with the unusual problem of competition from the Soviet press. Many issues of *Literaturnaya gazeta* (The Literary Gazette) and other publications openly discuss things that were previously monopolized by the Russian free press. Quite often these topics are treated so thoroughly, so openly, and with such talent and wit that nothing remains to be added. By comparison, the kind of revelation that the free émigré press has specialized in seems trite at best, at worst childish nonsense. Our journal has not remained untouched by this unusual competition. But we seem to be handling it. As far as we can tell, interest in our publication has not dropped off. On the contrary, it seems to be growing. Part of the explanation is that our journal is not a rabid anti-Soviet publication. It goes without saying that we are opposed to the Soviet regime. But we are not as fixated or categorical as other émigré journals. We try to use an analytical approach to what is now happening in the Soviet Union.

JG Some see your journal as being pro-Gorbachev.

BK I wouldn't put it quite that way, although the journal is broadly sympathetic to *perestroika*.

JB But that is a very strange position. An exile journal that sees its goal as supporting the Soviet government.

BK That never was and never could be our goal. Of course we don't support the Soviet government in the political or social sense. That would indeed be strange.

JG But you support the policies of the head of that government.

BK We sympathize with what we believe deserves sympathy, approval, and encouragement. On the other hand anyone who reads our journal knows that we criticize Gorbachev and the people that surround him. Many of our issues are devoted to an analysis of Gorbachev's contradictions and inconsistencies. Of course our journal seems more tolerant than other émigré journals, which completely refute *perestroika, glasnost,* and everything else in the Soviet Union. Moreover, we do not share the well known and respected premise that Russia is one thing and the Soviet Union something entirely different. We do not support the thesis that Soviet power, communism, the regime, or anything else was forced on Russia from without. I feel that such a view is too facile. It is easy to claim that the country was enslaved by the Bolsheviks, foreign influence, or anything else of that sort. But things are more complicated than that. That kind of thinking, which reduces everything to a common denominator and repudiates anything that contradicts it, has never appealed to me. Our position manifests a certain lack of principle, if you can call it that. I think that we—those living in the twentieth century—should have a more comprehensive vision. That applies to artistic thought more than anything else. We must always remember that there is a multitude of possible ways of looking at anything. As for the journal, it goes without saying that we do not accept communism. Any decent human being is anticommunist. What else can you say? We all think that way, and to brag about it is ridiculous.

JG Let's go back to our writers. Before we began this interview we were talking about Joseph Brodsky. You spoke of the influence exercised on him by a sense of group-belonging.

BK I consider myself a fan of Brodsky's, and my admiration for his work goes way back. Brodsky is perhaps the only postmodernist—as I understand that word—in contemporary Russian literature. To try to define postmodernism is to get lost in a maze. There are as many definitions of that term as there are people who have defined it.

You mentioned "group-belongingness." I used that word not with regard to his poetry, but with regard to certain of his views on literature and on poets—those he accepts and those he rejects. But none of that has to do with his poetry. I have several interviews in mind, one of which was published in our journal. It seemed to me that his preferences in poets bore the imprint of the group of poets that he mixed with in his youth. I think that Brodsky is the first and, perhaps, the only major poet in Russian literature who is not a lyric poet. That's an important point because it leaves its mask on all of his work. The lyric tradition is alien to Brodsky, perhaps even anathema. Many readers censure him for this. It was for this reason that someone accused him of not caring about others, of being a misanthrope. He really does lack the emotional response to the minute events of man's inner and outer world characteristic of the lyric poet. That explains his dislike of Blok and the lyric trend in Russian poetry on the whole. Brodsky represents a different branch of Russian poetry. He is the heir of the acmeists, who, in general terms, discarded the lyric tradition. Lyricism is alien to Brodsky. He is an essayist-poet—but in a special sense.

Before I continue, we should agree on what we call essayism. Essayism is a certain way of looking at the world. Although, for the most part, Brodsky is oriented toward Anglo-American culture, he reminds me of a certain figure in German literature, albeit a prose writer. I have Gottfried Benn in mind—Benn the essayist, not the poet. It's impossible to translate any of Benn's essays into Russian or even to retell their content. Something similar is true of Brodsky, whose work is not easily memorized. And the fault for this, or the reason—I don't consider it a fault, although for many it is a sign of something antipoetic—lies in the complexity of his syntax and his endless enjambments.

JG That's part of his intentional prosiness.

BK No, it's something different, and it contributes to the originality of Brodsky's poetic thought, which is saturated with external elements. It is the complex vision of a man who observes reality from several angles simultaneously, a man who makes wide use of word play and who tries to allow for associations at the level of language, culture, history, the lore of the forced-labor camps, and the like. For him this is not a game at all, but a means of absorbing reality. Whether that reality is imaginary or the "real" thing is a different question. This is the origin of the complexity and multifacetedness of his language, both of which are characteristic of the postmodernist tradition.

It is the source of his baroqueness. Of his semantic flourishes. Finally, it is the source of Brodsky's complexity of syntax, tamed only by his strict observance of the strophe. It's no coincidence that his syntax goes hand in hand with a strict, strophic division of verse, without which his poetry would become a dense, impassable forest. Strophics blaze a trail through that forest, allowing the reader to move forward. And that complexity of perception is a great victory, for few have achieved that effect in verse. Normally it is considered the domain of prose. In your interview with him he made a wonderful off-the-cuff comment to the effect that prose is second-rate literature—compared to poetry. Of course, it wasn't a serious comment and isn't true. No one knows what should be considered first or second class. But it's typical that Brodsky's main poetic strength comes from prose.

Brodsky has managed to convey a quality peculiar to modern man—an internal rigidity in the midst of a fleeting and incredibly complex world. His poems constantly convey the image of a stunned person sitting in the midst of things, sounds, sparks, and the play of light and shadow. For example, in one poem he describes a man sitting in the dark on a hot night. He's taking everything in—the sound of music, patches of light. He discerns a huge number of details which in their turn lead him to reminisce. But in the midst of all that he himself has become frozen, numb. For many that kind of inner numbness is a sign of a poet's inner lack of warmth, of an icy soul. But it, too, is characteristic of modern man. Thanks to this inner immobility, modern man, oppressed by colossal amounts of information, manages to preserve his individuality. This quality of Brodsky's can't be found in any other contemporary Russian poet.

Brodsky—or those who write about him—likes to emphasize the importance to his work of English metaphysical poetry. That, in my view, is dubious. In any case Brodsky's poetry is not metaphysical at all. A metaphysical poet can't be ironic, and irony is Brodsky's way of finding a common language with the world. It's like the ravings of a psychologically ill person—it's his way of staying in contact with the world.

JG Earlier you praised Gorenstein. Could you talk a little more about him?

BK As a writer Gorenstein is out there on his own. He doesn't belong to the "thaw" generation and was practically unknown as a writer while in the Soviet Union. He was known as an author of screenplays. One of his stories was published in the Soviet Union. As a writer he seems to have blossomed in emigration. But "blossomed" is the wrong word for Gorenstein. He works in isolation, and as far as I know his work isn't reviewed much. I would rate him probably among the best émigré writers, although he doesn't adhere to any of the literary principles that I have adopted for myself. He is a highly undisciplined writer. He is extremely wordy and inclined to a kind of gloomy philosophizing, although I have to admit that that's one of the things about his work that attracts me. Perhaps you've noticed that his heroes tend to philosophize a lot. But, before your very eyes, that philosophizing imperceptibly turns into authorial speech. This brings us to an important issue concerning Gorenstein in particular, and literature on the whole— the issue of the relationship between the author and his characters. It's not always easy to tell where the author ends and where a character begins, or where one character ends and another begins. For each of these figures there exists a certain time frame. There's the time frame of the person sitting at the table and writing, the time frame of the author within the work, and finally the time frame of the characters. Reading Gorenstein makes you start thinking about this issue. The other authors we've talked about don't examine these kinds of issues and don't make us think about them. For them time is not an issue. They limit themselves to the Newtonian concept of time and to a uniform version of reality. Gorenstein is not like that. One other thing about Gorenstein: although he is interested in religious and philosophical issues, they are material for him, rather than an end in itself.

JG What do you have to say about Siniavsky?

BK I think that Siniavsky is one of the most talented writers in the émigré community. I am talking about Abram Terts (Siniavsky's pseudonym). That is Siniavsky the prose writer, not Siniavsky the literary critic, although the latter is also interesting and talented. Siniavsky's prose is not really my cup of tea, and I can't say that I am an unconditional fan of all his work. He is an uneven writer. However, writers should be judged on the basis of their best work. Siniavsky is a true aesthete, something rarely found in Russian literature as a whole, let alone in our generation. He would sell his mother into slavery for a good turn of phrase. He is deeply, well if not amoral—that's too strong a word—then immoral. In that sense he belongs to the century that seems to attract his attention the most. Flaubert once wrote something that is extremely applicable to Siniavsky. I'm quoting from memory so that this is more of a paraphrase than a direct quotation: if everything that happens to you and those around you is of value to you only as material for your literary work, then write away, for you have matured as a writer.

JG How about Voinovich?

BK Voinovich wins the reader over with an unusual harmony and beauty of style, with the transparent watercolor quality of his language. Not to mention his wonderful sense of humor, something that is rarely encountered in the émigré community. Just recalling a Voinovich character or one of his many elegantly crafted little sentences, turns of phrase, or observations is enough to bring a smile to your face. Compared to the other writers we've been discussing, he is at one with himself, and that explains the harmoniousness of his prose. From his language you can learn about phrasal beauty and affinity for the word. His best work remains *Chonkin*. He is a master of the short story. But, like the others, Voinovich is a completely different kind of writer from me. The problems that interest me evidently don't exist for him or don't interest him. He is basically a realistic writer, a believer in reality.

JG And you disagree with that?

BK I believe that reality is created by the writer, not described by him.

JG We haven't touched upon the older émigrés as much as I would have liked, for example, Merezhkovsky.

BK Merezhkovsky awakens emotional recollections. I read several of his books in a kind of intoxicated state when I was fifteen or sixteen. I'm talking about his philosophical religious treatises, not his novels. His novels made very little impression on me. They are mediocre. But since then I have moved in a different direction, and I don't think I would now have the patience to reread any of his work.

JG How about Nabokov?

BK Nabokov is in fashion these days. It's hard to find a name that is more bandied about. I find it difficult to come up with any simple formulation about Nabokov. At least two of his books delighted me—*Speak, Memory* and *The Defense.*

JG How about *Invitation to a Beheading?*

BK *Invitation to a Beheading* is a very interesting book, but. . . . This might be heresy, but I just don't consider Nabokov to be a great writer. One doesn't say of great writers that they are "talented." It would be strange to say that Pushkin was a "talented" writer. Talent isn't a category that we discuss when talking about great writers. One doesn't say that Tolstoy or Aristophanes or Musil was "talented." But Nabokov was talented, in the way that God would be talented if he weren't God. Nabokov was incredibly talented.

JG But not a genius?

BK He isn't a great writer, perhaps because he consciously set the concept of the "idea" aside.

Andrei Siniavsky and
Maria Rozanova

Siniavsky: literary critic and prose writer
(b. 1925); Rozanova: editor, wife of Siniavsky (b. 1930). After having published a series of stories and essays
abroad under the pseudonym "Abram
Terts," Siniavsky was arrested in 1965,
together with Yuly Daniel (pseudonym:
Daniil Arzhak), and imprisoned in a
forced-labor camp until 1971. In 1973
Siniavsky and Rozanova were permitted
to emigrate to the West. Siniavsky was
appointed professor of Russian literature at the Sorbonne, and Rozanova
founded the magazine *Sintaksis*. Siniavsky was not stripped of Soviet citizenship. In 1989 a book on his trial was pub-

lished in Moscow: *The Price of a Metaphor: The Crime and Punishment of Daniel and Siniavsky.*

Books by Siniavsky: *Sud idet* (Munich, 1960); *Fantasticheskie povesti* (Paris, 1961); *Liubimov* (Washington, 1964); *Mysli vrasplokh* (New York, 1966); *Fantastichesky mir Abrama Tertsa* (New York, 1970); *Golos iz khora* (London, 1973); *Progulki s Pushkinym* (London, 1973); *V teni Gogolya* (London, 1975); *Kroshka Tsores* (Paris, 1980); *Opavshie listya Rozanova* (Paris, 1982); and *Spokoynoi nochi* (Paris, 1984).

English translations: *Fantastic Stories* (Abram Terts), trans. Manya Harari (Evanston, Ill.: Northwestern University Press, 1963); *The Makepeace Experiment*, trans. Manya Harari (New York: Collins, 1977; originally published by Fontana Books, 1965); *On Trial: The Soviet State vs. Abram Terts and Nikolai Arzhak*, trans. Max Hayward and Leopold Labedz (New York: Harper, 1967); *For Freedom of Thought and Imagination*, trans. Laszlo Tikos and Murray Deppard (New York: Holt, 1971); *Unguarded Thoughts*, trans. Manya Harari (London: Harvill, 1972); *A Voice from the Chorus*, trans. Kyril Fitz-Lyon and Max Hayward (New York: Farrar, Straus & Giroux, 1976); *The Trial Begins*, trans. Max Hayward (Los Angeles: University of California Press, 1982); *On Socialist Realism*, trans. George Dennis (Los Angeles: University of California Press, 1982); and *Good Night* (written under the pseudonym Abram Tertz, New York: Viking, 1989).

———

College Park, Maryland, May 1983

JG I have many questions for you, Andrei Donatovich, and I don't know where to begin. I once asked Aksyonov what questions I should ask you, and he said, "Ask him why he shaves so poorly." (Siniavsky, who wears a beard, laughs.)

Let me start by asking you how you view contemporary Russian literature.

AS For the most part, favorably. Of course, I'm going on my own background, as anyone must, and for me that background was the Stalinist era, when it seemed that Russian literature had perished forever. Now, as it turns out, it did not perish. It continues to develop, albeit under very trying circumstances, but nevertheless with rather varied and interesting results, even in Russia today. And *now* Russian literature has had the chance to move abroad. So while I can't say I'm ecstatic, I'd have to admit that for the most part things aren't bad at all.

JG What if we compare modern Russian literature to Western European literature?

AS Well, I think Western European literature is probably somewhat more varied in form. But it seems to me that the Russians have brought in a number of important twists in both theme and form—the theme of the prison camp, in particular. The camp theme is not just a litany of endless suffering, although it may sometimes seem that way. The camp is also a world unto itself, a sort of microcosm that has its own twists and turns. And people like Shalamov, Solzhenitsyn or, say, Yevgenia Ginzburg provide extremely interesting accounts that not only illustrate the Russian national character, but apply to humanity in general.

JG What if we compare current Russian literature to that of the beginning of the twentieth century?

AS The beginning of the twentieth century was a flowering of Russian literature. It's my favorite period. But over the subsequent thirty or forty years the bridges connecting modern literature with the literature of that time were burned. And it is the rebuilding of those bridges that I myself see as one of the main tasks set before me.

JG I'm struck by how poorly informed new émigrés from the Soviet Union—writers, critics—are about earlier émigré literature, of the period between the two world wars, especially.

AS That's understandable. It's only fairly recently that émigré literature began to make its way into Russia. For a long time people didn't know anything about it at all. They might have heard mention of names like Nabokov or Bunin, but they hadn't read them. It's only now that people are becoming acquainted with émigré literature. When I first came into contact with the current émigrés, it seemed to me that aesthetically they were incredibly far behind the *beginning* of the twentieth century—somewhere back in the 1880s. Sometimes émigrés come to my lectures, and they don't understand a single thing, especially when I'm talking about poetry. Even Blok is beyond them; he's too hard. He's a lot easier for the French students.

JG Easier for French students than for Russian émigrés?

AS Yes. These émigrés, kindly old folks that they are, find it all very strange. It's as if they're still living in the presymbolist

age, not to mention later developments like the work of Mayakovsky, Khlebnikov, Pasternak.

JG Well, the nineteenth-century classical tradition of Russian literature remains very strong among émigrés, even today.
Writers like Solzhenitsyn and Maksimov seem to belong to an
earlier era.

AS Certainly. If we limit ourselves to realism, we might
ascribe two directions to the nineteenth-century literary tradition. For the sake of simplicity let's stick to prose. First, there is
what we could call a straight realistic sort of prose along the
lines of people like Turgenev, Lev Tolstoy, and Chekhov. That
tradition has turned out to be the stronger one, even today. The
other, to which I am much closer in spirit, I would call "exaggerated" prose: Gogol, Dostoevsky, Leskov. . . . It leads up to the
modernist literature at the start of the twentieth century—
Andrei Bely, for instance. In the early 1920s Russian prose takes
a very interesting turn and then stops dead.

Twentieth-century Russian poetry fared better than prose.
Poetry had developed earlier; it had already bloomed in a most
remarkable way. I think that, measured historically, twentieth-
century Russian poetry has turned out to be one of the oases of
world culture. Poetry was clearly ahead of the other art forms
of that time—along with painting. Prose lagged behind. And
then, just as modernist writing had begun to appear, prose was
put into the deep freeze.

Now, we do have some marvelous writers, whom I love—
Soviet writers of the 1920s, like Babel, Zoshchenko, Zamyatin,
and Bulgakov. But the literature wasn't allowed to develop
further. "Exaggerated" prose vanished in the Stalin era. I feel a
personal bond with *that* literary tradition and also with early
twentieth-century Russian poetry in the sense that Russian
prose at the beginning of the twentieth century developed
some of the principles discovered by its poetry. I don't mean
that the prose was poetry rewritten, but that attempts were
made to seek out analogous devices. That's where that condensed style comes from. Prose writing had achieved that same
condensed style you see in poetry, and then it disappeared. So
for me the connection between that early prose and the poetry
at the beginning of the century are very important.

JG Early Pasternak is clearly a part of that tradition, but what about the later Pasternak, after 1940?

AS The later Pasternak can't be included, although he did retain something from his earlier years. While I'm not all that fond of *Doctor Zhivago* as a work of prose, some of the nature descriptions and the attempts to describe the totality of history itself through the use of landscapes hearken back to *My Sister, Life,* even if the writing is more harmonious.

JG Let's talk about Slavophiles and Westernizers—Solzhenitsyn and Siniavsky.

AS I can, of course, only give my own feelings on the matter. Solzhenitsyn today has become the standard-bearer of Russian nationalism. Some nationalists, however, are more moderate than Solzhenitsyn, others more extreme. These try to stress Solzhenitsyn's more nationalistic views, some even criticizing him for being *too* liberal and *too* democratic. Nevertheless, because it has flared up so suddenly, Russian nationalism has become a serious and interesting phenomenon. There are so many aspects to the question, so many developments, so many different directions and so many journals. For example, in his letter to President Carter, Solzhenitsyn warns about the dangers of "Russophobia."

JG There are some who would put you in that category.

AS Oh, certainly. And without a moment's hesitation, from what I hear. On one occasion he even called me "Siniavsky, that famous Russia-hater."

JG Solzhenitsyn said that?

AS Yes, Solzhenitsyn. In his view of things the Russia-haters include the American public, American financial circles, even certain generals who dream of annihilating the Russian people, regardless of whether Russia is communist or not. They all hate Russia. And so do the dissidents, of course. Overall, you've got quite a few people there: the intelligentsia of the Soviet Union, the Jews, of course, and myself—all in one big happy family of Russophobes.

Solzhenitsyn is relentless in introducing his concept of an enemy, largely mythical, who has Russia surrounded. On the one hand, you have the Communists (they're also Russophobes as far as Solzhenitsyn is concerned). Then the Ameri-

ssophobes, and the "Yids" are Russophobes, and
uals are Russophobes, and the West is also some-
hobic. As I see things, this is just a new slant of the
"capitalists-have-us-surrounded" line. And that's very dangerous because it does to some extent parallel the official ideology.

The Russian people don't need to be told again that they're
surrounded by enemies; it's been drummed into our heads
enough already. Our enemies are everywhere. The Americans
are our enemies. Then Solzhenitsyn adds his contribution.
For him, instead of communism and the Soviet Union being
surrounded, it's: "Russia and we the Russian people are surrounded!" Then we have the more militant Russian nationalists
who support Solzhenitsyn.

JG For example?

AS The émigré journal *Veche*, which puts forth some, well,
even fascist notions—mainly of a socialist nature.

JG What do you think of the editorship of *Veche*?

AS His name is Yevgeny Vagin. There's a second editor, but I
forget who. But Yevgeny Vagin I know well. I spent two months
with him in a labor camp.

Then there's Shimanov, for example, who criticizes Solzhenitsyn from the right. He believes Solzhenitsyn is too much of a
democrat and that indeed the only thing wrong with the Soviet
regime is its ideology. All you have to do to assure world
salvation is to change the facade, replace Marxism with Russian
Orthodoxy—but keep the police state apparatus and the repression and then wait for the Russian Orthodox conquest of
the world. That's his view. Shimanov criticizes Solzhenitsyn for
wanting to give too much freedom to the nationalities within
the Russian Empire—national groups that want to break away.
He even goes so far as to say that the Russian Empire of modern
times represents something of a "mystical phenomenon" and
"humanity itself in miniature," as he puts it, led by the Russian
people—a proto-symbol of the future of mankind as a whole.

So you see, those are some of the fantasies, the new utopias,
which present a danger to society. Perhaps they're not so much
dangerous as simply bad for Russian culture. It's nationalism
that sets off the old drum-rolling patriotic battle cry, and off into
combat they go, anti-Westernizers fighting some mythical en-

emy. But the trouble is that anti-Westernizing for Russia in its current state is tantamount to anticulture.

JG What about Maksimov? Where does he fit into this scheme?

AS Unlike Solzhenitsyn, Maksimov has no set program. His thinking is closer to that nationalistic extreme, although he changes with the prevailing wind. Solzhenitsyn is a theoretician, an ideologue. . . . Furthermore his ideas aren't about to change. Maksimov, on the other hand, is more of an organizer for whom organizational hierarchy is very important. He has to be in charge. So Maksimov has turned himself into the organizer of a sort of émigré mafia—if you'll forgive me for saying so—a mafia based on money, threats, and also some warm feelings to give Russian émigrés someone to rally around. That's why Maksimov is given to threats and foul language in his writing and to buying off people and ideas. So that any argument I may have with Maksimov is on a local scale, rather than the wide historical plane which characterizes my disagreements with Solzhenitsyn.

JG Leaving Solzhenitsyn's political views aside, what would you say about him as a writer?

AS I very much like *One Day in the Life of Ivan Denisovich*. In my opinion it's his best work, and that may be Solzhenitsyn's undoing—that his first work turned out to be his best. And that's always hard. Artistically speaking, he does have some other good things. But the works I consider to be the best are *One Day in the Life of Ivan Denisovich* and, of course,—although it's not a work of fiction—*The Gulag Archipelago*.

JG What about *Cancer Ward* and *The First Circle*?

AS *Cancer Ward* is not bad. *The First Circle*, I think, is a bit weak. But I may be being subjective, since with the exception of *A Day in the Life of Ivan Denisovich*, where everything takes place in the space of a day, there are times when I find all this realism boring. In his later major works, like *August 1914*, there are a number of places where you can see the old-fashioned realistic tradition intertwined with an insistent preaching in an attempt to rewrite history. And as a result he really has to strain, sometimes quite a bit, and this can be particularly grating on a realistic style of narrative. While presenting prerevolutionary

Russia as a wonderful, even ideal country, Solzhenitsyn clearly sees that this Russia is hurtling into the abyss. That is where you start to see certain slips in logic. So I don't like *August,* except perhaps for the scene where Samsonov commits suicide. The rest is not my style.

Now, *Cancer Ward* is a good novel. I don't think that by saying so I'm contradicting myself in any way. I have nothing against traditional realism. Let it live long and prosper. God grant it health and good fortune. It's just that personally I can't relate to it. It leaves me cold. But I'm much more troubled by Solzhenitsyn's writing on public issues. It's his right, of course, to express those views if he wants. It's just that it becomes a matter for public concern.

JG Nabokov writes in his memoirs that in the 1920s and 1930s he and other émigrés in the West had all the everyday conveniences that other Western Europeans had, but for the most part they lived in isolation, maintaining their own separate kind of lifestyle. How long have you now been in France?

AS It'll soon be ten years.

JG And you don't speak French, do you?

AS Poorly.

JG So doesn't that all pertain to you too? It's a continuing tradition, isn't it?

AS In a way. Although people from the First Wave of emigration, as far as I understand, had their own community, their own émigré association. Today they still have an association, jokingly called the "Party Committee." But personally, I steer clear of that community and live my life alone. And that's fine with me. It gives me more time to work. Of course, we keep in touch with a few émigrés living in Paris and some French Slavicists. And the scholars and the émigrés we do see regularly are, in a word, people of a "liberal" inclination, which is how I would characterize myself. But that alone does not make up anything you could call a thoroughly Russian existence. The fact is that my wife and I are old, and we see our work in terms of Russian culture. For instance, we've just set up our own printing press, right in our own home. And we publish Russian books, and we're publishing a Russian journal. And that is such a lot of work that we can't afford to get overly involved in the

French mainstream. We realize, of course, that this is our inadequacy. But we limit ourselves to things like traveling. We like to absorb whatever elements or currents of Western culture we can. And not only culture, but geography, too. So I don't feel limited to some isolated Russian world. For me that's a very important plus. My life, my life as an émigré, that is, is connected with my trips to Italy, where I've been fifteen times or so—to different provincial towns. The variety I've discovered in Italy is amazing, not only in its historical monuments, but in the way the people go about their everyday lives, the way people live. We also visited Israel on two occasions, and we discovered an entire world there as well. So I don't feel as though I'm inside some kind of Russian shell, unable to see anything out there.

There is a sense of great expanses and naturally a desire to become part of it all. The fact that such opportunities are limited is another story. It's how I sometimes imagined it would be—even though I knew it never could be—if suddenly I had the chance to return to Russia, live normally, and publish wherever I want, in Russia or abroad, but with the condition that I could never go to the West. I don't know if I'd agree to that. And if I did agree, I would probably be more nostalgic about the West than I am about Russia now.

JG So then you feel you're "not so much an exile as an envoy," to borrow a phrase from the First Wave.

AS I think that's a bit bombastic. When people talk about envoys and messianic hopes, they are dreaming of returning. Emigration for me is the opportunity to do the sort of work I would like to do, but under different conditions. We are limited to some degree by various barriers such as language, but still it's a great opportunity.

JG Emigration is freedom?

AS It's freedom, and it also happens to be the piece of earth that I've landed on. So here I am. I might add, it's different for my wife Maria, who agonized and still agonizes much more over the separation from Russia. For me the move here was very different. Maybe it has to do with my having been in the camp. Not because that made me feel more negative about Russia, but because I got a sense of myself, not just as a private individual but as a writer. In Russia I could be seized by the scruff of the neck and thrown into a forced-labor camp. Just as unceremoniously they could yank me out of camp and take me to Moscow. Or exile me. Or "transplant" me to the West. It's a very mechanical process. But in the camp I tried to spend every free minute I had, even if I was just sitting on my bunk, writing *something*. Now I'm continuing to do the same thing, but under the best of conditions. The conditions change, but the principle remains the same.

JG   Being a critic doesn't interfere with the writing of fiction?

AS   No, I don't think so. Besides, that personality split into two distinct individuals—Andrei Siniavsky and Abram Terts—began long ago and continues today.

JG   Siniavsky the critic and Terts the creative writer?

AS   Well, Siniavsky's a critic, Siniavsky's a professor . . . while Terts is pure artist. Naturally, there are some points where they overlap, but psychologically and physically I don't see them as being very much alike. Siniavsky is an academic sort, rather mild mannered, contemplative, honest, probably a bit boring—an ordinary man. While Abram Terts is impudent and pushy, a thief. As a matter of fact, that's where he gets his name: *tertz*—"bandit." He even differs from Siniavsky in his physical appearance. Abram Terts doesn't have a beard, maybe just a thin moustache. He wears a cap pulled down over his eyes. Hands in his pockets. Sure to have a knife hidden there, and God only knows what else. Always ready to stab you in the side. That's what he's like, Abram Terts. That's my dark double, I'd call him. For me, of course, he's the more important of the two.

JG   The more important? So Abram Terts is the ventriloquist, and Siniavsky is the puppet?

AS   Well, Siniavsky is a gimmick for Abram Terts, if you know what I mean. A sort of human gadget so that this half-mythical, half-fantasy Abram Terts can exist. Terts is, of course, also a kind of literary mask, but one which expresses a very important side of me. Whereas Siniavsky could write a paper on any academic subject, Abram Terts is always on the lookout for something taboo. Imagine that someone said to me: "Describe life. Tell us a true-life story in a realistic way." I would refuse.

For me an essential part of being a writer is breaking taboos, both thematic and stylistic. And for me the artist's style is not the usual conversational or literary style.

JG What about your book *Tiny Tsores?*

AS That's Abram Terts making fun of Siniavsky. Using him as a guinea pig. A subtitle for *Tiny Tsores,* or maybe a blurb on what the book's about, might call it the true story of how Siniavsky murdered his five brothers.

Actually, *Tiny Tsores* is a sort of experiment in theme, but also in language. I wanted to write in an exaggeratedly incorrect but elegant style. I think that's how I'd put it. Using verbal adverbs the way you can in French but can't in Russian: "Having opened the pocket book, thick wads of bills could be seen." These admittedly incorrect sentences run throughout *Tiny Tsores.*

But that's only one aspect. There's another aspect to *Tiny Tsores,* the human side, if you will—the theme of man's sinfulness. Tiny Tsores doesn't actually kill anybody, or if he does, he certainly doesn't mean to. It isn't his fault. But he has this guilt. We don't have to murder someone physically to feel guilty. That is part of man's makeup. Despite himself, he causes pain to others.

That's one aspect. The other, perhaps more important, is that Tiny Tsores is a variation on the theme of the artist. Tiny Tsores is the fate of the writer. In his relation to humanity and society, the writer is a criminal. He's an outsider. He's held responsible for all the world's misery. It's as if he were cursed from birth.

Many of the things I've written, nearly all of them, strange as it may seem, revolve around the fate of the writer, the fate of the artist. And the theme of the artist. That can even be said of my earlier work, for example, my short story *Pkhents.* A Martian, a being from another world, is the artist. Tiny Tsores is also an artist. Gogol is an artist. Pushkin is an artist. Siniavsky (laughs) is an artist. So you see, that's how it is. That's my central subject.

JG You said that to be an artist one must break taboos. Perhaps Siniavsky/Tiny Tsores is what the Soviets call an "internal émigré," a rebel who violates all the artistic taboos.

AS Yes. He violates the rules, in this case, the rules of the literary language. Everything he does goes hand in hand with the comic and the grotesque. Tiny Tsores thinks himself a writer, and yet he's devoid of everything except his language. Everything else is bad. His language is beautiful. Yet at the same time he writes in a hideous style.

JG Do you know how the authorities established Abram Terts's true identity?

AS Not exactly. I know that they spent a long time looking. Keep in mind that we first started sending manuscripts to the West in 1956. They were published in 1959. That wasn't our fault. The person who smuggled out the manuscripts and had them published held them up so as to first clear the way for Pasternak's *Doctor Zhivago.*

JG Who brought out the manuscript?

AS Hélène Zamoiskaya, an old French friend, whom I had met back in the years I was a student. I met her in 1947 at Moscow State University. And we're still friends to this day.

After it was published, the KGB began an investigation, and I was given some idea as to their progress. For instance, I learned that the Soviet ambassador to France asked the publisher where he got the material, who gave it to him, how it was gotten out, and so on and so on. So they were on the lookout.

It even became necessary to lead them down the wrong track, into some wild goose chases. It was a real detective story. It's the Abram Terts psychology: here's a thief who's committed a crime, and they're hot on his heels, closing in on him. We gave them false leads through the French. We pretended that the author lived in Leningrad, that the manuscripts had been smuggled out through Poland. But then, of course, they found out. I don't know exactly how.

It was the courier they had to identify. They had to find the route being used. There were attempts to bribe some foreigners, particularly French and American, to establish the route. They had to establish the courier's contacts in Russia, and usually the contacts of a person like that are limited to a small circle at Moscow State University. The rest was easy. Our rooms were bugged, Daniel's and mine, for at least six months, and I think it was more like nine months.

JG Did you find out about that then?

AS Not at the time. During interrogation they quoted a conversation Daniel and I had had when we were alone. It was even stylistically correct, so it's obvious they had a tape.

JG Could you describe your arrest and the camp?

AS We were ready for it; my wife was also fully aware of what was happening, but she did not back away. But even though we realized that they would get me sooner or later—and we were only trying to delay that unhappy moment—it nevertheless came unexpectedly. I was arrested on the street in broad daylight. I was on my way to a class at a Moscow Art Theater studio, where I also taught at the time as a part-time lecturer. I heard a voice behind me: "Andrei Donatovich?" I glanced back but didn't see anyone, so I turned my head around further. They're so agile at that sort of thing that right then and there, all in one smooth sweep, I was shoved into the open waiting car. Even though it was midday on a crowded street, no one even noticed that someone had been arrested. Then it was straight to the Lubyanka Prison and the interrogations.

JG It's like the Galich song about Daniil Kharms, the writer who disappeared without a trace.

AS In the song Kharms went out for some tobacco, and I went out for a lecture. And was arrested. They began with all sorts of leading questions and then moved on to direct accusations. At first I tried to deny that I was Abram Terts.

Thanks to all their efforts, they knew exactly what had been going on. I also fell into a sort of logic trap. For several days I denied I was Abram Terts, and they said, "Why are you so stubborn as to resist this way when *you* know you're Abram Terts, and *we* know you're Abram Terts. We know such-and-such and so-and-so and have gathered facts X, Y, and Z. Fine, let it be your way: don't agree that you're Abram Terts. But that must mean the thought frightens you. That you consider it a serious crime." So they lead you on like that, slowly but surely. And then I realized it was stupid to deny the facts, so I took the position which I held up till the very end and at the trial. I admitted the facts but did not admit guilt. Then, of course, they put a lot of time and effort into pressuring me to admit my guilt. That's very important for them. You see, a person who has admitted his guilt has in a way knocked himself out of the game, even more so if he's recanted. Naturally, they give him a shorter sentence. Now they even let people go free. It's to their benefit. But if I had admitted my guilt, that would have been committing suicide in a metaphysical sense: I would have been killing Abram Terts.

JG Yes, but others have recanted: Shalamov, Father Dudko. . . .

AS Well, Shalamov was during Stalin's time. I don't know. I mean, the circumstances under Stalin were totally different. [Shalamov recanted in 1972—long after Stalin's death.—Ed.]

And as for Father Dudko, well, he confessed, although that's a different and rather involved question. He obviously overestimated himself—he thought he could carry the burdens of the prophet, and it proved too much for him. And I think from a Christian standpoint it was wrong of him when, realizing that he might be arrested, he proclaimed that he and others like him were, in his words, "going to Golgotha." There was even a sermon called "Russian Golgotha." It was Christ who went to Golgotha. Even when the Apostle Paul was to be crucified, he asked that he be crucified upside down so as not to be equated with Christ. And here is Father Dmitry Dudko exalting himself. Anyway, some of the things he did were just unacceptable. And afterward apparently he couldn't take it.

I think too that Russian nationalism is also to blame. If you look carefully at the statement he made on television and then in the press, it's not something the KGB just dictated to him. Some of it was dictated, but there are places where the words are his own. For instance he says: "I realize now that the West hates us and that we have to solve our own problems. That danger threatens us from the West. The West is alien to us, and I was wrong to appeal to the West."

What's happening is that a Russian priest is starting to compromise himself using nationalism as a justification. He's known to be a nationalist. That's why he was so crazy about Glazunov and went around singing his praises as the greatest artist the world has ever seen. Anyway, that's Father Dmitry Dudko.

I knew him slightly. He has little education—no education at all, in fact. And that has something to do with it.

Everyone has his weak spots. The KGB puts tremendous pressure on people, not physical, of course, but psychological, threatening a maximum sentence while at the same time offering the opportunity to get off with a shorter one. In my case, they threatened to arrest my wife. She would be sent to a camp, and our son Yegor, who was eight months old when I was arrested, would be put in an orphanage, where he too would perish. So, they say, *you* choose. What do you consider more important?

I was a mature adult by the time I was put in prison. As a matter of fact, I turned forty while in the Lubyanka Prison. I had been active for ten years. I knew what I was risking. It would have been stupid to retreat. I think too that in a situation like this it's important to be true to yourself. And for me it would have been a lie to admit some sort of guilt for art. Moreover (I learned this only later), ours was the first public political trial—with the possible exception of the Penkovsky trial—since the Stalin era. So you can see, deep down in my consciousness were the show trials of the thirties where the accused were always repenting. And I loathed all of that. So it would have been stupid if I had repented. It would have been unnatural.

What then is natural? I really *am* a proponent of pure art. Even if I have political motives, I don't believe you can try a writer for that. In the interrogations everything was reduced to long and sometimes ludicrous theoretical arguments. I might have read a short story to someone. That counted as agitation and propaganda, as "distribution" of material. So I asked if Gogol's having at one point read a chapter of *Dead Souls* out loud to Aksakov was agitation and propaganda against serfdom. Well, the only thing they could answer, of course, was "You're not Gogol." So I usually won the theoretical arguments.

JG What was it like in the camp?

AS The camp was fine.

JG Not like Ivan Denisovich's camp? Not like Shalamov's?

AS Well, that's not the point. That's not the point at all. Physically it was hard. Very hard.

JG What did you do while you were in the camp?

AS Hard labor and nothing but. Various jobs. I hauled sawdust. That's really nasty work because the sawdust kills your breathing. I hammered crates together. But most often I worked as a loader, just a loader. Something would come in, and I'd have to unload it.

JG Your health evidently is not the best.

AS I came through okay. Except for my teeth. I lost them all. That was a result of being fed very poorly. No vitamins. From a purely physical standpoint it was very bad. Hard labor and the same food all the time. They'd give us a little piece of meat twice a year—on the anniversary of the October Revolution and on May 1, International Labor Day.

JG And the rest of the time?

AS The rest of the time we'd get soup or variations on soup, fixed one way one time, another way another time. Psychologically, of course, it's very hard on a man when he thinks about his wife and small child. You give up all hope for yourself too. And you're sure never to go back to your work, so you're through as a writer. Your name has been dragged through the mud in all the papers. You're imperialist scum, a second Smerdyakov, and on and on it goes. Not very pleasant to hear. But the most important thing is you're finished, so it would seem. This is your life's calling. That, incidentally, is when you start to resist. That was why I continued writing as Abram Terts in the camp.

The world I ended up in, the world of the camp, the milieu of the camp prisoner, is a fascinating and varied world. It's like being in a fairy tale. And the fairy tale is my favorite genre, especially when it's cloaked in realism and not just some kind of romantic dream come true. It was as if I had found my reality, my fantasy-reality, if you know what I mean, something which I had earlier created in my head and which turned out in the end to be real.

Even from the standpoint of information it was an extremely interesting world. I learned much more about my country than in all the previous years, despite the fact that my wife and I had traveled all over the country, even to the most remote places. The camp provided a far more vivid picture since it was selective, that is, that I was put in a camp for highly dangerous state criminals. That's the official name.

JG Were they mostly criminal offenders or political?

AS Both, since officially the Soviet Union now has no political criminals. And I didn't have the right to say: "I am a political prisoner." That's forbidden. There's only one sort of law—criminal law. But there are varying categories of criminal offenders. And I was classified as a "highly dangerous state criminal." That means political offenses: agitation, propaganda, terrorism, espionage, treason. There were also real criminals there who, for one reason or another, had been charged with an additional political crime. People who, for instance, had printed leaflets reading "Down with the Communist Party." The authorities would instantly add on to that a charge of violation of article 70, a political charge. Some people had done these things out of despair. Others to save their lives. If someone lost a card game and was not able to pay his debt, fearing that the other thieves might kill him, he would pull some such stunt and become a political criminal—so as to be sent off to another camp. There were all sorts of things like that.

There were also a lot of people serving sentences simply for religious reasons, and there were many different interesting sects. I got to know all those people very well and became friends with many of them. With only the rarest of exceptions the other prisoners treated me very well. The fact that I had been criticized so much in the press had something to do with it.

JG They could read the papers?

AS They get papers in the camp.

JG *Pravda, Izvestia?*

AS Yes, radio too. And they all knew about me before I arrived. They practically lifted me up onto their shoulders! They realize that the more a person is criticized in the Soviet press, the better a person he must be. Because the papers said that I wasn't remorseful, the other prisoners realized that I wasn't an informer or a provocateur. They were impressed that I was a writer. Of course, they had never read any of my books. They probably would have been horrified if they had. But a writer who was imprisoned because of his books must have been writing the truth. So they treated me very well.

JG Did the camp have meaning for you as a writer?

AS It did. Although it did not affect my outlook. As I said, I was a fully grown man when I went in. It affected me in that it broadened the fabric of my life. For me camp was, to use a fanciful phrase, an incredible encounter with my own people and one that included a concentrated assortment of people—the best and the worst. There were real criminals there too—murderers, people who had collaborated with the Germans, and so on. And because of that I suddenly felt that I was mingling with my own people, as a manifestation of that people. Abram Terts had unexpectedly found himself standing on what for him was the native soil of the criminal world. And in that sense I think that the camp enriched me for a long time to come. So I often remember the camp with a feeling of gratitude, even though it was a very difficult time.

JG Gratitude?

AS Yes, gratitude.

JG How is it that your religious views play such a modest role in your writing? And how do they square with the frank discussions of sex, for example?

AS Well, I don't consider myself a religious writer, you see. I think that one's religious views and experiences are mostly a private, personal matter. I am not one for mixing private religious convictions with public activity, especially politics. For that reason I am opposed to the theocratic state, strongly opposed. If religious motifs find their way into my work, it's only to a modest degree. I think that overall, God is best talked about less, that religious fervor can become hypocrisy, and can alienate. That is, it can lead not to religious feeling, but to anti-religious feeling. This is how we feel when we read the religious novels of certain authors.

JG Which ones?

AS Those of Feliks Svetov, for example.

I often use sex or frank discussions of sex first and foremost, I suppose, to emphasize its inherent inadequacy or sin, perhaps, or the comical aspects of sex. I have no erotically stimulating passages in my work. Just the opposite—my style takes a sharp downturn toward the grotesque, sex as the grotesque. I think that my treatment of sex would have been more appropriate in medieval literature, let's say, than total silence on sex. If you look at some of the medieval writers, you find obscene language and just this kind of abasement of sex.

MR I wonder if I could interrupt you from time to time.

JG Of course, Maria Vasilievna.

MR I'm not quite sure where you found all these "frank discussions of sex," as you put it.

JG For example, in *Unguarded Thoughts.*

AS That's exactly where you find this abasement of sex, that Christian disgust with sex, I would call it.

MR I would call it a Kantian approach. Do you know how he defines sex? An amalgam of absurd and awkward movements.

JG Andrei Donatovich, describe your development as a writer and as a critic. Do you see yourself going through stages?

AS As a critic my development has been very academic. The book about Rozanov bears witness to that. I wouldn't mind writing several more such books.

JG The fact that Maria Vasilievna's last name is Rozanova didn't influence you to write the book about Rozanov?

AS No, I loved Rozanov even before that. But one of the first questions I asked when we met was "Are you related to Vasily Vasilievich Rozanov?" Then I bit my tongue when I realized that Vasily Vasilievich died in 1919, and she was born in 1930.

As far as criticism is concerned, I would like to write a series of scholarly monographs on those areas of Russian culture which have not been well covered or on which I have something new and original to say. I have many such articles in the planning stage—on Archpriest Avvakum, the Russian national faith, Yury Tynianov, Nikolai Zabolotsky. And Isaak Babel. I'd like to write a book about him. It's because we're now living in the West, and we have our own press as well as the material on Russian culture, that I feel there is a gap in Russian culture—a very wide gap. And I feel a need to fill that hole.

Of course, my development as a writer has taken an entirely different direction. It is still running along Tertsian lines, that is, somewhere between realism and fantasy. There is a tendency toward the taboo or the risqué. There is the play of abrupt stylistic changes and the use of the grotesque.

As far as I can judge about myself, I would say that my recent development has been toward the literary baroque. This can be seen in my book *In Gogol's Shadow,* where I have long, complicated, winding sentences, even entire passages, one right after the other.

I even see it as a visual effect, since under Maria's influence the visual arts have become very important to me. I like music, but I don't know much about it—I'm no aficionado. But painting and architecture—those are the forms closest to me, and so at times I perceive even literary style on a visual plane. And that's why I say that I seem to be evolving toward the baroque. Whereas once I tried to write in short constructive sentences, so that every sentence would have a surprise in it, now more and more I tend toward longer, even somewhat elaborate, old-fashioned phraseology. Not old-fashioned realism, no. Again, I'm playing games with this baroque style, the same way I did in *Gogol.* The form in that book to some extent matched the content—I consider Gogol a baroque writer. I'm doing a lot of writing just now on that subject, and my styling is more baroque than Gogolian. I recently finished a new, rather long novel which also leans toward the baroque.

JG Which novel?

AS It's entitled *Good Night.* It is a long novel, my longest. I worked on it for several years.

JG The émigré scholar Dmitry Chizhevsky at one time had popularized the concept of the Slavic baroque, but it remained unrecognized for a long time in the Soviet Union. The first volume, as I recall, of the *Literary Encyclopedia* had a rather skimpy entry, but later the editors inserted a fairly long article on the Slavic baroque in Yugoslavia, Czechoslovakia, and various other countries.

Maria Vasilievna, yesterday you and I spent some time talking about censorship among émigrés. Perhaps you would share with us some of your thoughts on that.

MR My thoughts on that are bitter. Bitter and filled with disgust. While they were changing the videotape, Siniavsky and I had what you might call an argument between professionals. I said he was the boring Andrei Siniavsky, and I was his Abram Terts, since I'm willing to be the bandit in the family. I'm willing to take some of those neat, well-defined arguments he puts forth so quietly and politely and follow them to their nasty logical conclusion.

The fact is that emigration has taught me a great deal. It's an extremely difficult experience to go through, but one that's unbelievably beneficial. Only in exile have I come to realize just what sort of place my homeland is, even though I lived there forty-three years and believed I knew it very well. Even so, I never realized before my emigration that my country is the product of all of us. It was not invaded from the outside by Marxism, socialism, communism or any other evil *ism*. It is a society that we ourselves built, and we must look for the source of the evil not somewhere out there, but within ourselves. That's a conclusion I came to as a result of my experiences abroad. This is what I was getting at before—here, in the West, we, the Third Wave, have built the exact same world which we had fought against there and left behind.

JG Well, not entirely. After all . . .

MR The only thing we can't do is build our own Lubyanka. And the only reason we can't do that is . . .

AS . . . is that we live in a free country.

MR We live in a country . . . or countries where the government doesn't permit that. But if they did, we'd go ahead and set up our own Lubyanka in an instant. In an instant! Sometimes I tell Siniavsky that he should write a book. Unfortunately, Siniavsky doesn't write humor—you'd need someone with Voinovich's brand of talent. If Voinovich, for instance, wrote a book called *Private Chonkin in Emigration*, it would be very funny, very bitter, and very Russian. As it is, we've set up our own system of taboos which very quickly became defined.

JG Give me an example.

MR There are certain things that you're not allowed to say. For example, you're not allowed to say that Russian tanks invaded Prague. Prague was never invaded by Russian tanks, only by *Soviet* tanks. You can't say that we Russians are in Afghanistan. No Russian ever goes near Afghanistan, only Soviets. We make a distinction between Russian and Soviet which we never made there. There we knew that we were the Great

Russian State which would soon conquer the entire world. Here it's not permitted to utter the word Russian in any sort of pejorative context.

Then too, we quickly set up our own personality cults: the Solzhenitsyn cult, the Maksimov cult, and the Father Dmitry Dudko cult. Then we responded to all this exactly as we had done when we were in Russia. I know for an absolute fact that Vladimir Yemilyanovich Maksimov very much dislikes Aleksandr Isaevich Solzhenitsyn—as a writer. He once called Solzhenitsyn a graphomaniac. Maksimov doesn't like him as a writer, and he doesn't like him as a public figure—an ideologue. But whenever Maksimov speaks in public he begins with a quote from Solzhenitsyn and ends with a quote from Solzhenitsyn. Why? Because he has to. That's one of the canons of Soviet behavior, one which we brought with us and which we live by to this day.

But we can go further than that. Of course, we poor souls grew up in the Soviet Union, and we can't help but behave that way. But then look at the First Wave of émigrés, which was untouched by the Soviet regime. You'll see the exact same thing. Their writing is Soviet. Their approach is entirely Soviet.

JG Give me some names.

MR Gleb Struve, for example, who never lived in the Soviet Union, is completely Soviet in his approach. Or Ilovaiskaya-Alberti, currently the editor of *Russkaya mysl'*, and who has never set foot on Russian soil. Or Nikita Struve, who has never seen Russia, and yet has the exact same Soviet approach.

JG In what way are they Soviet?

MR Voinovich's *Private Chonkin* couldn't be published for years. No one would take it. Nikita Struve didn't want it. And why not? Because of the distorted image of the Russian soldier. How could you have a bow-legged Russian soldier, a bow-legged *Russian!* How could that be! And the first thing Struve did after he *did* finally publish the book was to publish a critique, a humorous critique, in *Vestnik RSKhD* (Russian Student Christian Movement Herald). In other words, he wrote an article in his own journal blasting it, and in purely Soviet-style clichés. So you see? And Nikita Struve has never been in the Soviet Union.

So the problem is not just in the Soviet Union, but somewhere in the depths of our Slavic soul. Something's wrong down there in the depths of our Russian soul. So I would look for the enemy within ourselves. And it's very unpleasant to look for the enemy within oneself. It's probably much more pleasant to isolate the evil "out there" and say that we have nothing to do with it. But if we want anything to happen in our country, if we want to see anything good come about, if we want to see the country try to get well, the first thing we have to do is to arrive at a correct and accurate diagnosis, even if that diagnosis is unpleasant.

Imagine you go to see a doctor, and you tell him you feel awful. You go to two doctors. One doctor says: "John, old friend, it's just a cold. Take a few cold capsules, drink plenty of water, go home and relax, and you'll be okay." The second doctor says: "John, it's cancer and it looks bad. You've got practically no chance whatsoever, but if you do A, B, C, and D, if we do this operation and that operation, then maybe that will give you a 20 percent chance of survival." Which doctor would be more pleasant to deal with? Naturally, the one who gives you the pills and sends you home. But after which doctor are you going to croak the quickest? After the first one.

JG Andrei Donatovich, in your *Strolls with Pushkin* you write: "After all, he's our Charlie Chaplin, a contemporary Ersatz Petrushka puppet, who got himself all dandied up and taught himself how to strut in rhyme." Roman Goul was displeased by your book, to put it mildly. He called it "A Boor's Strolls with Pushkin." And Gleb Struve, as I recall, also wrote a review in which he said that "while he had not read the book. . . ."

AS Well, there's a fatal misunderstanding here. The newspaper *Sovetskaya kul'tura* (Soviet Culture) lambasted *Strolls with Pushkin* in the March 5 issue, which curiously enough coincided with the thirtieth anniversary of Stalin's death. And they also had the same quotes, the same idea, that Siniavsky/Terts hates Pushkin, that he hates all Russian culture, that he's out to destroy it all, and so on and so forth.

First, I'd like to add something to what Maria said about our all being Russians. If a person builds his life around excoriating some enemy, he often becomes a mirror image of that enemy. If the Russian émigré community doesn't broaden its view to something beyond the wonderful Tsarist past and the abominable enemy, it'll never break out of its mold.

The other thing I wanted to say was that they have no sense of humor. When I write something like "Pushkin ran into the thick of literature on his slender erotic little legs," they think I'm trying to debase Pushkin. There were even times when they would ask, "How does he know that Pushkin had slender legs?" But the book is written *in praise* of Pushkin. I wrote it in the camp under very hard conditions. It was the first thing I wrote.

JG   Goul claims that you didn't write it while you were in the camp.

AS   I know. I'll have something to say about that later. But first, I want to explain *why* I wrote it in camp. I wrote it as my last will and testament. After all, being in the camp is like being on a deathbed, both literally and metaphorically. So *Strolls with Pushkin* was a continuation of my last word in court, which was basically that art serves no one. Art is independent. Art is free. To me, Pushkin is an example of pure art, an art which may touch here and there on public issues but which has its own intrinsic value. And I saw no better Russian symbol for that concept than Pushkin. At the same time I had no intention of writing a monograph on Pushkin. That would have been a joke. A dying man chooses to write a monograph on Pushkin! I felt I had to make it clear that that was Terts writing. I had to prove that he wasn't dead. The seamy language is Terts's.

So while in fact I'm praising Pushkin internally, the style is not one of deferential enthrallment. At times it is not deferential at all, but a purposeful combining of various styles, from Pushkin to Charlie Chaplin. Probably I saw a sort of example for what I was doing in Meierhold, who modernized classical productions, changing them around and staging them in new ways. And in Picasso, who would take classical motifs, say those of Poussin, and do them over the way he wanted, introducing cubism or anything else he chose. So that's what I had in mind. *Pushkin* was my blueprint for pure art and one which was in praise of Pushkin.

The current émigrés take offense at any sort of stylistic lowering, at any sort of ironic game, and I do a huge amount of game-playing. Once I wrote, "As Lomonosov said, 'You might not be a poet, but you must be a citizen.' But Pushkin broke that tradition." Well, my God, every schoolboy knows that Nekrasov said that, not Lomonosov. I wrote that in jest. So they decided to expose me. "Just imagine," they said. "He's a professor, and he doesn't know that!" They're out of touch, and they can't see it.

My opponents also claimed that either I hadn't written *Strolls* in camp, and that I was lying about the date and place, or else that the KGB had specially brought in materials and had arranged for me to write this vile book while I was in camp, so that later I would go to the West and poison Russian culture. In other words they were especially assigned to have me write this book. That's how much they hate Pushkin and Russian culture. Finally, there's a third version: that I was never in camp to begin with.

JG Then where were you supposed to have written it?

AS Oh, I don't know. Again it was supposed to have been a KGB plot to have me write about Pushkin. They cite several references in the book, such as one to an 1826 volume of the *Severnaya pchela*. There *are* some exact references. Not many, but there are some. And Goul and others gleefully pointed out that no camp prisoner could have gotten hold of an issue of the *Severnaya pchela*. But the fact of the matter is that any attentive reader, and not even necessarily a Pushkin expert, but any Russian intellectual, a person of letters and the humanities, could easily discern the source of the quotes: Veresaev's *Pushkin*, which follows Pushkin's life and works through statements of his contemporaries, from journals like the *Severnaya pchela*. When I was being held in Lefortovo Prison . . .

JG They say Lefortovo has a good library.

AS Yes, it does. And that was where I read the Veresaev book. I took notes and then used it all later. The Pushkin quotes were easy. I was sent a set, not an Academy of Sciences edition, just an ordinary three-volume one. I had that, plus my notes on Veresaev, plus my own Tertsian inventiveness. And that's how I wrote the book.

MR There's something else to that book. It's one of my favorite Abram Terts books. I like it for its sense of humor. It's very nice to think that Siniavsky wrote his most humorous book under the hardest of conditions in a prison camp! It was a wonderful surprise to get letters with excerpts, and instead of reading about the hardships of the camp, I would be reading these sparkling humorous fragments. That, I would say, is also something purely Tertsian: to cut right through the camp, not letting the camp get inside you.

My first meeting with Siniavsky in the camp was very instructive. I mean, it was awful. Here they had thrown my husband in jail, where he sat for a year and a half while the investigation was going on. And after that the trial. And only then was I permitted my first meeting with him in the camp. I had already met with other prisoners who had been released, and they had already told me about how badly they were fed, how hard the work was. So I knew all of that beforehand.

JG Where was that?

MR In Mordovia, in Potma. They had told me what I should take with me, what sort of food to bring, what would be best to feed him. And here I was prepared to meet this poor, miserable prisoner, emaciated and traumatized. It would be my job to help uplift his spirits. And then suddenly out comes Siniavsky, his head shaven but still with a beard, thin—he's been there a year and he's really very thin, scrawny. And instead of telling me how awful it all is, he says, "Masha, it's fascinating!"

His first camp (they kept switching him from one zone to another) was very small, and most of the prisoners were religious old men from all sorts of different sects. I got the impression that he felt that he had been given a very difficult but very interesting assignment.

AS At first Maria was even offended. She said: "You seem better off in here than out there."

JG Let's come back to your writing, Andrei Donatovich. You don't write for the man on the street.

AS That's correct.

JG Whom *do* you write for?

AS This may be somewhat exaggerated, but I would say that I write for myself, and for her. . . . I consider her my most important reader, and indeed she's the first to read anything I write, and then she tells me whether she approves or disapproves.

MR Also for our son and our dog Matilda.

AS No, I don't write for my son anymore. . . . I write for the open space out there, and for time. I perceive time as space too.

JG So you're not reaching out for a particular audience?

AS No, no, not me. I don't remember who, maybe it was Mandelstam who said that the reader the author has in mind is a product of the author's self-image. And I would say that that's how it is with me. No, I write for myself and for a few people spread around the world in time and space. I never felt the need to have a mass following. In fact, even when I had my work smuggled out, I wasn't trying to shock the West or to open the eyes of people in the West. No, my first goal was to preserve what I had written—which you can do only by publication. Once preserved, it will reach a few individual readers, a few individual friends—friends not in the immediate physical, but in the philosophical, sense. I realized that I would be greeted rather coldly from time to time after I emigrated. But I didn't suspect that the émigrés would come down on me so hard that they would want to kill me artistically.

JG Well, that was unavoidable. Just recently I was interviewing Andrei Sedykh. He was sitting in the exact same chair you're in now. Here's a man who has spent his entire life surrounded by Russian culture. He was Bunin's personal secretary. He edits the New York Russian language daily newspaper *Novoe russkoe slovo*. He's written a number of books of his own, known everybody. And when the interview was over, I asked him what places he had been to in Russia. It turned out that with the exception of the Crimea, he hadn't been anywhere. He had been evacuated in 1920, I think, and he had never seen Moscow or Petersburg. I asked him if he wouldn't want to make just one trip to take a look around. And he said: "You know, I might as well go to Peking." And so it seems to me that the bridge you're trying to build between that world and modern Russian culture is a very difficult bridge to build.

MR No, that's not what we're talking about. That's not the bridge we mean, not a bridge between Russia back there and the intellectual émigré community here. In fact, there is no real intellectual Russian émigré community.

AS Not any more.

MR What is the Russian émigré community but a gigantic graveyard? That's what it is, a graveyard. And what happens in a graveyard? Some of the people rest peacefully in their nice little coffins. Others can't. They can't calm down and rest, and so they crawl out and become vampires. And that's what's happened with the émigrés. Most of them are vampires, who just *look* like they're alive.

When we first arrived in the West, some of them, no, many of them, liked us very much. Siniavsky hadn't published his *Pushkin* yet, so they didn't really know just who this Abram Terts was. Just the opposite: we were well liked, invited everywhere. We would go and talk with people, and everything was just lovely—hearing this wonderful Russian, all the conversations and reminiscences . . . Bunin, of course, Zaitsev, Merezhkovsky. One person might remember someone from the past. Another might tell us about a person he once knew. It was very interesting. And then suddenly I realized that they were all dead! Very nice, but dead. And there was a bit of vampire in all of them. Then I realized that when a vampire attacks you, and he begins to suck your blood, he's not trying to kill you; he's not trying to harm you. It's an act of love. He's trying to bring you closer to him, to make you one of his kind, for when he sucks your blood, you too become a vampire. He accepts you as one of his own. *That* is the Russian émigré community. And that's why I'll sometimes say about a person we know, someone recently here from Moscow, but who has over a period of time begun to change, I'll say to Siniavsky: "Look, he's already being sucked into that world of dead men."

AS I want to explain something from a literary point of view. Sedykh was Bunin's secretary. Now, Bunin's literary tastes were most conservative. He considered Blok to be scum—Blok was crazy, a graphomaniac, and so on and so forth. And not only Blok; all the symbolists! And what about the others? To Bunin they were a gang of thugs and syphilitics. And that's what he wrote. About Pasternak, about Mayakovsky. That's how Bunin perceived them.

You say that in Bunin's time Sedykh saw a small part of the Crimea—and even that he can perceive only through Bunin's eyes. Nothing that is going on now is credible to him. Tradition must remain as it is. Anything out of the ordinary is an abomination. He doesn't know *what* to make of anything unusual that might be written about Pushkin. But I didn't want to write *just* about Pushkin. So many extremely subjective things had *already* been written about him—Tsvetaeva's *My Pushkin, Pushkin and Pugachov,* and the Mayakovsky Commemorative. *That's* the Abram Terts tradition, the tradition of Tsvetaeva and Mayakovsky. Now, what sort of perception could these old men have? How could they possibly perceive real modernism or the avant-garde? They know nothing of that.

MR There's a story about an exhibition of Russian nonconformist art that was put on in Paris. In Moscow, of course, the nonconformist artists are persecuted by the Moscow Artists' Union. If the union decides that someone's not acceptable, they close down exhibitions with bulldozers. So, all at once, these paintings arrived in Paris from under the very treads of the bulldozers. The pictures were hung in the gallery. There was an opening ceremony. The crème de la crème of the émigré community was on hand. And some older émigrés came to look at the paintings. After the exhibit a big argument broke out between the old émigrés and us, people in the Third Wave. We tried to explain about Socialist Realism and nonconformism. And since they didn't understand anything about form—it was something they couldn't conceive of—we tried to explain it all in terms of the battle of trends, the struggle for free expression. They listened. They listened and then they said: "Okay, take the paintings back to Moscow and carry on your struggle there. We can do without it."

AS "We don't want it! Where are the positive ideals?"

MR They point at Rabin's picture, and they say, "What's that? That's supposed to be Moscow?! That's Russia?! How am I going to teach my grandson to love a Russia like that? Now Vasnetsov—*that's* Russia!

JG So you reject the current émigré community in toto?

MR No, the argument between the Third Emigration and the old émigrés is one of style. It's one big stylistic argument.

Within the Third Emigration there is a completely different argument going on.

AS More often than not social rather than stylistic—on the issue of nationalism and democracy. That indeed is the main argument. And the nationalists are the ones who are winning because they have the support of the older émigrés. People from the Second Emigration for the most part support the nationalists. By tradition, based on their memories of the monarchy. You can prove that in print. Just look at the magazines *Chasovoy* or *Veche*. Some of the things they print in *Veche* are so unbelievably conservative that they might as well be fish fossils. They are purely monarchist or just plain fascist tracts. And what's even funnier is that while they exalt everything Russian, the language these pieces are written in is so *awful;* it's illiterate. It's absurd, that's all.

JG What's going to happen to the émigré community in twenty or thirty years when there is no First or Second Emigration, when there's just the Third Emigration, Russian-speaking but ethnically Jewish?

AS I'm convinced you can't create a culture in emigration. I had some illusions earlier, when I was still living "there," and I pictured the First Emigration as a kind of crowning end to the Silver Age. But when I got here, I saw what the Silver Age had become. There was nothing left of it! And now I think that nothing will remain of this emigration. You see, emigration is not a place where an independent culture can grow. It is a place of preservation. It is a place where a few individual writers can go on working. For that reason I don't perceive the First Emigration as having been a separate monolithic culture. Rather, it was place for Tsvetaeva, for Remizov, for Nabokov, and other people like that. But it is *not* some sort of monolithic cultural temple.

MR By the way, I think it's very indicative that Tsvetaeva and Remizov and Nabokov were all very much disliked in the émigré community. They forced Tsvetaeva out; they sent her back. Nabokov tried for a time, but then he left the émigré community and started writing in English. Remizov lived somewhere on the edge. But they didn't like him much either, and they never accepted him.

JG What would you say about Viacheslav Ivanov?

AS Well, Viacheslav Ivanov is different. He was probably too intelligent for the émigré community, too far removed and too abstract for them. He lived, so to speak, for the world, for world culture as a whole. I guess you could put it that way. He was a different type of person. In many ways he had always been that way, even before.

JG But surely I don't have to go through all the names, people like Shestov and Berdiaev. You can do that better than I can. Do you really want to cross all of them out and say they created nothing, that they couldn't do anything just because they were on foreign soil?

MR They were able to create as individuals. . . .

AS Shestov and Berdiaev are another story. The one thing that the First Emigration did do for Russian culture was to preserve Russian religious philosophy, which these first émigrés brought out with them and which continued to grow. Berdiaev here was better than Berdiaev before the Revolution. And Shestov here was better then Shestov before the Revolution. Indeed, the most interesting and the most valuable contribution of that period was religious philosophy and religious thought. That was of great value to Russian culture. But as far as literature is concerned, it's a matter of a few individuals. I'd put Khodasevich in that group. A few individuals, but not any sort of unified culture. Even so, the First Emigration was a far greater cultural force than the Third is today.

Admittedly we may possess one advantage: we don't view ourselves as being cut off from modern Russia. We don't see it as being something completely different. Let me give an example: just because I came here and Yuly Daniel stayed there, that doesn't mean that there's been any basic change in the way we feel about each other. There isn't that psychological barrier. And I'm not talking about any physical barrier. During the twenties you could still cross the border back and forth. But the psychological barrier that existed then between the émigré world and the motherland is gone now, in practice as well as in theory—since we see each other. Of course we don't go around announcing it. It's done partly in secret. But there are Soviet writers who come to the West and make attempts to meet with us—and on their own initiative. I've met more Soviet writers here than there!

JG "The emigration of defeat or the emigration of hope"—to which do you belong?

AS To begin with, I think that hope comes out of defeat. In other words, emigration is a certain experience one has to go through. And you'll either perish, which is not at all beyond the realm of possibility, or you'll make something out of it. Victory is out of the question. Hope? Hope for what? That we'll go back and conquer Russia? That they'll turn to us? That will never happen. Never. You see, culture is its own purpose, just like art. You may be able to preserve some remnants and develop them further here, but that doesn't mean that anything will ever change in Russia proper.

Washington, D.C., to Paris, by telephone, August 20, 1990

MR John, if I were you, I would ask everyone the same question: do you want to go back, and if not, why?

JG I already have asked some.

MR And what do they say? Do they want to go back?

JG They seem to want to keep their foreign passports, their apartments in London, Berlin, New York, their foreign pensions (if they have any), and have a place in Russia to visit.

MR Then what about all their shouting about being exiles? It's wonderful that Solzhenitsyn's works have returned to Russia and that everything he's written will be published, but now it is forbidden there to criticize him.

Personally I don't want to return for fear of death from irritation. It's impossible to work there. True, you can talk now, and that's a great blessing. But there are still a lot of limitations. Besides, while freedom of speech is a lovely thing, it isn't everything. There's nothing for me there.

JG What are you going to do with your journal *Sintaksis?*

MR I think a lot about that. Now that *Kontinent* and *Vremya i my* (Time and We) are going to be published in the USSR, perhaps one journal should remain as a Parisian bastion of free thought.

JG Andrei Donatovich, if Russian writers haven't returned home, at least their books have. What will happen to literature now?

AS There will be such an incredible process of enrichment that the average reader will have a hard time not being overwhelmed. Soviet literature is going through a period of stress. They publish indiscriminately. Everything is up for grabs. Now they have to publish a book backlog of seventy years! For literature this is a very trying situation, but also a very rewarding one.

JG Will emigration become an incidental fact for literature?

AS On the one hand, émigré literature is flowing into Soviet literature. On the other, the division between West and East has not yet come to an end. There still are a lot of writers who cannot be published. The émigré world may well turn out to be a saving place for them.

For me, the location of the writers' bodies is of secondary importance. The location of their souls and intellects is what is crucial.

JG Their souls are with Russia while their bodies remain in France?

AS Yes, something like that (laughs).

My wife and I never manage to travel to Russia without terrible scandals. The authorities don't want to let us in. We wait for months for visas—on a *Soviet* passport!

JG Would you like to say something about your novel *Good Night?*

AS I'm afraid to. It may be published in Russia in a few months. But everything there takes place on a semiconspiratorial basis. The publishers beg me to keep my mouth shut.

There was a terrible scandal over *Strolls with Pushkin.* The journal *Oktyabr'* (October) printed an excerpt of five and a half pages from the book, and there was a commotion that reminded me of the attacks on Akhmatova and Zoshchenko. Igor Shafarevich even compared the book to Rushdie's *Satanic Verses!* It's all a throwback to Stalinism.

Sasha Sokolov

Novelist (b. 1943). Sokolov, who was born in Canada and is a Canadian citizen, was a journalist in the Soviet Union and also worked as a gamekeeper. He emigrated in 1975. His first novel, *A School for Fools*, was written in Russia, but not published until after he left the country.

Books: *Shkola dlya durakov* (Ann Arbor, 1976); *Mezhdu sobakoi i volkom* (Ann Arbor, 1980); and *Palisandria* (Ann Arbor, 1985).

English translations: *A School for Fools*, trans. Carl R. Proffer (Ann Arbor: Ardis, 1977); *Astrophobia*, trans. Michael Heim (New York: Grove Weidenfeld, 1989).

Washington, D.C., May 21, 1986

JG Your curriculum vitae lists a paper you read called "How and Why I Left Russia." Why in fact did you leave?

SS It's simple. I wanted to be published. I knew I wanted to write, although I didn't know exactly what; I was only twenty. But I had written a bit. I had only a lazy notion of what it would end up looking like, but I knew I would write, and I realized full well that no matter what I wrote, it could never be published in the Soviet Union. So I had planned on leaving from the start and was always looking for a way out.

That came when I met an Austrian girl who agreed to marry me. We went through a long battle, first to get married and then to get a visa. Chancellor Kreisky and Brezhnev wrote to each other. The two countries' foreign ministers had several exchanges. I suddenly was allowed to go to Vienna. I was given a month-long visa, but I and everyone else connected with the matter knew perfectly well that I would never return. On the flight out I could only look back in disgust and anger.

JG Twenty years ago you helped start an organization called SMOG (a Russian acronym for "Courage-Thought-Image-Depth").

SS Yes, SMOG was an organization of young Moscow poets. It came into being at the height of the Khrushchev thaw. There were about thirty members, including some bright, talented people who had just come to Moscow from the provinces. A similar movement was going on in Leningrad, but the Moscow organization became the most well known and the most respected. It won the admiration of established writers, and the Writers' Union even tried to set up links with SMOG's founders. There was Vladimir Oleinikov, a noteworthy poet, Leonid Gubanov, who, unfortunately, has since died. Then there was Vladimir Batshev, although he was more politically oriented.

SMOG started with poetry readings at Mayakovsky Square on weekend evenings. This spread to readings in Moscow salons, student dormitories, and research institutes. The readings themselves were spontaneous events, but they were a springboard for SMOG.

I remember the freezing January evening when we met and agreed to write a manifesto. This turned into an amusing document, rather akin to the Futurists' Manifesto. We included such expressions as "I'm jumping off the ship of modernity" and other admitted clichés. And instead of kicking Pushkin and Lermontov off our ship, we threw out Yevtushenko and Voznesensky. At the time they were the ones in the limelight.

JG But that was years ago.

SS That's true. Now Voznesensky and Yevtushenko appear abroad and are better known in the West. Their popularity in Russia has greatly fallen off as a result of their dubious pronouncements. And their frequent trips to America help them out a great deal. For some reason I do not understand, they are often invited to speak at universities. No one doubts their talent. What dumbfounds me is that the people who invite some of these poets are dealing with the direct representatives of a bloody regime. They might just as well invite Pinochet's court poet or the supporters of apartheid. But even that is really no comparison. It would be more like extending a welcome to Nazi Germany's state poets.

JG What happened to SMOG?

SS It was disbanded in December 1966, after the first big human-rights demonstration on Pushkin Square. Some of the demonstrators were sentenced to internal exile, some were jailed, and some were thrown into psychiatric wards. It was a brief page in history, but an interesting one.

JG Your novel *School for Fools* was written in stream of consciousness style. A friend of mine, who didn't like the novel, made the argument that stream of consciousness was nothing new and that Russian writers were just reliving what had been done here fifty years ago.

SS This was an American?

JG Yes, and a writer as well.

SS All right. Stream of consciousness has been around since Joyce. But stream of consciousness per se is not the issue. Realism with all its attendant literary devices is centuries old. And whether you view realism as a separate movement or as a set of literary devices, it has been around a long, long time. But that doesn't mean it should be avoided.

Russian literature has yet to experience stream of consciousness, although both Tolstoy and Bely used a version of it. Literature, in fact, is unimaginable without this type of writing. It is simply a dam bursting.

No one calls Tolstoy one of the first Russian modernists, although in *War and Peace* entire pages—largely of battle scenes— are written in the stream of consciousness manner. In these scenes Tolstoy achieved what we call that fourth dimension of prose. He makes the reader feel as if he were right there on the spot. His is a cinematographic kind of prose, which brings the events and characters to instant life. Soviet critics, in particular, keep away from that side of Tolstoy. They view him as a realist with his feet planted firmly on the ground. Not that stream of consciousness could be called a crime.

JG I want to ask you to do something rather difficult: retell the plot of your novel *Between the Dog and the Wolf*.

SS Difficult indeed. It's like Faulkner: you need at least two, maybe even three or four readings before you can do it. Most people say that after the second time the fog begins to lift, and by the third everything becomes clear.

I myself haven't reread the book recently, so I would have trouble retelling the plot coherently. Basically it's about a young huntsman, Yakov. . . .

JG You were also a hunter. . . .

SS Yes, I spent two years on the upper Volga. Anyway, the hunter lives alone, drinking his life away, looking out of the window and writing poems. These interrupt the narrative from time to time. His father is a traveling one-legged knife-grinder, who has been all over Russia. Like nearly all other Russians, the son drinks, and drinks heavily. Part of the narrative is told in the form of the father's letters to the local police chief. The other part is told through the son's poetry.

One evening Ilya is walking home on crutches from a nearby village. It's dark, and while crossing an ice-covered river, he comes across a dog, which in his drunken state he takes for a wolf. He grabs the dog by its collar and begins hitting it with his crutch. Cruelly beaten, the dog finally breaks loose and runs off. Ilya believes that he has won his fight with the wolf. The next morning the local huntsmen learn that Ilya has beaten up one of their hunting dogs. That night they go to his house, find his crutches on the porch, and steal them. That is just the beginning of the ill will between Ilya and the hunters. Ilya then kills two more of their dogs, and finally, they push him into a hole in the ice and drown him. It is all within the realm of possibility. I once worked with a huntsman who was shot because he had killed two dogs which other hunters were using to hunt out of season.

JG   For me the plot was as elusive as the title.

SS   I had some help with the title from Nabokov through Carl Proffer. Unfortunately, I never knew Nabokov personally. When he asked Carl Proffer what Sasha Sokolov was working on after *School for Fools*, Carl told him that I was writing a novel to be called *Between the Dog and the Wolf*. Nabokov asked if I knew that Pushkin had written some lines about a dog and a wolf in *Eugene Onegin*. I had only a hazy recollection of the Pushkin quote, but once I found it, I decided to use it as the epigraph. That turned out to be the one concrete piece of advice from Nabokov I ever used.

Pushkin took the expression "between dog and wolf" from a Latin poem. It refers to that time of day when a shepherd can no longer distinguish between his own sheep dog and the approaching wolf.

JG   One critic commented that *School for Fools* and *Between the Dog and the Wolf* are two totally different works, like two separate languages of one language system. Do you agree?

SS   Yes, that's only natural. Each author, I believe, speaks with not one, but several voices. In that sense writers are an abnormal phenomenon. Well, not only writers. All creative people share that ability. To a certain extent it's an unhealthy characteristic, this double or even triple personality.

You put yourself on a certain wavelength, and at once you find yourself in a new kind of laboratory. Before you sit down to write, you have to create a mental and emotional atmosphere. Once you begin to breath in that atmosphere, you absorb it, and then everything comes out the way it's supposed to. The style is right. You need time to switch styles. I would find it not only boring but absolutely impossible to start a new book in the same

style, the same spirit, without changing my mental "interior."
Each time I start a new book, I want to change keys.

JG Is that the only reason your writing changes, or is it
because you vary what you write?

SS The changes in my writing have nothing to do with what
I want or what I write. They are the result of life-long evolution.

JG I would just like to quote from your *Palisandria*: "cogs and
gears, ratchets and springs, pendulums and tongs, every piece
in the Kremlin chronometers moved in monotone. Thermome-
ters, nozzles and droppers hit their mark. Every instrument left
its imprint: all glistened or shone, all were in perfect motion or
were completely still, all ticked or was totally silent." That's a
description of your own intricate work, isn't it? The American
Slavist D. Barton Johnson writes that your novels are not narra-
tives but rather compositions of highly polished word structure. How do you respond to that?

SS I have no objections. I don't think a writer's creative work
has to fit into a premolded genre. There can be new genres. And
while I don't believe that the novel is dead, I would like to see
some sort of new form of writing.

JG But is he correct in saying that narrative plays a relatively
weak role in your writing?

SS Yes, he is. I'm not that interested in the narrative. That
has more to do with my own philosophy. I believe that life itself
has no plot, and if the novel is the mirror of life, as Stendhal
said, then why should each novel have a plot, beyond perhaps
a few coincidences, such as happen in life itself? But even that's
not what literature is about. That's not what the novel is supposed to be. "Literature is not about life": Brodsky expressed
that idea quite well when you interviewed him.

JG Again from *Palisandria*: "And yet history is on the whole a
Kantian 'thing in and of itself.' If you discard the clearly apocalyptic tone, the first thing you notice is that it's no accident that
history is bursting with events which are scrupulously ordered,
yet unknown and unknowable. Taken separately they dumb-
found you. You cannot see where they are leading you. Consequently you're in a state of nervous anticipation: you expect
things to go wrong. You look at the road ahead and you look

back just to get your bearings. All the same, ours is a world, not of fear and superstition, but of modern learning, and you have to live in it somehow or other, just like everyone else. And so you make a conscious decision to form a credo. For myself, I have decided to believe, and I swear by this, that history is the inexorable, albeit gradual process of disintegration." You view your novels that way, don't you?

SS Perhaps. It seems to express my attitude toward history, as seen through the prism of my hero. We hear his words and dreams, but what comes through are my own attitudes.

JG Yet there's still that Kantian "thing in and of itself." Are your own works such "objects"?

SS No, I was talking about history, as seen through the eyes of the hero. But I know there is an element of a "thing in and of itself" in my novel. So no, I don't have any objection to that approach. I don't have any particular feeling one way or the other on things like that. I just do whatever I can.

JG Is Sasha Sokolov a Russian writer or a cosmopolitan writer? I see the influence of Borges, Joyce, Kafka, and perhaps Nabokov. On the other hand, your themes are Russian.

SS I think that first I am a writer of the Russian language, who is operating in a kind of cultural vacuum.

People will now accuse me of saying that the West is devoid of culture, but that's not at all what I mean. What I *am* saying is that a writer needs a field, a force field, as it were, in order to be productive. And emigration, especially at first, is very difficult because you have no contact with that force field. As a Russian I feel an attachment to the land, to Russia. The Russian soil exerts a strong pull. That's true of the land in places in the West too. Israel, for example, and Vermont also hold on to a person and nurture him with some sort of life-giving juice. I believe that. I feel it.

Then there's a cultural field, or at least culture is part of the force field as a whole. My work is in Russian literature; I write in Russian. But it's hard for me to surround myself in that environment. I have to try to recreate that field for myself, to surround myself with the Russian language, and that takes no small effort.

I think I'm a writer of the Russian language, but not Russian literature. I barely give literature a thought. It doesn't interest me. Even when I was living there, I had stopped thinking about Russian-Soviet problems. I was mainly interested in the creative process.

JG You end up with a cruel contradiction: attachment to a language detached from its literary traditions.

SS There is much in Russian culture that I never accepted. And much of what is interesting I discovered here. I began to write prose out of revulsion for what I had seen and read there. But *something* there remains an essential part of me. So that I am, to some degree, a split personality. My feeling of revulsion set me out on new, more interesting paths. I never knew contemporary Russian literature very well. I knew the classics, but I could not get interested in Soviet writers. There are a few exceptions. To take an example, I always found Kazakov fascinating and thought-provoking. My tastes and the tastes of many writers of my generation were influenced by Western writers. There's a very good phrase in Ageev's novel *A Novel with Cocaine.* The hero keeps on repeating, "You've got to be a European." I've always felt that it's long been time for Russian writers to start heeding that piece of advice.

Lenin said: "Before Count Tolstoy there were no real peasants in Russian literature." That was said a long time ago. But since then, there have been far too many real peasants.

JG Do you mean the so-called Rural Prose?

SS For the most part, yes. I could never stand that toil-hardened sort of writing. Herzen, Bunin, Lermontov, Pushkin—they were the Europeans. As a matter of fact, Brodsky has some interesting thoughts on that subject. He says that Russian literature reached a crossroads between Dostoevsky and Tolstoy and chose Tolstoy. That's an interesting way of looking at it. A friend of mine, Valery Afanasiev, says that that split came much earlier, when Russian literature had to decide whether it would follow the lead of Pushkin or his nursemaid Arina Rodionovna. Unfortunately, for the most part, it followed Arina Rodionovna. The "Natural School" bears witness to that. Of course, all of that's fine and good. But a new age has dawned, and you can't go on making people wear traditional Russian baste sandals. We have to seek out what is new. We have to look at where Europe is going, or Latin America, where literature has already moved from the twentieth to the twenty-first century.

JG You speak of new literature in the same breath as a return to the European tradition. Your own prose is filled with archaisms, which suggest a longing for the past. Is that just style, or is it something ideological?

SS No, I don't yearn for the past. My use of archaisms is all by way of parody. I think that it is just a feature of modern prose . . . perhaps more than just a feature, a movement in contemporary literature, which we could call pan-irony. Yerofeev's novel *Moscow-Petushki* is an example of that: a parodied, cynical send-up of everything.

JG I want to quote you something Igor Yefimov said in my interview with him. When I interviewed him, I asked him if there were any writers he would not publish. He said that Sasha Sokolov was an interesting writer in every sense, but he said: "There's a style which shuns all rationality, the visible and physical world, and concentrates exclusively on the demands of the aesthetic. To me that is a retreat into the self. It's as if an acrobat, growing tired of battling with gravity, were to find himself in a weightless state in which he must do his somersaults. He would be able to do marvelous leaps, like the astronauts we've seen flying circles around a floating toothbrush. It would be stunning, but it wouldn't be acrobatics.

"I see Sokolov as a writer who is determined to defy common sense, to wrench the narrative fabric apart. He has fought against rational narrative with such deftness and such ferociousness that he is left with nothing but the connective tissue. And he adamantly refuses to give that fabric any kind of literary clothing. As far as I'm concerned that goes against the grain."

SS Well, that puts me in pleasant company. Nabokov was accused of the exact same things. And Pushkin was criticized for insensitivity to intonation and for lack of depth, for sacrificing content for form. This recalls the famous slogan "Art for art's sake." Or, to use the language of the Gospel, "Let he who hath ears hear." Words have meaning. At least I hope that mine have some sort of meaning. Each word is a symbol and has

meaning both separately and in the context of any given composition. And those who want to read my work, and who know
how to read it, those who are on my wavelength, will find the
same as they'll find in any other contemporary work. The only
difference is that my language is a bit unusual.

Yefimov and I are of different schools of thought. I belong to
a different generation. We're not that far apart in age, but the
difference in literature is there, and that's what leads to these
gaps in understanding. Yefimov belonged to the Leningrad
Gorozhane group, whose members loved people like Andrei
Platonov. Platonov's not a bad writer, but he should not be used
as the be-all and end-all of literary adoration. The *Gorozhane*
group saw him as their model. They also liked the *Oberiuty* and
a number of other writers, but their pantheon is quite limited,
and in my view that's not how things should be. As for Platonov, I repeat, you have to be European, and Platonov is no
European.

JG Let me continue with what Yefimov had to say. I men-
tally compared your work to that of Borges, whose narrative
element is stronger. After you read something by Borges, it's
easier to retell what is going on than in your work. Yet your
styles seem to have quite a bit in common.

SS But I was never influenced by Borges. Or by Nabokov or
Joyce. No critic has ever doubted the influence all those writers
were supposed to have had on me. But I had never read any of
them at the time. What more can I say? Anyway, literature has
undergone a great deal of development. Take Beckett, who has
very little action in his work. He's my trump card. I can always
refer the critics to him.

JG I recently gave a talk at a symposium on literature in
exile. Some of my colleagues were discussing Argentine writers
who had left for Venezuela and now consider themselves émigrés. We mentioned Dante, who left his home city of Florence
to live a hundred kilometers away. Then there was Gertrude
Stein, who moved to Europe, but could always come home,
which she did when she felt like it. Is this kind of emigration the
same as exile from Russia, or is it qualitatively different?

SS There is a qualitative difference; the situations cannot be compared. I think all of us émigré writers secretly dream of a Russian Taiwan. If there were a chunk left over somewhere, Alaska or the Crimea, say, things would be a lot easier. Maybe we wouldn't even live there. I wouldn't want to live there, but I would visit once a year, for a month at a time. I could recharge my language, that linguistic force field, which makes writing so comfortable. That need to be surrounded by the language is so easy to forget about when you're *there*. You begin to notice it only after you've left . . . just as you begin to see other things as they are.

There's another qualitative difference about living in exile, which has nothing to do with the people themselves. From the moment you emigrate you become part of an ethnic minority, which is something unknown to a Russian living in Russia. Not that it becomes a problem in the social sense. But it is a problem in the creative sense, because you suddenly realize that the vast majority of the people around you turn a cold shoulder to your attempts, relentless as they may be, to make yourself known as a writer. There are already plenty of writers who are perfectly comfortable in their own language. Sometimes you sit somewhere in the Midwest writing all day, and suddenly you look up from the paper and glance out the window, and what do you see? Unfamiliar automobiles, houses, people. All those objects, those people—they're from another culture. You become horribly aware that within a radius of perhaps several hundred miles not a soul speaks Russian, and therefore not a soul can understand a single word you've written. . . . Even after you've sat there pouring over your work, sweating, laughing, crying; it's all so otherworldly. And whether you like it or not, you become a cosmopolitan. Literarily and spiritually you are forced into becoming an international writer. In the end it's a good thing. You learn to look at things from without, outside of your own Russian hide. You live in another dimension. It's a tremendous experience.

I realize that I can only advise my colleagues in Russia to try emigration, but I could name many who would agree with me, South American writers in particular.

JG Sasha, one last, very quick question. Whom do you prefer to have as readers—Russians, Americans, or Europeans?

SS   Anyone who isn't tone-deaf. I have readers in America, naturally fewer than in Russia. But now I am writing more for American readers or Westerners in general. And what's important here is translation. I think more and more in terms of which books have been or are going to be translated.

The Moralists

4

Fridrikh Gorenstein

Prose writer, scenarist (b. 1932). Gorenstein, whose father was executed and
whose mother avoided a similar fate
only by going into hiding, was raised in
an orphanage. He managed to publish
little of his fiction in the Soviet Union,
but wrote the scenarios for several successful films, including *Solaris* and *Slave
of Love*. In 1979 he contributed to the almanac *Metropole* and emigrated in 1980,
settling in Berlin. A three-volume set of
his works is currently being prepared for
publication in Moscow, and his play "In-
fanticide" (Detoubiitsa) is to be staged in
both the Vakhtangov and Maly Theaters
in Moscow. Seven of his books have appeared in French translation.

Books: *Iskuplenie* (Redemption) (Tenafly, N.J., 1984) and *Psalom* (Psalm) (Munich, 1986). His *Fellow Travellers* was published in English by Harcourt Brace Jovanovich in 1990.

West Berlin, November 12, 1988

JG   Fridrikh Naumovich, you display a great affinity for the archaic, especially in your book *Psalm*. Neither in the literary nor in the philosophical sense does this book belong to the Russian or Western European literary traditions. It derives from the Old Testament. Why is that?

FG   It's because of the material. In other books I draw upon other traditions. In the novel *Place*, my other main work, I use the classical novel tradition. The material at hand dictates the form of a novel, and in the case of *Psalm* I decided to look at Russia and its history through the prism of the Bible. I change my style according to the material at hand. I have been reading the Bible for a long time now, and each time I learn something new. We can learn from its style as well as from its merciless courage in the revelation of human failings. It is also filled with self-revelation. That kind of courage can't be found in most popular folklore. This may be why Jewish folklore grew into the Bible. Jewish folklore lacks a balance of positive and negative heroes; there are only monsters. But here we see man in his complexity of the good and the evil resident in him. Evil often grows out of good, and good out of evil.

JG   Did you plan to write the book in that style from the very beginning, or did the manuscript change as you worked on it?

FG   The manuscript didn't change as I worked because I always plan my work ahead of time and spend much more time in the planning stages than I do actually writing, even in the case of such large book. I spent at least six months in the planning stage and had enough material to have written three or four books the size of *Psalm*.

The Soviet Radio Committee was helping people find relatives who had disappeared during the war. A search was announced, and listeners were encouraged to write in letters telling of their lives. Some of the letters were read on the air. But the most interesting ones were given to me by one of the technicians. At the time I still didn't know what period of history I would describe, and those letters helped me to decide on the structure of the book. I decided to use the form of parables, starting with the collectivization and the war and ending with the 1970s. So there you have it: the natural combination of idea and happenstance, a normal occurrence when your energies are concentrated on one project.

JG   And what exactly led you to the biblical style?

FG   I have been interested in biblical themes for a long time, primarily because the Bible is a textbook of culture. I perceive it more as a cultural work than a religious one. That's just a personal thing. In the ideological arena I think the Bible can be used against those who continue to misinterpret the ideas expressed in it. I say ideas because one of the themes of the Bible and one of the reasons it is not accepted by many is that it reveals the false path Christianity has taken since the time of Christ, a path which in many ways contradicts the teachings of Jesus of Nazareth.

In Germany the publishing industry obviously hasn't accepted my book, because I set the goriness of history within a biblical framework. The theme is not limited to one generation, but extends into the future. In *Fellow Travellers*, a book I wrote here in the West, German atrocities are described in even greater detail. From what I understand, German publishers have read the book and probably would like to publish it. It's already appeared in France. It describes events in a more sociological framework. But in Germany, the biblical style becomes penetrating and merciless. Criminals have no hope in this world or in the other. The Old Testament is as unforgiving as the judgment of God portrayed by Lermontov. All may be forgiven and forgotten in the courts of men, but God will not forgive and will render judgment on all. That is one of the reasons my book has run into difficulties here. But that was what I intended when I wrote it.

JG   The book's subtitle is "A Novel in Meditations." It consists of five parables, each of which has its own philosophical introduction. Would you really describe it as a novel?

FG   What other genre could it be? For me a novel is a narration that encompasses various aspects of life. I don't know any other form of writing. I consider it a novel structured around parables. What else could it be called? A Solzhenitsyn-style "knot"? A poem? What would you call it?

JG I don't have an answer to that question. That's why I asked you.

FG I tried to write the parables in a biblical rhythm. All prose has a rhythm. If you can detect that rhythm, then the prose comes to resemble music. Nowadays craftsmanship doesn't count. All that counts these days is inspiration and fabrication, so rhythm doesn't play as important a role as it used to. But thanks to circumstance I have always been outside the mainstream, and the great books and the great masters have been my teachers. They taught me rhythm, rhythm, and rhythm. I learned the old kind of rhythm, and not at literary institutes or in literary circles or in the so-called Leningrad School. I became an involuntary student of life. I wouldn't wish the kind of life I have lived on anybody. I hope my son won't have to live as I have.

JG To what extent does the religious theme in the book develop as a result of the world created within the book—as a result of its rhythm—and to what extent is this theme your personal philosophy?

FG The ideas reflected in the book are those I believed in when I was writing. But while people's ideas may change, those in books are written in stone. So it would be incorrect to say that my ideas coincide with those described in any of my books absolutely. I have achieved some distance from my own spiritual state in which I wrote the book. I am pretty much out of touch with that state now and am literally undeserving of that book. I am busy with other things, and I no longer know the Bible as well as I did when I wrote the book. And I don't have to. In that way a writer is different from a philosopher.

JG Well, there is a school of literary criticism that says that an author is merely one of the few or many readers of a given book and that he has no claims to any special status.

In the context of Russian literature in general and Russian émigré literature in particular you would be considered one of the outsiders. What kind of impression does contemporary

Russian literature make on someone like you, perceiving it both geographically and artistically from the outside?

FG Well, like the rest of world culture, Russian literature is not going through the best of times. We are witnessing a spiritual decline that has to do with various social phenomena in the world today. The last remnants of spirituality, tension, and—most importantly—craftsmanship were lost in the 1930s. I'm not one of the fans of the 1960s. That period was responsible for the liberation of consciousness, but it also put a brake on literary development in terms of spiritual values. And more importantly in terms of craftsmanship. The sad fate of the second "thaw" reveals the failings of the first.

Everything is now on the wane because literature has taken on the responsibilities of journalism, and that always has a price. We can find wonderful journalism in Dante's work, but it's only one of his many levels and sources. I feel an affinity with Dante. He tried to take revenge on his life. He understood that the more artistically he wrote, the more powerful his work would be. To a certain extent my work is also ruled by a desire for revenge.

JG I see that you have a German translation of García Márquez's *A Hundred Years of Solitude* on the shelf.

FG It's my wife's shelf, not mine. I'm not a fan of his.

JG I also feel that book was overpraised. But it occurred to me that it might contain some things for which you would feel an affinity. Is that not the case?

FG No, the book is very much linked to modernism. That's why García Márquez is popular. In a way he belongs to the Kafka school. I like Kafka, but for completely different reasons—for the echoes of classicism in his work. García Márquez and other successful contemporary writers have adopted the modernistic aspects of writers like Kafka and Dostoevsky. They probably are some of the best writers around, but I feel put off even by today's best writing. I don't really like American literature—Faulkner and the rest—although I've read them. I don't feel an affinity for all of Nabokov's subject matter, but I understand that it's real literature. It's on a professional level. And that's important. I don't like everything that Bulgakov wrote. I don't think that *The Master and Margarita* was his best work. It's too satirical. I think his best book was *The White Guard*. And I don't like everything that Platonov wrote. I like the short story "Fro" better than *The Foundation Pit*. Its language has a too harmonious and fairy-tale quality to it.

Language is very important to me, and I feel that it has been lost in contemporary culture and life. It has absorbed too many bureaucratic and criminal elements. I have done a lot of work on history and have written a play about Peter the Great that is about to be published. And I am amazed at how much the language has lost since then. In those days robbers spoke the same language as the boyars. It was a nonstandardized, unprocessed, and very poetic language. Perhaps the Russian language reached its peak in Pushkin's time, when a kind of harmonic blending of popular and aristocratic elements took place. *Eugene Onegin* couldn't have been written in the language spoken during the reigns of Peter the Great or Ivan the Terrible, but the language was still vibrant and rich. I don't like Russian anymore. I don't like Solzhenitsyn's language. I'm not a fan of his literary work in general. I'm not talking about his political views, which are his own affair. But his literature has a black-and-white quality and is written in a kind of language that is foreign to me. It's difficult for me to read his work.

JG Perhaps that explains the intentionally archaic quality of *Psalm?*

FG The archaic quality wasn't intentional, but flowed from my perception of the world. The language of *Redemption* is not archaic at all. It is a language of long sentences and many commas—and, where necessary, of short sentences. To me, rhythm is very important. It is why poets often cannot write prose. They don't feel the rhythm of prose. Neither Brodsky nor Mandelstam sense the rhythm of prose. Only Pushkin and Lermontov could. If you cannot sense its rhythm, you can't write prose. You will end up writing essays. Rhythm is the vibration of the heart and soul. Rhythm beats in time with the heart.

JG And each work has its own rhythm?

FG That's right, and to sense it is the hardest thing in the world.

JG   And rhythm is the unifying element at the heart of any work?

FG   Yes, but it has to be learned. It cannot be constructed, it happens subconsciously. Like a heartbeat—it's either normal or abnormal.

JG   Do any émigré writers have that sense of rhythm?

FG   Voinovich has a sense of humor which lends his work rhythm, although he doesn't put any thought into it. I want to stress that his work is humorous rather than satirical, because anyone can make use of satire, but humor and lyricism are the fundamental building blocks for any literary work. And it's humor and lyricism that are lacking even in Solzhenitsyn's best-known work.

JG   Would you like to attempt to formulate the difference between the rhythm of poetry and prose?

FG   That's impossible. Rhythm is born instinctively, not logically.

JG   Does the rhythm of short prose works differ from that of larger genres?

FG   Of course. In short works the word plays a more important role. It seems to depend on purely geometrical correlations—not that I'm any theoretician. A hole the size of a centimeter seems large in something that is only a meter long. In something a kilometer long it is insignificant. There is an important relationship between the word and the size of a work. The musical phrase used to be tied in with mathematics. In ancient times music and mathematics belonged to the same scientific sphere, if I'm not mistaken. Have you ever heard that?

JG   There have been attempts to work it out theoretically.

FG   And it seems to me that logic plays a greater role in the rhythm of poetry than in prose.

JG   What about prose?

FG   In prose the main element of rhythm is instinct. The rhythm of poetry is more immediately evident. In poetry it can even be removed, whereas in prose that's impossible. And it's impossible to live without rhythm.

JG   Free verse now dominates poetry in the English language, whereas Russians often don't even acknowledge free verse as poetry. Perhaps the distinction between poetry and prose is more clear-cut in Russian than in English. But then there are Turgenev's prose poems.

FG Yes, they are prose poems, if they are poems at all. Perhaps we should call them poetic prose instead. But they are the exception. You can use that style to describe an idea, thought, or scene, but not to build a character. Lermontov doesn't use it in this way. The works in which character development is important are written according to the rules of prose rather than poetry.

JG I find that the musical element is stronger in Russian poetry than it is in poetry in English. Perhaps what you said about differing stylistic roles for poetry and prose is truer of Russian literature than of English and American.

FG That's true of contemporary literature in English, but not of English or French literature as a whole. That's why I don't really like contemporary Anglo-American literature. But the musical element is the basis of Shakespeare's sonnets or Baudelaire's work, which has a great deal in common with Russian poetry. It is, in fact, a model for it. The same is true of German literature.

JG So your taste in foreign literature also tends toward the past?

FG You could put it that way. But in a hundred years we'll see who's ahead and who's behind the times. In a hundred years the avant-garde may turn out to be the rearguard. Even if it has many talented writers, the avant-garde is a fad. I don't want and don't have the right to deny their talent, since I don't know much about avant-garde literature. It might be truer to say I don't know it because I don't like it. I feel an affinity for Shakespeare and Baudelaire and often quote them. They are enough for me. I don't have to understand the whole world. For instance, I don't need African literature. I think that one of the tragedies of the modern world is the desire to understand everyone and everything. There's not enough time and everyone loses out. I am quite satisfied with the European biblical literature I was brought up on and which I love.

JG In the Soviet Union you wrote movie scripts. That is a kind of theater in its own right, don't you agree? Is the creation of a movie scenario totally unrelated to that of a literary work?

FG Those are different genres, John. You started out talking about theater and then switched to screenplays. These are two completely different things. I wrote screenplays as well. I think that any dramatic literary work is prose. For me even *Hamlet* is prose.

JG But *Hamlet* is written in poetic meter.

FG In Russian it's only partly poetic. Although I love the theater, on the whole I find reading more interesting than watching something on the stage. Even the best performances are not as enjoyable to me as reading. I mean reading something as prose. I wrote a play called *Berdichev* about the inhabitants of a Jewish town. It is one of my favorite plays. I was going to write it as prose, but something told me that the material lent itself better to drama. Something told Pushkin to write *Boris Godunov* in prose form. Drama and prose are closely related. Even when drama is written in verse, I perceive it as prose.

JG Why don't you see a connection between theatrical works and screenplays?

FG As a professional scriptwriter I have separated that genre from prose writing. Yury Trifonov, who was a talented prose writer, wrote several bad screenplays. They were uninteresting because he wrote them as if they were prose. Screenplays have a different rhythm. In order to write good screenplays you have to be able to feel the rhythm of film. Of course my experience with the visual image has helped me in my prose. But Lev Tolstoy had no background in film. Nonetheless, with little alteration, much of his work would lend itself to that medium. All the same, I think that even though screenplays seem closer in form to prose, they are actually further from it than drama. The rhythm of a screenplay involves editing. The screenplay writer has to be able to sense that editing.

JG Do you think that the Soviet reader will understand *Psalm?*

FG There are people who hate it but haven't written reviews of it.

JG Can you explain what you mean?

FG I think it's a social phenomenon, especially among Russian nationalists. But no one except Boris Khazanov has written anything about it. The émigré community has tried to silence it, as they have all my work.

JG Why is that?

FG Ever since the 1960s there has been a pecking order consisting of a few basic writers. Obviously I'm not part of that pecking order. *Psalm* was reviewed by both the liberal and conservative press. However, in the émigré press, it got no mention at all.

JG Perhaps that goes back to what I said earlier about the book being too unusual for Soviet readers and consequently for émigré readers as well. Perhaps only the Western reader is open to that sort of literary work?

FG That depends on what Western reader we're talking about. The West is not an organic whole. The eclectic French reader may be more open, the German reader—probably not, but I don't really know how German readers will react. Italian publishers approached me on their own, but once they had read the book they beat a hasty retreat. When I appeared in New York, the room was half full. Part of the audience was a bunch of old men who were hostile from the start. I felt like showing them what I thought of them. A few questions were asked. When I began to read an excerpt from the book, they got up and left in a very demonstrative way. Silence was always the main weapon used against me, both there and here. Silence is more effective than denunciation. Denunciation is used only when silence fails. That's ridiculous here because the émigré community itself is up in the air. They can't give me anything, can't take anything from me. That's the advantage of living here.

JG Almost without exception Russian émigré publications bring little or no income, so the émigré writer depends on translations for income, slight as it may be. Why then does it matter what the émigré community says or doesn't say?

FG In theory it doesn't matter at all.

JG Or are émigrés the primary source of information about Russian literature and thus call the shots?

FG At the outset they have some effect because they're connected with Slavists such as yourself, and you are the people who ultimately determine which émigré books get published. Carl Proffer brought some of my work to the West but refused to publish it. I decided that if the liberals wouldn't publish it I'd go to the conservatives. So I approached Possev in West Germany. They also refused to publish *Redemption*. And when they read *Psalm*, they tore their hair out. They're all Russian nationalists, you know. Then some Ukrainian émigrés bought the two books, read them, and said they were anti-Slavic. For me that was a compliment. I think there are very few true lovers of literature about these days.

JG Maria Rozanova wrote somewhere that the émigré reader fails the test of the educated reader.

FG Yes, that's the émigré reader for you. It all reeks of some kind of ideology or party loyalty, which is always the case with people who are unsure of themselves, unless they're completely disinterested. But that isn't important because a book's existence doesn't depend on the reader's opinion. Some books need lots of readers, but *Psalm* doesn't.

JG The figure of Dan the Antichrist is present throughout *Psalm*. Although he participates in the action and would seem to be the common thread that ties the parables together, his role seems to be more that of the silent observer. He has been doomed to eat the tainted bread of exile. Is Dan you?

FG No. I am never a character in the pure sense in any of my works—even autobiographical ones—since one of the main postulates of literature is the idea of transformation. I am as much Dan as I am the small girl Sashenka in *Redemption*. There are moments when I experience Dan and become him, just as I become Maria Korobko when I experience her life. It's a transformation during which I myself cease to exist as a person. I don't know what to call that sensation. It's like being possessed.

JG So the work is cut off from the author, but not necessarily the reverse?

FG Writers are cut off from the actual work as well as from the feelings they invest in it. They're cut off from themselves, but they're also cut off from the characters they create. It resembles man's isolation from God. A true work of creation is always cut off from its creator.

JG That's a typically romantic notion. Writers and artists are "inspired" and create as a result.

FG It's not just a matter of inspiration, but of professionalism and craftsmanship. One of the drawbacks of the literature of the 1960s was that authors identified too closely with their characters.

JG Let's take a classical work of Russian literature such as *The Death of Ivan Ilyich*. Ivan Ilyich *is* Tolstoy.

FG No, he isn't Tolstoy. Tolstoy took Ivan Ilyich and *poured* his own feelings into him. There's a large gap between someone like Gogol and Khlestakov. The idea of transformation is what modern literature has lost. Today's literature is too journalistic and author-bound.

JG What has changed for you since you emigrated?

FG There haven't been any substantial changes.

JG So it doesn't matter whether you're here or there?

FG No, it does matter.

JG I mean for you as a writer, not personally.

FG As a writer too. I have a new view of Russia from here. I felt safer here when I was writing certain things. There are several things I have written here that I wouldn't have written there. And understanding certain of the West's pros and cons helps you understand Russia better. You understand not only why things are so bad there, but also how those bad things can be overcome. Russia isn't an ideal world. It's a world with many negative aspects. But in a way that gives you some hope for salvation. When you encounter something bad here, you experience this very ambivalent feeling of inescapability because there is nowhere to go.

JG And you had hope there?

FG Yes. And as soon as I left everything changed there. But I'm better off here because I can defend myself. And a sense of stability is good for my world view. Everything comes with time. *Psalm* and *Place* had to be written there. I think it's quite possible that I would never have written them here.

JG Do you have any favorites among your own works?

FG Yes, *Berdichev*. It's not about my life, but about a world I carry with me. It's about the world of my childhood, a world in which I lived for only a very short time. I'm not from Berdichev. I was born in Kiev, moved from place to place, worked in mines and on construction sites. But it's a kind of historical motherland that I also write about in *Fellow Travellers*. By the way, *Fellow Travellers* was written in the West and for the time being has been received better than my other work. It is obviously pervaded by some kind of unconscious Western influence, even though I was writing about Russia.

JG If your Jewishness is so important to you, how is it that you ended up in Germany?

FG I received a grant here.

JG But you stayed even after the grant ended.

FG I needed Germany. I find it interesting and want to write about it. I already have enough material about Germany.

JG A novel?

FG I'm thinking of writing a novel, maybe even two. I think about life here. This is an advanced country with a crippled psyche. An analysis of this country is important for an understanding of humanity. I understand myself in terms of this triangle—Russia, Germany, and Judaism. I love France, but I don't know whether I would be able to write about it. But I have a sense of Germany. I mean they were on my heels when I was only nine years old. But they didn't manage to kill me. And I came here. . . . In many ways they have remained the same as they were. This country is at a spiritual roadblock. Just recently something unique happened here.

JG Do you mean the incident with Philip Enninger, the former president of the West German parliament who was forced to resign in 1987 after a speech that many felt was anti-Semitic?

FG Yes, he was preparing a speech in honor of the victims of a pogrom. And suddenly he started screaming all kinds of Nazi slogans. And he understood what he was doing. It's like some kind of devil screaming from inside.

JG And Enninger is Germany?

FG He's their president. He understands everything—intellectually. After all, he's been to Israel. And suddenly something started screaming inside him. I don't think he even knew what he was saying. It was like some kind of delirium, even though the text had been prepared ahead of time. I would have started writing about Germany a long time ago, but I still have a lot of material about Russia. I'm afraid that it will go stale. It was here that I began my work on Russian history, and it has helped me understand the modern world better. Nowadays Russian and

Soviet historians write the truth. At least a part of the truth. But there are no truthful works of literature. I wouldn't have been able to write the kind of play I wrote here about Peter the Great or Ivan the Terrible. There's your view from without. Germans and Russian are two hypostases. They are very closely related. Historically, one is the teacher, the other the pupil. Germany is the most Slavicized country in the world—in spite of its hatred for the Slavs. And I don't feel confused or foreign here, because Germany is tied in with Slavic life. That also stems from the mass murders. The convergence of the scientifically planned genocide of the Germans with the wild character of the Slavic element led to very effective results. There is no doubt that without the mass support of the local population the Germans would not have been able to make such short work of it. I even think they were the ones who actually began the genocide.

JG Who do you mean by "they"?

FG It was the Western Ukrainians and the Balts who in effect started everything. The Germans had made the preparations, but it was the locals who actually took the first step. By the time the Germans came the murders were already under way. I show part of that in *Redemption*. In *Psalm* I show the reasons for it, where the chief guilt lies—in the defenselessness of the victims.

Washingtion, D.C., to Berlin, by telephone, August 12, 1990

JG What do *perestroika* and *glasnost* mean for you? I just asked that same question of Zinoviev, and he said they had no significance for him.

FG They have significance for me in that my plays are going to be staged—not without a certain reluctance—in the Maly Theater and the Vakhtangov Theater. Of course, they have significance! How could it be otherwise! And my prose works will be published—a three-volume set. Even so, they're trying to kill me with silence.

JG Here or there?

FG Both here and there. It's the same liberal crowd. Zinoviev is one of those for whom war is like a mother. And he's not the only one. *Glasnost* and what have you have been a blow to them. For many the fact that they were outlawed or semi-outlawed, especially in the 1960s, was an important element in their very existence. Take Solzhenitsyn. I think he's lost more than he's gained from being published in the Soviet Union. His outlaw status was a tremendous advantage for him. Or take the Taganka Theater. Without their political problems and semiforbidden shows the theater would have been radically impoverished, to put it mildly. I don't have any of the hidden text that they did.

JG Do you want to remain in Germany?

FG I don't want to remain, but as a writer it gives me a lot. Nabokov lived here for eight years. Besides, I'm planning to write a book about Germany.

JG So you don't want to return to Russia?

FG If I hadn't left then, I'd do so now. Russia is the country in whose tongue I work. Now my books are returning there.

I have a reputation in France, and only in France. My seventh book is appearing there, and a play was staged. If I had my way, that's where I'd live. John, you wouldn't recognize Berlin now. What with all the people who've come from Eastern Europe and East Germany, the city is a mess.

Aleksandr Zinoviev

Prose writer, philosopher, logician (b. 1922). Zinoviev was a professor of logic at Moscow University. While still residing in the USSR, he published six books and some two hundred articles in the Soviet press, but no literary works. When he published *The Yawning Heights* abroad, a book satirizing Soviet society, he was expelled from the communist party and fired from his job. In 1978 he emigrated and settled in Munich. In 1990 Zinoviev's Soviet citizenship was returned to him.

Books: *Ziyaushchie vysoty* (Lausanne, 1976); *Svetloe budushchee* (Lausanne, 1978); *Zapiski nochnogo storozha* (Lausanne, 1979); *V predverii raya* (Lausanne, 1979); *Bez illyuzii* (Lausanne, 1979);

Zhelty dom (2 vols., Lausanne, 1980); *My i Zapad* (Lausanne, 1981); *Kommunizm kak real'nost'* (Lausanne, 1981); *Gomo sovetikus* (Lausanne, 1982); *Moy dom—moya chuzhbina* (Lausanne, 1982); *Nashei yunosti polyot* (Lausanne, 1983); *Evangelie dlya Ivana* (Lausanne, 1984); *Idi na Golgofu* (Lausanne, 1985); *Para Bellum* (Lausanne, 1986).

English translations: *Foundations of the Logical Theory of Scientific Knowledge* (Reidel, 1973); *The Yawning Heights*, trans. Gordon Clough (New York: Random House-Vintage Books, 1980); *The Radiant Future*, trans. Gordon Clough (New York: Random House-Vintage Books, 1981); *Logical Physics*, trans. O. A. Germogenova (Boston: Reidel, 1983); *The Reality of Communism*, trans. Charles Janson (New York: Schocken Books, 1984); *Homo Sovieticus*, trans. Charles Janson (London: Gollancz, 1985); *Logical Physics*, trans. Charles Janson (London: Gollancz, 1985).

Munich, November 4, 1988

JG Let's start by talking about your life in the Soviet Union.

AZ I was born way out in the country, but my family moved to Moscow as a result of the collectivization. The conditions we lived in were so terrible that it's hard for me even to think about them. The first time I had a bed to myself and three meals a day on a plate of my own was when I was sent to prison in 1939. Before and after that I was cold, hungry, and dirty. As a result of living in those conditions and seeing how badly others lived, by the time I was sixteen or seventeen, I had become a confirmed anti-Stalinist. I even belonged to a terrorist group whose goal was to kill Stalin. We planned to pass by the Lenin Mausoleum during a demonstration and create some sort of diversion during which we would shoot him and throw bombs.

JG That would have been suicide.

AZ That's right. But I was in such a state that I was willing to sacrifice my life. We even had a backup plan to wire me with explosive devices and detonate them as I stood by the Lenin Mausoleum.

JG When was that?

AZ That was in 1939. But we had difficulty getting weapons, so we postponed our plans to the spring of 1940. However, our assassination attempt never took place because that year I was provoked into making a speech against collective farms and the cult of Stalin. I was kicked out of my institute and the Komsomol and was sent to a psychiatric ward, where I was found to be sane and arrested soon after. I was put in the Lubyanka, the central prison of the KGB, and held there for a short time, during which I was interrogated every day.

I had already come to the conclusion back then that communism doesn't eliminate inequality, injustice, violence, or any of the other cancers that it attributed to other forms of society, but merely changes the face of such phenomena. My interrogator didn't believe that these were my own ideas and decided to find those who were responsible for them. So they decided to move me out of the Lubyanka and keep me under the surveillance of a KGB officer (back then it was called the NKVD). It was supposed to look as if I had been freed, while in reality an officer would follow me at all times, trying to unearth my coconspirators and mentors. But on the way out there was some kind of mix-up, and I was left unsupervised for several minutes. I seized the opportunity and fled—just walked off. After that I traveled around the country trying to avoid the authorities. Then an all-points bulletin was put out on me. It was unusual, after all, for a person to flee from the KGB. I call that my first year of horrors. I traveled around Siberia and the northern parts of the country getting work on construction sites where I could.

JG All of this without identification papers of any kind?

AZ At that time there were lots of people in my situation. Many criminals hid out in that way. The Volgograd authorities took me into custody and asked for my papers. I told them that I was a student, but for reasons of health I was not currently matriculated for classes. I said that my papers and all my money had been stolen. They believed me and suggested that I go north to find work. At that time they were taking on anybody for northern construction sites. I worked there for a time, but fled when people started to take an interest in who I was. By then I had an official work record in my pocket, so I set off for Siberia. When I reached Omsk, I found work at several construction sites. Gradually I obtained all kinds of papers, many of which were forged.

In the fall of 1940 I returned to Moscow, where I lived in a friend's shed and worked as a porter at the railway station. Soon after a search was conducted, and all the porters were taken into custody. We were given a choice: either go to jail or volunteer for the army. They were drafting everyone they could get their hands on. By that time it was obvious to everyone that there would be war with Germany.

JG Obvious to everyone except Stalin, it seems.

AZ It was probably obvious to Stalin as well, but he wanted to delay the war as long as he could since the country wasn't ready for it. The element of surprise that everyone talks about was surprise at how quickly we had been dragged into the war.

In the army I served first in the cavalry, then in a tank division, and finally in the air force. Immediately before the war started I was assigned to a tank division on the frontier. I knew that we would get into the war. For a while I worked in a classified section of the Division Headquarters and later in the corps headquarters, since I could draw all sorts of maps and knew German. I started the war in the infantry and was wounded several times. But I refused to go to the hospital, since at that time it would have been senseless, even life-threatening.

JG Why was that?

AZ Say that I had gotten a shoulder wound at Orsha. If I had gone to the hospital, I would have ended up a POW since, a couple of days later, the hospital would have been captured by the Germans. That's why those with light wounds avoided the hospital.

At the end of 1941 I was sent to aviation school. I went to two different ones. The first prepared me to be a fighter pilot, the second—a bomber pilot. Then I served in various aviation attack units where I completed quite a few missions, was shot down a number of times, and was awarded several medals and decorations.

In 1946 I was demobilized and worked for a while as a civil aviation pilot. When my unit was transferred north, I returned to Moscow and entered the Philosophy Department of Moscow University. I supported myself by working as a porter, laboratory assistant, and ditch digger. I also taught military preparedness, math, logic, and psychology in a primary school. Life was rough. It was impossible to live on the stipend I got from the

university. In 1951 I graduated from the Philosophy Department with honors, began to study in graduate school, and
wrote my dissertation.

JG What was your topic?

AZ The logic of Marx's *Das Kapital*. My dissertation made
quite an impression in philosophical circles and typed copies
were passed from hand to hand. That was the precursor of
samizdat. But then the authorities banned the dissertation, and
only those who could get special permission were allowed to
read it. Later the period of liberalization or de-Stalinization
began. I was asked to join the party to help fight Stalinism
within party organizations. In 1954 I did just that.

For a time the country waged a war against Stalinism, especially within the party itself. The West has overlooked that
period. Khrushchev's famous speech at the Twentieth Party
Congress was the culmination, not the beginning, of the struggle against Stalinism. Former Stalinists became anti-Stalinists,
and my own anti-Stalinism lost its point.

I retreated into academia. When my work began to be published in the West, I regularly received personal invitations to
international meetings, but I was never allowed to go. I was
nominated for a state prize but the party higher-ups passed me
over. After that I was nominated to the Academy of Sciences
but was passed over once again. One of my papers was discussed at a meeting of the Presidium of the Academy of Sciences, which was attended by many well-known scientists. A
decision was made to support the new school of logic that I had
already founded and that had many followers. But in order to
obtain substantial support, I was supposed to display my party
loyalty in a meaningful way. It was suggested that I publish an
article in the journal *Kommunist*, in which I would state that I
was a Marxist developing the Marxist approach to logic. I refused, and soon after that the Academy of Sciences' decision
was forgotten. That was the beginning of a difficult time for me.
One of my problems was a conflict with the editorial board of
the journal *Voprosy filosofii* (Questions of Philosophy), of which I
was a member. The journal's editor was a Brezhnev lackey.

JG What was his name?

AZ Ivan Frolov. He's a member of the Academy now, and

one of Gorbachev's closest aides. In one issue of the journal he increased the number of allusions to Brezhnev so that they outstripped those to Stalin in the journal *Pod znamenem marksizma* (Under the Banner of Marxism) in the worst years of Stalin's rule. In protest, I quit the editorial board. After that I lost the patronage of the liberals who served the higher party organs.

I was the chair of a department at Moscow University and had two dissidents working for me, and I was asked to fire them. I refused, and that lost me all official support for good. My colleagues used my noncompliance to destroy the school of logic that I had founded and to make difficulties for my protégés. In the true Soviet spirit, my protégés immediately began to betray me. I found myself completely alone. But every cloud has a silver lining. As a consequence of losing my position in the university, my students, and my classes, I started to have a lot of free time. I decided to make use of it and avenge all the wrong that had been done to me.

JG Using literature?

AZ Using the word. I had two choices. I could either write a sociological treatise criticizing communism or a work of fiction. I chose the latter and began to work on *The Yawning Heights.*

Writing was not a new idea to me. I had written fiction all my life without any hope of getting it published. After the war, I had written a long short story, which I showed to Konstantin Simonov. He liked it a lot, but suggested that if I valued my life, I should destroy the manuscript. I showed it to another writer who simply informed on me to the KGB.

JG What year was that?

AZ 1946. After that I stopped trying to enter the arena of officially sanctioned Soviet literature. I began to write my first novel *The Yawning Heights* when I was fifty-two. By that time I already had an understanding of communist social structure. I also had a great deal of experience with oral genres—jokes and table talk—and academic work. I had given public lectures, many of which made their way into *The Yawning Heights*. So, by the time I started, I was thoroughly prepared to write a book. I had written dozens of them in my head. Now all I had to do was get them on paper.

JG Do you mean books of a literary nature? Or do you mean books on logic? Or politics?

AZ All of the above. You could say that I invented a new literary form, which I call the sociological novel. All that meant was that I wrote fiction based on research in sociology and philosophy. If I had simply written an academic treatise, no one would have read it.

JG So that your main stimulus was ideological rather than creative?

AZ The main stimulus for my work was very simple. I had acquired so much intellectual and emotional baggage that I had to purge myself. I just wanted to hurt them, the establishment—the authorities and the society. Wanting to deal a blow to society when I was seventeen, I decided to assassinate Stalin. Now I was a fifty-two-year-old man, and the blow had to be much harder. And I hit that society where it hurts. I revealed its essence, its internal mechanism. I portrayed the administrators of that society and its leader in a way that made them objects of ridicule. I had been gifted since childhood with an ironic, satirical bent, and I had gone on to display and hone it all the time in one way or another.

The KGB quickly found out that I was working on a book and had me tailed. Every time I entered even a public toilet, a KGB agent would follow me in to see what I was doing. I realized that the only way to end this was to write as fast as I could. I needed to outrun the authorities so that they wouldn't be able to keep me from completing the book. In six months I had finished the book—which turned out to be very large. I wrote day and night, sometimes for twenty hours straight, without ever going back to make corrections. My wife Olga typed out each page on onionskin paper as I wrote. And those sheets were immediately sent off to the West.

By the time the authorities had decided to take stronger measures against me, it was too late. The book was already in the West, published in Switzerland in 1976. It was immediately reviewed, for the most part favorably. It was called the first book of the twentieth century. I wasn't a professional writer or a member of the Writer's Union, and I didn't have to get the book approved by a censor. I wrote with absolute freedom and in my own voice—in the voice of the person I had come to be by the age of fifty. That was why the book was unusual.

JG How do you define the genre in which it's written?

AZ Literary critics couldn't come up with a suitable generic slot for it. When I was asked what genre it belonged to, I replied that it was a book.

Heights is based on the scientifically developed theory of communism. That, in and of itself, is nothing unusual. But I also used all of the literary devices that I had at my disposal: poems, anecdotes, jokes, satire, humor, as well as serious, dramatic, and tragic elements. In other words I used every kind of literary tool. The result was a synthesis of artistic forms. When I was writing the book, I thought that each page might be my last. As a result the book can be begun in any place and in any direction. Yet together the parts form a coherent whole. The book is held together by a unity of ideas, idea development, and characters. The heroes are ideas rather than people. So it did not matter who expressed what ideas in which situations. The main thing was to get the idea on the page. Therefore, positive ideas were sometimes put forward by negative characters and negative ideas by positive ones.

What my characters looked like was of no importance to me—what color eyes they had or where they lived. I left that kind of description out completely. I think that, for the modern reader, that kind of description is a complete waste of time. In a normal, traditional novel the author writes that the character is tall with blue eyes and blond hair and is wearing a sport jacket. He enters the room, turns to the right, turns off the light, walks to the window, and pulls the drapes. To me that's just a waste of valuable space, and I got rid of it. In its place I substituted detailed descriptions of ideas and their adventures. As a result the book is very concentrated. Traditional novels contain one or two ideas for every several hundred pages. My book has dozens—sometimes even hundreds—of ideas on every page, so they are quite difficult to read, especially the first one. But I think that reading should be hard work.

As soon as the book was published, I was fired from my job and stripped of all stipends, awards, and honors—including my military rank. Everyone backed away from me.

JG But you must have been prepared for that?

AZ I had assumed it would happen. But these were people whom I had known for decades and who didn't stand to lose anything. They immediately broke off all contact with me.

JG In a demonstrative way?

AZ In a very demonstrative way. Perhaps they are ashamed now, but at the time they were beside themselves with rage. My friends in the institute demanded that I be handed over to the courts, while the KGB officer handling the case told them it wasn't their business. In other words suddenly the KGB was defending me from my liberal friends. Why was that? The answer is quite simple. I had dared to do what they only dreamed of doing. I had risked everything that I had acquired in my fifty years of life. I was a professor, held an important position, was a member of the Academy, and was well off. And I lost it all at a stroke. What bothered them most of all was not that I had published a book in the West, but that it had been successful. Dozens of copies made it back to the Soviet Union and, in spite of the ban, the book began a triumphant, albeit illegal, tour of the country. People would come from distant cities just to see me. One of my guests had copied the entire book in microscopic handwriting. The result was about the size of an address book.

JG I wonder where that copy is now.

AZ A Western journalist wanted to buy it for 500 rubles, but the owner refused.

JG I understand that people were frightened and backed off. But aggressive censure is a different matter.

AZ It wasn't just fear. People recognized themselves in the book's characters.

Two years after the book was published we were living under strict surveillance in the Soviet Union. There was always at least one KGB car outside our house. Anyone who came to visit us was photographed, sometimes even filmed. The KGB even set up a special watch point in our apartment building. All our rooms were bugged, and we were followed everywhere. I had been attacked several times, so I never went out unaccompanied. We had nothing to live on. We sold all our books, furniture, and things. A few people helped us out.

JG What about royalties for *The Yawning Heights?*

AZ So as not to be accused of receiving money from the CIA, I categorically refused to accept any royalties. Moreover, it wouldn't have been very easy to get such payments through. A few people helped us out. Some sent small amounts of money anonymously, others did it openly. One member of the Academy, Pyotr Kapitsa, became a fan of mine and sent me money openly. But of course it wasn't enough to live on.

The surprising thing was that our relatives stayed with us. That was unheard of. My son, a police officer, came to stay with us. He had been warned that if he came to see me he would be expelled from the party and fired at work. That was precisely what happened. For a long time after that he made his living as a blue-collar worker. My daughter was immediately fired and expelled from the Komsomol. To this day she doesn't have regular work. But my brother suffered the most. He was a military lawyer and a colonel. He is an unusually honest and conscientious person. He had a good reputation in the military and had been involved in solving some famous crimes. He had been transferred to Moscow, given an apartment, and appointed general. He was told to condemn me publicly. He refused, saying that he was proud of me. The very next day he was discharged from the army and expelled from Moscow. All our relatives stuck by us. I have a number of brothers and sisters, and not one of them uttered a word of reproach. And things were made difficult for them for many years because of us.

Our apartment began to be frequented by dissidents—Venedikt Yerofeev, Georgy Vladimov, and others. They had all responded enthusiastically to the publication of my book. For two years we literally lived under house arrest, with all sources of income exhausted. I kept being charged with parasitism and taken into custody. People in the know have told me that Suslov demanded I be put on trial: "we have been struggling with dissidents, but we have overlooked the chief bastard." By "chief bastard" he meant me. He even said that people like me should be shot, and he demanded my arrest. And, indeed, I faced a seven-year prison sentence and five years of internal exile for anti-Soviet activity.

In *The Radiant Future* and *The Yawning Heights* I criticized Brezhnev outright. I not only criticized him, but made him into a laughing stock. I described him as "a commander who had lost the battle," "a researcher who had made no discoveries," and "a senile old man."

JG A second suicide attempt?

AZ Right! But after the publication of *The Yawning Heights* I felt great relief, as if I had purged myself. Before the book's publication I had asked my wife Olga to decide whether or not we should publish it. I was prepared to accept the consequences, but I didn't know if she would want to. She agreed to share whatever awaited us. But there was an unexpected turn of events. One of my good friends, who was a personal friend of Andropov's, told me that Andropov liked my books. He had insisted in the Politburo that, instead of being sent to prison, I be allowed to leave the country. In the end Brezhnev, who was always inclined to compromise, took the middle road. He decided to let me go to the West, but first to strip me of Soviet citizenship. While I was still in the Soviet Union, Roy Medvedev told me that I had been deprived of citizenship. I was told to leave the country within five days, but we never filed any emigration or travel papers.

JG Were you already thinking of emigrating when you wrote *The Yawning Heights?*

AZ No, I didn't consider emigration at any time. I am Russian to the bones. Not all Soviet people are Russians. But I am. Leaving the country was the harshest punishment they could have thought up. I hadn't planned to emigrate and didn't want to. I had expected to go to jail or, at best, to be exiled to Siberia. But I never expected that I would suddenly be told to leave the country. While I was in Sheremetievo Airport, I kept hoping that at the last minute a government representative would come up to us and say that our departure had been canceled.

JG You said that you are "Russian to the bones." I take it you feel that there are others who do not fall into that category.

AZ The overwhelming majority of Third-Wave Soviet émigrés are not ethnic Russians. They are Soviet, but not Russian. Most of them are Jews. There are also a lot of Ukrainians and Armenians. The number of Russians who emigrated during that time is incredibly small.

JG But Russian is the native language for the majority of émigrés.

AZ I'm talking about ethnic Russians. A Tartar doesn't become a Russian just because he's grown up in Russian society. I'm talking about the Russian national character.

JG Do you consider Voinovich to be a Russian writer?

AZ Ask him.

JG But I would like to know what you think.

AZ I can't answer for him. I am speaking for myself. I am an ethnic Russian with the traits of the Russian national character.

JG What about Galich? Was he a Russian?

AZ Galich was an ethnic Jew.

JG Not Russian?

AZ He's not Russian, but Jewish. In the West people use the word "Russian" when they really mean "Soviet." But there are different ethnic groups. It's one thing to be Kazakh, Kalmyk, Jew, Georgian, Ukrainian, or what have you. It's quite another thing to be Russian. I don't want to say that Russians are better or worse. But a Russian is a Russian. We have a different destiny, a different way of bringing up our children, a different way of life. One characteristic of Russians is that they feel very attached to where they live. And for that reason Russians suffer a greater sense of nostalgia when they emigrate than do those of other ethnic backgrounds.

JG Are you haunted by nostalgia?

AZ My first years of emigration I spent in a state of shock. I was fifty-six years old, and we were living in completely alien surroundings. I was used to a certain way of living. All of that fell apart here, and, for about four years, we were miserable. By the end of 1982 I was on the verge of a nervous breakdown. I contemplated suicide. Although I have now gotten over that, I can't say that I have adapted to life in the West. I never will. It's too late for that.

JG So you think that emigration is harder for ethnic Russians than it is for Russian Jews?

AZ Absolutely. Take a look at Jewish émigrés. They leave the country in rather large numbers, and they have a support system. Jews have a greater sense of solidarity than Russians. Russians don't have much solidarity.

JG   I don't think anyone could say that there is a great deal of solidarity in the Third Wave. They are constantly fighting with one another.

AZ   They fight in the Soviet Union and in their own families as well. But they still share ties. They form groups and socialize with one another. They have created a kind of microcosm of Soviet society here in the West. They simply brought all their Soviet baggage with them.

JG   Soviet, not Russian?

AZ   Soviet, not Russian. As I said, solidarity is not a characteristic Russian trait. Russians don't support one another. I have been supported by Jews more than Russians both in the Soviet Union and the West. The older generation of Russian émigrés greeted me with hostility.

JG   How did that hostility make itself felt?

AZ   In many ways. For the last ten years I have been surrounded by false rumors, slander, and name-calling. I can't name one Russian-language publication in the West that wouldn't want to discredit me.

JG   Could you be more precise?

AZ   I have been called an agent of the KGB. Rumors have been spread that I am returning to the Soviet Union. The first Russian-language review of my book in the West, which appeared in *Novoe Russkoe Slovo* (The New Russian Word) was incredibly base and vulgar. Nor did it make sense. One Western publisher said that if I had been anyone else, after what had happened to me, I would have been carried on the crowd's shoulders. Then he found out that I was an ethnic Russian. "Too bad," he said, "if Zinoviev weren't Russian, he would have monuments to him in every city of the world." Do you see what I mean? There wasn't a murmur in the Russian-language press about my awards. The first time I had a chance to appear before the latest generation of émigrés was only last year in New York.

JG   Do you ever write anything for the émigré press?

AZ   Very rarely. I have just started to publish occasionally in *Kontinent*. I can't say that my path through emigration has been strewn with roses. Quite the reverse. On the one hand I have enjoyed some success. I have traveled around the world and given papers in dozens of cities. There have been television films, my books have been translated into many languages, and the press I have received has been wonderful. But the response to me in the émigré community has been more hostile than friendly.

The Third Wave is very heterogeneous. You might say that there are the "enlisted men" and then there are the "generals"—those who publish newspapers and magazines and who are writers themselves. In other words, there is the intellectual and political elite. But it has been the "enlisted men," the everyday people, whose response to me has been positive. I have acquired a large number of fans within the émigré community here in the West. And most of them, by the way, are Jewish. But the émigré "generals" have greeted me with a great deal of hostility. Sakharov himself greeted the publication of my book with hostility. We bumped into one another once by accident and didn't even exchange greetings. In an interview with a French journalist, he said that my book was decadent, that I didn't have the right to write about what had happened because I hadn't been in prison. Solzhenitsyn also greeted the book with hostility. When he was compiling a list of books that should be sent to the Soviet Union, he crossed out my name. And he forbade YMCA Press to sell my book. YMCA Press can sell my books only under the counter.

There are many reasons for that kind of reaction. I appeared out of nowhere, upsetting a kind of accepted order. They were also annoyed by the fact that I hadn't gone through samizdat, which would have allowed them to exert some control. It irritated them that my book had enjoyed such unusual success and that I have always been independent. For ten years I have lived in the West, I have never received a cent from anyone. We have always lived entirely off my literary income, which is really slave labor. To scrape out a meager existence, I have to write a minimum of two books and dozens of articles a year. I never know what will happen next year or what I will live on. I never know whether I'll have any offers. This is in contrast to other émigré writers who get help from all kinds of organizations, do

work on radio, and so on. I was never offered those opportunities.

JG I'd like to ask a purely financial question. Does your basic
income come from translations of your work?

AZ In the West the relations between publishers, distribu-
tors, and stores are so complicated that it is impossible to follow
what is going on. And Russian émigré writers find that they are
totally dependent on these people. I get no more than 5 percent
of my income from Russian-language editions.

JG You recently gave an interview to Vladimir Tolz at Radio
Liberty in which you more or less said that Gorbachev is a new
Stalin.

AZ Not exactly a new Stalin, but something similar. The fact
is that there are two possible kinds of leadership in a communist society—the Stalin kind and the Brezhnev kind. Gorbachev
displays all the symptoms of the libertarian style. He's trying to
initiate change from above—by forcing people to live as the
authorities want them to. If Gorbachev is still in power a few
years from now, the whole world will finally see what really
lurks behind this *glasnost,* liberalization, democratization, and
the like. I am analyzing the situation, not offering any concrete
advice. I can view the Soviet Union objectively. I can explain
what is possible in the country and what isn't. But I don't go
further than that. Can Soviet economic activity ever reach Western levels? No, it's impossible, and that can be proven like a
theorem. Will Gorbachev and his followers overcome the current crisis? Yes, they will. But the result will be nothing like
what is being promised.

JG So what do you think will happen?

AZ The country will come out of the current crisis. With the
help of the West, industry—especially the military—will to
some extent be modernized. In five to ten years the armed
forces of the Soviet Union will double. The USSR will talk to the
West in a different voice—from a position of power. All the so-
called democratic and liberal tendencies will be wiped out in the
course of a day or two. No one will even remember that they
ever existed. The regime will become stricter; discipline in the
workplace will be increased. Many people will be sent to those
parts of Siberia where no one wants to go. That's what will hap-

pen. There are no other alternatives. And if Gorbachev stays in power, he will create his own cadre of higher authorities who will stand above the normal party apparatus. The country will accept a compromise somewhere between Stalin and Brezhnev—a kind of modernized Brezhnevism that is closer to Stalinism.

JG So you think it will be worse than under Brezhnev?

AZ Of course. The Brezhnev years will be remembered as the most liberal period in our history.

JG And Gorbachev will be responsible for all of this?

AZ If he remains in power. If he is removed, others will do it.

JG Let's go back to literature. I'm going to play the role of devil's advocate. Some say that Zinoviev is talented, but he doesn't write fiction. He writes sociological treatises. Viktor Shklovsky wrote that one can use a samovar to hammer in nails, but that's not what it was made for, and it ends up the worse for it. How would you respond to that?

AZ I would say that literature can take more than one form. In prerevolutionary Russian literature there was a trend that literary specialists call Sociological Realism. Saltykov-Shchedrin and Chekhov belong to that school. I know that many Soviet émigré writers are willing to recognize me as a thinker but not as a writer; they leave me no place in literature. I am, above all, a writer. I am a writer who uses the results of his sociological research. My books are works of literature in the highest degree. The fact that it is a new form of literature is a different issue. I have to add that for the time being nobody—not just Russian émigré writers, but Western writers as well—can understand this new form. There is no one else writing in the same way. I don't say that it's better or worse than other genres. I'm talking about kind, not quality. At the moment I'm the only one writing in this style, and that irritates everyone. But if you were to try publishing one of my books in large numbers in the Soviet Union, you would see that within two weeks I would become a recognized writer—not a philosopher or sociologist, but a writer. The fact is that there exists in the Soviet Union a well-educated average reader with a highly developed aesthetic sense. There is nothing like that here. Moreover, there are now about a thousand people writing in Russian in the West, and they all consider themselves writers. In fact their work can in no way be described as literature. There is no comparison between their work and mine! In the end history will judge. Time will tell.

JG Do you ever worry that since your books are so tied up with politics and sociology, they have to be published as soon as you've finished them? Are you concerned that if too much time goes by they will lose their topicality and be out of step with the times?

AZ That doesn't frighten me—if only because I'm not ambitious. If my books are forgotten, it won't be because they're out of date. As long as communism is alive and well, they will continue to be pertinent. Considerable efforts will be made to suppress my books. But they deal with sociology, not current politics, and sociology deals with the universal and timeless aspects of human life.

JG What literary tradition do you feel you belong to?

AZ I feel I belong with writers like Rabelais, Swift, Anatole France, and later Kafka, Orwell, and Zamyatin. In classical Russian literature there is Saltykov-Shchedrin and, to some extent, Chekhov. Kozma Prutkov is well known in Russia, but unheard of in the West. There is also a book by Fyodor Sologub called *The Petty Demon*. I don't write about love, the adventures of the young and old, or nature, but about social phenomena. Try writing a novel about power without mentioning the mechanisms of power. It won't work. The time has come when knowing how to craft a phrase is not the only quality necessary to make a contribution to literature. A high level of training in the areas dealt with by literature is now equally important.

JG If I wanted to classify you, could I put you in the same bag as, say, Solzhenitsyn?

AZ I wouldn't advise you to do that. Not because I would be offended by it; I think very highly of Solzhenitsyn as a writer. I'm just a different kind of writer. I have a scientifically developed theory of communist society.

JG And Solzhenitsyn doesn't?

AZ No, he doesn't. In my opinion his understanding of the social structure of communism is dilettantish and completely false.

JG But those are not artistic criteria.

AZ They are artistic if taken together with other criteria. I introduced a scientific style of thought to literature. Solzhenitsyn and I also differ in language, imagery, and in the literary devices we use. If a literary specialist is interested in my work, he will soon notice these things. Classification is, in any case, of secondary importance. Solzhenitsyn reviews history in the hopes of rewriting it. I'm not interested in that. Solzhenitsyn's work looks toward the past. Mine looks toward the future.

Washington, D.C., to Munich, by telephone, August 12, 1990

JG Since we last talked, Aleksandr Aleksandrovich, some things have changed. You have received Soviet citizenship. Did you ask to receive it? And how did you learn about it?

AZ I certainly never asked, and I learned when someone called me from Radio Free Europe/Radio Liberty.

JG So you could get a Soviet passport now, if you wanted to?

AZ I could but I don't want to—at least not yet.

JG Has perestroika changed anything for you in your personal life?

AZ Precious little.

JG You said you would be the last of the émigrés to be accepted.

AZ That is exactly what has happened. Aksyonov, Voinovich, and the others have all traveled there and have been published. A number of my books—including *Yawning Heights*—are scheduled for publication in late 1990 and 1991, but not yet—except for one thing in Estonia and a couple of complimentary articles in Russia, one in *Izvestia*. So I really am the last.

JG But don't the changes taking place in the USSR change your attitude in any way? During our last interview you viewed Gorbachev in a very negative light.

AZ None of my views have changed in the least. All that is taking place confirms my predictions. The Soviet Union is going through a crisis, but a crisis is not a collapse; it will be overcome, and the Soviet Union will return to its normal state of affairs.

Natalya Gorbanevskaya

Poet and journalist (b. 1936). Gorbanevskaya, whose verse was circulated in samizdat, became involved in the human-
rights movement in 1968 and founded
The Chronicle of Current Events, a publication which kept track of Soviet vio-
lations of human rights. After demonstrating against the Soviet intervention
in Czechoslovakia, she was placed in a
mental hospital. She emigrated from the
USSR in 1975 and settled in Paris in 1976.
There she works as a journalist for *Kontinent* and *Russkaya mysl'*.

　　Books: *Stikhi* (Verse) (Frankfurt-am-
Main, 1969); *Polden': Delo o demonstratsii
25 avgusta 1968 goda na Krasnoi ploshchadi*
(Noon: The Case of the August 25,
1968, Demonstration) (Frankfurt-am-

Main, 1970); *Poberezhie: Stikhi* (The Coast: Verse) (Ann Arbor, 1973); *Tri tetradi stikhotvoreniy* (Three Notebooks of Verse) (Bremen, 1975); *Angel derevyanny* (Wooden Angel) (Ann Arbor, 1982); *Chuzhie kamni: Stikhi 1979–82* (Alien Stones: Verse 1979–82) (New York, 1983); *Peremennaya oblachnost': Stikhi* (Occasionally Overcast: Verse) (Paris, 1985); and *Gde i kogda: Stikhi* (When and Where: Verse) (Paris, 1985).

English translations: *Red Square at Noon,* introd. Harrison E. Salisbury, trans. Alexander Lieven (New York: Holt, Rinehart and Winston, 1972); *Selected Poems,* trans. Daniel Weissbort (Oxford: Carcanet Press, 1972).

Paris, December 17, 1988

JG After the demonstration of August 25, 1968, why weren't you imprisoned immediately?

NG At that point I had two small children, one of whom was only three months old. I took him with me to the demonstration. I don't think that would have prevented my imprisonment if the demonstration and my part in it hadn't been surrounded by a great deal of public outcry. For that reason they decided to wait until the controversy died down, and I was arrested only in December 1969. In the interim I continued to publish the *Chronicle of Current Events* and wrote a documentary-style story, entitled *Red Square at Noon.* I think I would eventually have been arrested in any case, since they were still dying to lock me up for my part in the demonstration. I was subjected to psychiatric evaluation, found to be psychologically unfit, and sent to a psychiatric prison in Kazan.

JG What was the actual diagnosis?

NG "Latent schizophrenia"—one of their favorite diagnoses. Actually I was fairly lucky because two weeks after my arrest Vladimir Bukovsky got out of prison and began in earnest to investigate repressive psychiatry. In addition, two of my friends—Vera Lashkova, a former political prisoner, and Tatiana Velikanova, who was eventually to become a political prisoner—sent an open letter in my defense to Western psychiatrists. Furthermore, of all the evidence on psychiatric repression gathered by Vladimir Bukovsky, my case was perhaps the most well documented. He even included in his book a copy of the actual medical certificate. Not only a specialist, but any layman reading that diagnosis could see that it was utter nonsense.

Thanks to Bukovsky's work, a wave of protest against repressive psychiatry arose in the West. As a result Bukovsky ended up in prison, but I was soon freed, having served two years and two months, which is nothing in the Soviet Union.

JG You were in a hospital the whole time?

NG No, not exactly. I was in a psychiatric prison. That's what they call it: a "special psychiatric hospital" or psychiatric prison, and I see no reason to call it anything else. I was there for about a year, but I would have preferred to serve three or even seven years in a regular camp.

JG Were you given injections?

NG No, but I was given Haloperidol, an antihallucinogen with side effects similar to the symptoms of Parkinson's disease. Since none of the political prisoners I knew had been diagnosed as hallucinatory but practically all were given those tablets, I think the medicine was intended as an instrument of torture, that is, precisely because of its excruciating side effects. The symptoms of Parkinson's disease differ from person to person, but in every case the physical and psychological suffering is extreme.

JG What made them decide to use a psychiatric diagnosis against you? Many dissidents weren't put through that.

NG In 1969, when I was arrested, there had been an increase in the number of people found psychologically unfit. But I had been in a psychiatric hospital for two weeks in 1959. At that time I had been diagnosed with possible schizophrenia, but the doctor who observed me later said he thought a mistake had been made, and I had experienced nothing more than a temporary psychotic episode. A little more than a month before my arrest, I was summoned back to the psychiatric hospital for a review of my case. Once you seek psychiatric help in the Soviet Union, your name remains on record for the rest of your life. I received a call from the hospital; they said they wanted to delete my name from their records, and I was asked to appear before a large commission.

Later I was told that my name would not be deleted from the

records in case I should need help again. But the commission's conclusion was that there was no evidence of schizophrenia. Five weeks later I was arrested and sent to the Serbsky Psychiatric Institute. Before my arrest, I don't think the authorities were quite sure whether I should be sent to a camp or a psychiatric hospital. I think that because of the assistant prosecutor's words at my interrogation: "You will spend the rest of your life in camps or psychiatric hospitals!" Perhaps the eventual decision was partly my own fault for telling my so-called cellmate that the one thing I feared was psychiatric prison.

The Serbsky Institute representative was Daniil Romanovich Lunts, and the diagnosis read as follows: "Latent schizophrenia is not out of the question. Involuntary treatment at a special psychiatric hospital is recommended." It was all very simple. The case was closed, but the document didn't disappear. I made fun of that phrase in *Noon*, since it was a perfect capsule of humor, albeit black humor. That, I think, was why the Serbsky Institute felt it a matter of pride to change the wording in my medical history: "not ruled out" became simply "latent schizophrenia."

To this day I don't think anyone could tell you what latent schizophrenia is. At the trial my lawyer informed Lunts that, according to the textbook of legal psychiatry, the medical certificate must specify the specific type of schizophrenia. Lunts calmly answered that I suffered from a nameless form of schizophrenia which had no obvious symptoms.

JG Now that reform has come to Russia, would you consider demanding some kind of apology or even compensation?

NG What good would that do?

JG If nothing else, it would be interesting to see what sort of response that would bring.

NG There are people who are much worse off than I. I don't think that anyone who knows me personally or is familiar with my poetry, my contributions to *Kontinent* and *Russkaya mysl'*, or my work at Radio Liberty has ever thought for an instant that anything was wrong with me. So what good is a retraction? The same people still work at the Serbsky Institute. If the authorities demand it, the Serbsky Institute will obediently follow directions, just as they did before, and they will retract the diagnosis. What do I need that for? Let them shoot themselves instead.

I saw some people in the women's ward of the Kazan Hospital who had been driven to the verge of insanity. They seem to have disappeared without a trace, although they are probably still in prison. Those are the people Gorbachev should release and compensate. I have a wonderful life in Paris. What difference would it make to me?

JG Let's go back to the *Chronicle of Current Events*. You must have needed a lot of people to gather the amount of information required by that kind of publication. The more people who participate, the greater the chance of leaks. How did you manage to keep it all quiet? I don't think it has to be secret anymore.

NG You're right, it doesn't have to be a secret. In 1969 I think all of Moscow knew that I was publishing the *Chronicle*. The only question was when I would be arrested. Since I knew I would be arrested, all I had to do was to find a successor. But that turned out to be more difficult than I imagined. One idea was to hand it over to Galya Gabai, but her apartment was constantly being searched. Once she took some material for the *Chronicle* home, and her mother was forced to throw it into a pot of soup to keep it out of the hands of the KGB. That was in November 1969. After that Galya said she wouldn't be able to take over for me. I started work on it again, and after a while I was arrested.

JG Perhaps you weren't arrested immediately because they wanted to track down your ties and relationships with other people?

NG I think they knew perfectly well whom I associated with.

JG In that case your successor would have run into difficulties, no matter what.

NG I received material indirectly from people all over the Soviet Union. In one of the issues of the *Chronicle* I gave instructions on submissions. I explained that people should pass their material on to whomever they had gotten their last issue from and so on down the line. The main thing was not to try to follow the material through the chain or someone might take you for an informer.

I was arrested on Wednesday, December 24, 1969. I had found someone who was thinking of taking over the *Chronicle*, and he was supposed to come over that night to see how the publication was put together. Material for the eleventh edition, which was supposed to come out in a week, was in my desk. That day my apartment was searched. In the pocket of my winter coat I had notes on a hunger strike in the camps from an interview with the wife of a political prisoner. So much material was found during the search that they stopped filling out the statement, stuffed the rest of the papers into a folder, sealed it, and said that the statement would be completed in my presence and in the presence of other witnesses. That never happened, and I had the impression that the envelope never left my desk. Some of my friends were present during the search, and, as I was led out, I managed to signal to them to clean out the desk. Furthermore, I put on a jacket instead of my winter coat and indicated with my eyes that the coat, which had not been searched, should be taken care of. All that material was left in the apartment and wound up in the hands of those who continued to publish the *Chronicle* after I was arrested. The eleventh edition came out on time with a lead article about my arrest. I never learned what happened to the envelope, whether it was left untouched or if it had just seemed that way to me. The material had been collected by all sorts of people, all with different handwriting. If it had fallen into the hands of the KGB, it would have provided evidence against many people.

JG It's surprising they weren't more efficient.

NG You know, two months earlier, when I was about to leave for the Chitinsk and Irkutsk regions to visit my exiled friends Pavel Litvinov and Larisa Bogoraz, I had been searched. My knapsack was already packed and my handbag, in which I had put a whole stack of samizdat material, was on the couch. They searched my knapsack and found a few pages of samizdat between some phonograph records. Then they took the handbag from the couch to look inside, but for some reason forgot to do so. So I managed to take all the samizdat material with me. The fact is that their operatives are not very good. They try to convince you they know everything, and all they have to do is collect confirming evidence. But they actually know very little. You need to worry about yourself more than about them.

JG Did you try to distribute material by sending it to the West or by passing it from hand to hand?

NG I tried for the most part to distribute it within the country. We would send a few copies to the West just so that the material would reenter the Soviet Union through Western radio broadcasts.

JG But Western radio stations have a far greater audience than you could ever have hoped to reach within the country through written means.

NG Yes, but we didn't need that many copies for that. In any case, so much is broadcast over the radio that it's hard to know what's important. It would have been one thing if people could have tape-recorded the broadcasts, but back then there were practically no tape recorders around. The machines were huge, and tape recording was much more dangerous than typing. Several hundred issues of the *Chronicle* made their way around the country.

JG How did you duplicate it?

NG On the typewriter. We would just copy it over and over.

JG Did you do some of the typing yourself?

NG Yes.

JG With carbon paper?

NG Yes.

JG How many copies at a time?

NG I would get seven copies on fairly thin paper. Later we started getting twenty copies on very thin paper, although the last couple of copies were almost completely illegible. Each of these was then retyped several times in Moscow and other cities. When things got more repressive, copying became more difficult. But even so, we would get out several hundred copies of each issue.

Another method was to photograph the pages and print them on photo paper. We got more copies that way, but they came out very thick. All the same, it was a popular, if expensive method. It was hard to find the proper film and paper. After prison I used to buy photo paper in Leningrad, where it was easier to get, and bring it to Moscow.

JG What is the connection between your verse and your political activity? After all, your poems reflect your life, if only in tone.

NG If I didn't write poetry, I would be an entirely different person, and it's possible that the events in my life would have unfolded differently. If I hadn't started writing poetry, I probably would not have gotten involved with the *Chronicle,* taken part in the demonstration in Red Square, or started my work with samizdat. All of it goes together. I think my world view has been shaped through the writing process. Poetry is not an extension of my personality but the basis of all I do and am. My poems come into being of their own will, not because I want them to. If it hadn't been for poetry, I don't think anything would have remained.

JG You live in the West now and lead a fairly normal life. Does your current work differ in any way from what you used to write?

NG It is natural for poetry to change over time. After all, I am no longer twenty, as I was in 1956, or thirty-two, as I was in 1968. It's natural for my poetry to change along with me. And I think that it helps me even now.

JG Could you be more specific?

NG I don't know how to put it more concretely. It's very difficult for me to talk about poetry. There are some permanent aspects to my work that haven't changed at all. One is that I've always been short-winded. I write long poems only very infrequently.

JG Your poetry is not just some kind of verbal game. It always expresses emotion. And if your emotions have changed, then your way of expressing them must have changed too, don't you agree?

NG You're right when you say that my poetry is not a verbal game. But I'm not sure it's accurate to say my poems directly express my emotions. The fact of the matter is that I recognize what emotion is expressed in a poem only when I have finished writing it. I write a poem when I hear a melody in my head, not as a result of some emotion I have just experienced. My poems are usually written while I am walking or driving somewhere. To write, I always need some kind of motion. The first line pops into my head, and I have no idea what emotion the poem will express. But the melody is always present, perhaps because melody is the highest form of emotion. In that sense I can agree with you. But it is impossible to define a melody in exact terms.

One melody may be more dancelike, another may be longer. Some of my bitterest poems appear in dancelike melodies. So I can't say that a given poem expresses some specific emotion. On the contrary, my poetry gives me the opportunity to find out what my emotions are. And I don't think that my emotions have changed very much over the last thirty-odd years.

In one major way, I have changed since 1956, when I wrote my first real poetry. I think I have become more reserved. In any case, when I read my former verse, I sense a restraint that wasn't a part of my personality when I was younger. Perhaps it's simply a matter of having destroyed some of my earlier work. When you hear a melody, there's a temptation to seize it immediately. Otherwise you have to listen to it over and over again and unravel the thread of the music. But you want to write immediately. So you write a poem on the spur of the moment, and then you realize it's all wrong and has no real voice of its own. It's like what Winnie the Pooh says: "Those are improper bees, and their honey is probably also improper." My proper poems are those in which I have listened long and hard to the unraveling thread of the melody. I don't want to say it depends on God, angels, a gift from heaven, or anything else like that. I'm not sure where it comes from. Perhaps it's more like musical composition, which depends on a good ear. It's no accident that I love music and that it plays a greater role in my work than it does in the work of any of my contemporaries. I think it's all tied in with a love and trust for music and the melody I hear when I write.

JG   Many of the writers I've interviewed have talked about a feeling of being cut off. They live in isolation, without the opportunity to participate in the mainstream of literary activity. Do you feel that way?

NG   I just work so hard that . . .

JG   As a journalist?

NG   Yes. But as it turns out, I don't have the time or energy for anything but my journalistic work and a circle of close friends. I'm constantly having to get together with people, often with Poles since I do a lot of translation from Polish. Recently Gustaw Herling-Grudzinski's book, *World Apart*, was published. I'm glad that it has finally come out in Russian. The book, which is about the camps, first appeared in 1951 in English, then in 1953 in Polish, then in many other languages. And now it has come out in Russian, which for me is a major event. It is a wonderful book, not just as a testament to what happened in the camps, but as a literary achievement as well.

I also translate quite a bit on Polish events for *Kontinent* and *Russkaya mysl'*. In point of fact, my journalistic contacts have left very little time for a literary life.

JG Tell me a little about the political orientation of *Kontinent* and *Russkaya mysl'*.

NG I would like to quote Lech Wałeşa. He said that what he wants for Poland is pluralism. There should be an open forum for ideas in which each of us can have our own opinion. I often hear complaints that Maksimov expresses his own opinion in his column or writes too many editorials, although he is the editor of the journal and has that right.

JG Yes, but there are people who aren't published in *Kontinent*.

NG That's because they don't want to. Name me anyone who has ever wanted to be published in *Kontinent* and can't.

JG What about the Siniavskys?

NG They don't want to. They went their own way. Siniavsky's last article lay around for a long time while we waited for his permission to publish it. Then, when they were planning to publish the first issue of their own journal, Maria Vasilievna complained that they had to put their house up as collateral in order to finance the journal. Maksimov offered to devote fifty pages of each issue of *Kontinent* to a "free forum" to be edited by Siniavsky. Siniavsky would be allowed to choose anything he wanted for that section, and his own articles would be published in addition. Bukovsky and I went to negotiate with him ourselves. But Siniavsky said that he didn't need anything like that. The only people who aren't published are those who don't want to be. Or graphomaniacs like Vadim Belotserkovsky, whom nobody is obliged to publish. Siniavsky simply doesn't want to be published in *Kontinent*. An article of his about Galich was lying around after he left, and we wanted to publish it. But he withdrew it. It was the last article he had submitted. That was a long time ago.

JG I can name others. What about Maksudov? He wrote a rather long article in which he attacked Maksimov, calling him a dictator and a Bonaparte.

NG What he submitted was not an article, but a twenty-five-page letter to the editor. Any paper has the right to choose what letters it will publish and not take up space that would normally be occupied by an article with a letter as long as an article.

JG Then there was the incident with Mihajlo Mihajlov.

NG Mihajlov's article was sent to every member of the editorial board since Maksimov felt that in theory he should publish it. Having sent the text around and even translated it for some, Maksimov surveyed the members of the editorial board. Mihajlov was offended and left the journal. I have to admit that I was against the publication of his article. Maksimov was just about ready to publish it, but I was against it. The article was a diatribe against Solzhenitsyn. If you want to attack Solzhenitsyn, there are many publications in the émigré community through which you can do so. But *Kontinent* can get along without that kind of stuff.

I think Mihajlov has recently changed many of his views and is once again closer to us. At one time it was fashionable to attack Solzhenitsyn, and everyone thought they could make their literary reputations that way. I don't know why Siniavsky, who had established his literary reputation, felt the need to do that. I personally owe a lot to Siniavsky since he was a big supporter of my early work. But as far as I'm concerned, his literary reputation has gone down the drain. It's too bad, but that's life.

JG You feel that Solzhenitsyn's detractors criticize him only as a way of building their careers? After all, they have their own ideology, their own way of thinking.

NG Their ideology and way of thinking consist of the repetition of certain quotations, not from Solzhenitsyn, but from those writers who they feel belong to the so-called Solzhenitsyn party.

JG Whom do you have in mind?

NG All of them. Shimanov, for example. Now they say that the *Pamiat'* society belongs to the Solzhenitsyn party, although that organization's views are those of a strictly National Communist party. That's a fundamental difference. And Solzhenitsyn has been attacked as a chauvinist, anti-Semite, imperialist, and opposed to the self-determination of nations. All you have to do is calmly read Solzhenitsyn's work to see that is not true. But his detractors are so blinded by their anger and so-called ideology that they are no longer able to read.

JG The mission of the émigré press used to be clear: to publish material that couldn't be published in the Soviet Union. But times have changed, and every day we are more surprised at how much can now be published there. How has that changed the orientation of a journal like *Kontinent?*

NG It greatly increases the demands put on us. We continue to receive material from people in the Soviet Union, so it's clear that some people still don't feel their work can be published there. We need to pull ahead of the Soviet press again. Right now the dynamics of *glasnost* are being felt by all, but it is not the same as complete freedom of speech or complete truth. *Glasnost* is merely a broader reading of the notion of freedom. It's similar to a quarter-truth becoming a half-truth. But we can go beyond that, and we'll do that by continuing to publish the material we receive.

JG This will probably be a difficult question to answer, but how much of what you now publish could also be published in the Soviet Union and how much could not?

NG I don't know. Some things could be published with no problem. A lot of the poetry published by our journal over the past fourteen years is now appearing in Soviet journals. I don't think that even today the essay of Nobel laureate Claude Simon, "Invitation," published in the fifty-sixth issue of *Kontinent*, could be printed in any Soviet publication. Neither do I think that my article on Poland, published in issue fifty-seven, could come out in a Soviet publication. Some things could appear in the USSR, but their authors still prefer to submit their manuscripts to us, although it is tempting to be published in a million copies. I know that some writers think that it's better to try to get a million copies of their work published there and to send their work to *Kontinent* only if that doesn't work out.

JG Recently there have been several statements in the émigré press like the Cologne Statement, for example. Has anything changed as a result?

NG The Cologne Statement expressed both skepticism and, as they say in the Soviet Union, a "constructive" program. It was the kind of constructive criticism they say they want but don't really like to get. While they entered into a real polemic with the *Letter of Ten*, which was written in haste and didn't put forth any real program, even if it did contain some very important points, they responded to the Cologne Statement with some little piece in *Literaturnaya gazeta* (The Literary Gazette), in which they didn't even explain what they were responding to. They simply noted that the enemies of *perestroika* had regrouped. The Cologne Statement explored the issue of how to make *perestroika* into more than a mere rearrangement of walls in the same house, how to make it into the true reemergence of the country on a humane and democratic footing. It discussed the need to dissolve the empire, as well as other issues. It really did advance a more developed program, but there was no response. Why shouldn't it be published there? Why not give millions of people the opportunity to discuss these issues? I'll tell you why. They simply can't allow attempts to undermine the party's monopoly of power.

JG Several of the authors of the *Letter of Ten* evidently regret that they signed it.

NG The Cologne Statement is a more thoughtful document.

JG Do you see any more fundamental differences between the two documents?

NG Yes. The *Letter of Ten* was addressed to the West. It listed a number of points and stressed that we needed to verify certain things and not just take everything on faith. The Cologne Statement was for the Soviet people.

If anyone regrets signing the *Letter of Ten*, that's their own business. No one forced them to sign. They only regret it now that new opportunities have opened up for them there.

JG Do you think it's possible that *Kontinent* could ever be published in the Soviet Union?

NG Not in the Soviet Union, but perhaps in Russia. But I'm afraid it would be without my participation. I'm a Parisian now. But I think that people could be found to do that work. And I'll be their Paris correspondent.

The Realists

5

Vladimir Maksimov

Novelist, playwright, poet, and editor (b. 1930). Maksimov was an established writer in the Soviet Union, having published his first collection of poetry in 1956 and his first novel in 1961. The galleys of his first verse collection had been ordered destroyed in 1954. He was also an editor for the magazine *Oktyabr'*. When his novels *Seven Days of Creation* and *Quarantine* were rejected by the censors, their publication abroad led to his expulsion from the Soviet Writers' Union in 1973 and emigration to France in 1974. In January 1975 he was stripped of Soviet citizenship. He is the founding editor of *Kontinent*, a magazine created in 1974 to express the views of Soviet and East European dissent. In 1990 Maksimov's Soviet citizenship was returned to him.

Novels: *Sem' dnei tvoreniya* (The Seven Days of Creation) (Frankfurt-am-Main, 1973); *Karantin* (Quarantine) (Frankfurt-am-Main, 1973); *Proshchanie iz neotkuda* (Farewell from Nowhere) (Frankfurt-am-Main, 1974); *Saga o Savve* (The Saga of Savva) (Frankfurt-am-Main, 1975); *Kovcheg dlya nezvanykh* (An Arc for the Uninvited) (Frankfurt-am-Main, 1979); *Zhiv chelovek* (Man Survives) (Frankfurt-am-Main, 1979); *Saga o nosorogakh* (Saga of the Rhinoceri) (Frankfurt-am-Main, 1981); and *Zaglyanut' v bezdnu* (To Peer into the Abyss) (Paris-New York, 1986).

English translations: *Man Survives* (Westport, Conn.: Greenwood Press, 1975); *The Seven Days of Creation* (New York: Penguin, 1977); *Farewell from Nowhere*, trans. Michael Glenny (New York: Doubleday, 1979).

College Park, Maryland, 1983

JG Vladimir Yemilianovich, your biography reminds me of Maksim Gorky's. You left home after the fourth grade, were in and out of orphanages, and then wandered about. Like Gorky, you were self-educated. Then came emigration and even some editorial clout—again experiences similar to those of Gorky. You write that you were very much taken with Gorky in your younger days. Could that be due to the life experiences you share?

VM No. As a boy I hadn't yet gone through those experiences. It was reading Gorky that pushed me to leave school and follow in his steps. I don't know to what extent I managed that. Gorky drew social conclusions, radical social conclusions, if you will, based on what he experienced and went on to become a part of the most extreme wing of Russian social democracy: Bolshevism. I, on the other hand, was born into an atheistic family, and yet I came to religion. So one set of experiences led to two quite different results. After my wandering, my "life experiences," as you put it, I lost interest in Gorky, and I came to totally different conclusions. I still like a few of Gorky's plays, such as "Yegor Bulychov" and "Counterfeit Coin." There's something to them. Or some of his prose works, *Matvei Kozhemyakin* and *The Threesome*. Or even *The Life of Klim Samgin*. It's not that good a book, but it has much to say about the times. But on the whole, I've lost interest in Gorky. My experiences led me to Dostoevsky and through Dostoevsky to religion. That's how it was for most of the intelligentsia. We came to religion through literature, for the most part through Dostoevsky and the Russian religious philosophers.

JG That's an ideological disagreement. What about art itself?

VM No, it's a disagreement over principle. My manner, as even most of my critics note, leans toward Tolstoy and large historical perspectives. To a certain heavy-handedness. There is none of that in Gorky. His is a very slippery, superficial prose. When you look at Gorky's words close up, they are usually empty. There's nothing supporting them. By adding ornamentation and authorial asides, he complicates things. Instead of saying that a lilac was blooming, he uses half a page to describe it. Chekhov pointed that out.

JG What about Gorky's autobiography?

VM His autobiography is somewhat different. He embellished it a bit. His grandfather was not a pauper. He was from a fairly wealthy family. According to informed sources, Gorky made up a lot of his life story.

JG Tell me about how you grew up. What was your childhood like?

VM Quite ordinary. I can name a dozen or more contemporary writers, starting with Astafiev, for example, who went through the same life school: we were the thirties generation that saw the war at an early age. Parentless and without supervision, these postwar children were not a rare occurrence, as in Gorky's time, but a mass phenomenon. Therefore my background—and I always emphasize this when I talk about my novel *Farewell from Nowhere*—is typical. It's the background of an entire generation of people involved in contemporary Russian literature. Writers as different from myself as Vasily Aksyonov or, say, someone just a bit older such as Bulat Okudzhava came from similar backgrounds.

JG What was your childhood like?

VM I was born on almost the lowest rung of the social ladder. My father was a peasant, who later became a worker. He left the village to join the army, and he never went back. That was very typical. My mother was a railroad worker. Both were party members. My father was first jailed not in the purges of 1937, but in 1927—for being a Trotskyite. He had marched alongside Trotsky in one of his demonstrations. But my father was barely literate. He was jailed on a number of occasions, and then in 1937 he was imprisoned for good.

Even my name was changed. My father had named me Lyova, after his teacher Lev Trotsky. My real name is Lev Alekseevich Samsonov. I was renamed Vladimir Maksimov in the orphanage, and it was all legalized later.

JG Why did they change the "Samsonov"?

VM Because I was placed in the orphanage and then in a youth colony under a false birth certificate listing Maksimov. When I left, I had reached legal age and was issued a passport based on my birth certificate. The change was later made official, and since then I've lived under the name Maksimov. So I lost my father quite early. My mother was a simple worker. Life was hard. Conditions were tough. I read a lot. Between twelve and fourteen Gorky made a big impression on me. I decided to make my own life, to look for my own happiness. I went south. I wandered around the Trans-Caucasus region, doing a little bit of everything: I tended livestock, was a manual laborer, harvested grain. Then I spent time in several colonies for juvenile delinquents in Central Asia. I ran away. After the last colony, Sheksnin, I was recruited to go diamond mining up north.

My life was not so much unusual as colorful. And yet, since the age of twenty-one, it has been quite stable. At twenty-one I started work on a newspaper, and since then I have lived by the pen; I know no other profession. All my adventures took place between the ages of fourteen and twenty.

JG You write that at sixteen you were sentenced to seven years imprisonment.

VM Yes.

JG What for?

VM I got caught up with a bad crowd, as is often the case. My crime was called parasitism, vagrancy, living without definite work. In other words, earning one's living illegally, which is the usual way in the Soviet Union. A very strict edict had been issued to deal with social elements like me. So I was sentenced to seven years. But I was released fairly quickly. Moreover, I was in a juvenile colony.

I spent eight months there and then another six in the hospital, and after that I was released. Then everything went back to normal, and, as I mentioned earlier, I went north. I worked on mining expeditions on the Taimyr Peninsula. Then I became director of a civic center in Igarka, a northern port. It was a club for riverboat workers. I put on amateur performances, plays, and what have you. After that I took off again—this time to work on a collective farm in the Kuban region.

It was there I wrote my first poems. I signed them, "A worker from the 'Red Star' Collective Farm." They were published by Vasily Litvinov, who then worked in the Kuban region. He is now the literary criticism editor at *Novy mir*. As soon as I began to be published, I was offered a job on the regional newspaper. After that I moved to the regional Komsomol paper, and then to the district party paper in Cherkessk, in the Stavropol region, where I once met Gorbachev. I also was a radio correspondent for the Cherkessk Autonomous Region.

Then I left for Moscow. I started working part-time for *Literaturnaya gazeta*, where I began to learn something about real literature, as opposed to patriotic hackwork. I learned first and foremost from Naum Korzhavin. For those who remember, Naum Korzhavin was the Solzhenitsyn of his day, a paragon of how a writer should live and think and how he should relate to his profession.

You see, I had already published two books of terrible pro-Soviet verse. But that was nothing out of the ordinary. People thought it was how literature was supposed to be. We didn't think of it as lying, even though we saw through it all. Vasily Aksyonov and I were talking about that just the other day. He began in the same way, even though both of his parents had been in labor camps and he's a sincere and honest man. It was the way things had to be.

And so at *Literaturnaya gazeta* I got to know Naum Korzhavin and Bulat Okudzhava. Bulat had just arrived from Kaluga. He worked for a time as an editor at Young Guard Publishers, and then he was hired as poetry editor for *Literaturnaya gazeta*. I learned a lot from him there. I finally began to get hold of real literature. Western literature too, original works. It was like a school for me, not even a school, but rather the beginning of the education that brought me to where I am today.

JG I understand it was Paustovsky who got you involved in the collection *Tarusa Pages*.

VM I wouldn't say that it was Paustovsky himself. I was taken to him by people at *Literaturnaya gazeta:* Bulat Okudzhava, Naum Korzhavin, and Stanislav Rassadin. Rassadin was a fairly major critic. He may even be at *Voprosy literatury* today. Boris Balter, another critic, was also there. They took me to see Paustovsky. That is to say, I went along with them to hand in some manuscripts, two short novellas: *We're Settling the Earth*, based on my work experiences on the Taimyr, and *Man Survives*, based on my life as a wanderer.

Paustovsky selected *We're Settling the Earth* for inclusion in the collection he was putting together, *Tarusa Pages*. I'm grateful to him for using the story. I never knew him closely, even though all my biographies list me as having been discovered by him. It was I, in fact, who discovered him, with the help of my friends at *Literaturnaya gazeta*.

He had his own disciples at the Literary Institute, in particular Lev Krivenko, now dead, also a good prose writer, Boris Balter, and Benedikt Sarnov, a critic. Those were the people from our generation with whom he was genuinely intimate.

JG Tell me about *Tarusa Pages*.

VM In retrospect, I can't say that it was anything special, unless you realize that some of the things published now could never have been published earlier, even in the most liberal of times.

No matter how one regards Solzhenitsyn, he raised the ceiling of the permissible. After Solzhenitsyn, everything seemed less terrifying. And it was only under that ceiling that so-called rural literature was allowed. But other factors also contributed. Something like 90 percent of the ruling class in our country is made up of former peasants, who have an unconscious longing for the past. Even the worst of them lived through both famine and collectivization. Other former villagers may experience nostalgia, but it is the ruling class which decides what is to be allowed and what isn't. And that's why "Rural Prose" made it.

Take Tvardovsky, for example. He first published *One Day in the Life of Ivan Denisovich* in *Novy mir*. I assure you that if Ivan Denisovich had been a worker, the story would never have gotten into print. But Tvardovsky was a peasant with a peasant psychology. His heart ached for the peasantry. His family had been victims of the kulak campaigns. They were all hauled off to Siberia. That is why, as you may have noticed, there was practically no "urban" prose in *Novy mir*. Bitov could not be published. Tvardovsky never wanted to publish Kazakov. I could name a whole set of other marvelous writers: Fazil Iskander, for instance. Tvardovsky didn't let quality urban writing in, only mediocre stuff. Anything good in *Novy mir* was peasant literature. The heroes were peasants.

And so if we go back to *Tarusa Pages*, it doesn't look all that threatening. But in 1961 it was a major event. It was the first to include Tsvetaeva, as well as a number of prose writers like Balter and Okudzhava. But if you leaf through the whole *Tarusa* collection, half of it is junk. There were a lot of Soviet things there such as a script by Otten and Gladkov. David Samoilov, Vladimir Kornilov, and Boris Slutsky were published for the first time in it—paradoxically by a regional publisher.

JG That sort of thing often happens in Russia.

VM Even so, it was strange: it's a small world. The director of the publishing house turned out to be my patron from Cherkessk, who at the time was the regional party boss for propaganda and agitation. Sladkov was his name, Vasily Fyodorovich Sladkov, I believe. He had been very kind to me. He took me under his wing and promoted me as a local writer. But when his wife fell ill, he was transferred to Kaluga, where he was made director of a publishing house. He agreed to go, and there he rotted away with the rest of us.

What's interesting is that they brought two truckloads of *Tarusa Pages* to Moscow and started selling them on Dzerzhinsky Square. The more people bought, the bigger the crowd grew. The books were snatched up. Everything that was unsold was seized and apparently destroyed. Then there were the reviews. When I reread them, they didn't seem that biting. They criticized this and that, but on the whole they weren't all that bad.

The whole collection was translated into all the Western languages. I remember how we gathered in Otten's house on Gorky Street waiting for the arrival of the books from Kaluga, and Slutsky said: "Comrades" (he had remained a Communist—an idealistic one). "Comrades, this is literary history in the making!" It seemed a bit high-flown at the time, but now we can see that it was an historical event—and not a minor one either. Together with the *Literary Moscow* collection, it was a watershed.

JG You now live in Paris, and in your *Saga of the Rhinoceri* you display a fairly scornful, even scathing attitude toward Western culture. I quote: "Horn to horn, nostril to nostril, frothing at the mouth, legion upon legion, they circle around. On a lone man the sweater seems more like a toga lined in raspberry red. He stands on a tiny speck of land which grows smaller and smaller under the thunder of their hooves. They surround him from all sides, each casting a bloody eye on this doomed fool who refuses to give way. 'Take my hand, Eugene. We shall fall together beneath their hooves, but we shall not give way. We wish to die as human beings. We who are about to die salute you.'" What is this—a description of Western culture?

VM First, it's a certain genre—satire. Secondly, it's not about Western culture; it's an interpretation of Ionesco's play "Rhinoceros," although it's based on real life and couched in publicistic terms. Ionesco said it all—in a different form. If you've seen the play, you know that that's exactly the way he puts it, nostril to nostril. All are transformed into rhinoceri. It has nothing to do with the West as such but with certain forces in the West, destructive forces, working—sometimes unconsciously—toward the downfall of civilization.

I have always been shocked at the way in which the "enlightened" West simply rehashes turn-of-the-century Russian intellectual thought. I have read about the liberal justice system in America and about how the educated classes claim that man is formed by social conditions. But these people are not even the educated classes. They are the intellectuals, and that's some-thing else entirely. And you'll pardon me, but we've heard it all before. We in Russia went through the exact same thing: our juries also turned criminals loose. And they too explained away every disorder as arising from social conditions. But experience shows that this isn't true. Changing social conditions doesn't change people. For instance, Russians have always thought of Russia as a drinking country. But now it's a fact that she drinks ten or fifteen times more heavily than before—and I don't mean that metaphorically. Crime has also multiplied.

JG How can you know about crime for sure? The statistics are kept secret.

VM We have a general idea. Liubimov recently told me about a rehearsal of *Crime and Punishment.* He had planned for Porfiry to come forward and address the audience and say that the world had to be changed, but that the change had to come from within ourselves. It's straight out of Dostoevsky. The actor, a fairly decent one too, said: "I won't do it."

JG Why not?

VM Because it was a reactionary line. The government is supposed to do everything. "But it's Dostoevsky!" Liubimov exclaimed. "So what if it's Dostoevsky?" the actor answered. "My own mother was a reactionary, and we're not on speaking terms." At that point Liubimov should have said: "I'd like to meet your mother. She sounds like an interesting woman."

So you see just how naive the West is? That kind of phi-losophizing went on in backwoods Russia. Why should we go through it again? *Saga of the Rhinoceri* is aimed at the destructive tendencies of the West, because we know from experience where it will all lead. People tell me: "You émigrés are a bunch of know-it-alls, always lecturing everyone." But we don't lec-ture. It's an intellectual process. We just want to impart our experience. You are repeating the same mistakes. For some the West is the *New York Times* or *Le Monde.* But that's only a part of the it. Freeborn Americans themselves, almost 60 percent of them, demonstrated that they feel the same way we do by voting for President Reagan. And while no one in the Soviet Union was ever born free, we've come to realize the danger.

The Gulag is an extreme instance. Paradoxically enough, that may make it also the least dangerous, because although its victims are many, it can be exposed quickly.

I go to Sweden, and, forgive me for saying so, I come back in horror. How can such a prosperous country be heading for the same fate under the banner of reform? Sweden leads all other Western countries in suicide, alcoholism, and birth defects. What's happened to a nation like that? I'm told that in a free country you have to have permission to repaint your roof the color you want or to put in a new window, or that in subsidized housing you need permission from the authorities to change the lock on the door. And at the same time any alcoholic can get a live-in nurse to help him through his hangovers. You know that something there has to be rotten.

That's what I'm against. It's not the gulags alone, but this whole process which is destroying human character. Whether it comes about through gulags or supermarkets is unimportant. That's what *Saga of the Rhinoceri* is about. I repeat: I have said nothing new. Ionesco's play was written something like thirty years ago. And he said it all quite succinctly, but in a work of art. My *Rhinoceri* is a pamphlet, the work of a publicist.

JG You published the note that Maria Rozanova wrote to you. I'd like to read from her note:

> Vladimir Yemilianovich, I'm afraid I have to say that the appalling tone of *Saga of the Rhinoceri* really tops the deck. I would think that the time has come for you to beat a retreat. I take the liberty of recommending the following course of action:
> (1) Apologize publicly.
> (2) Suspend serialization in *Russkaya mysl'*.
> (3) Withhold *Saga of the Rhinoceri* from publication in *Kontinent*, no. 19.
> P. S. Forgive me, but I am sending a copy of this note to *Russkaya mysl'*.

VM That's the true voice of pluralism, democracy at its best! No matter how much I object to something, I would never dream of sending a colleague a letter telling him what or what not to publish. These people seem to lack a sense of humor. They don't realize that to write a letter like that is an obscenity.

If you disagree, then speak up, state your disagreement! But to give me orders, and in language bordering on slang. What sort of cardsharp slang is "tops the deck"? What gall!

And it doesn't even come from a writer, but the wife of a writer. That is going too far. Some people expose themselves for what they really are.

I might add, by the way, that the Western reviews of *Saga of the Rhinoceri* were not merely positive; they were full of praise. Only the émigrés turned out to be more Catholic than the Pope. They know what's best for a democratic society, what to publish and what not to publish. I answered Rozanova's note. And you'll forgive me if I go ahead and publish anything I see fit.

JG Perhaps you would give me your view of these arguments among émigrés.

VM As the editor of *Kontinent* I would say that for Russian émigrés the situation has improved now that the journal publishes not only members of all the waves of emigration, but of the opposition in Eastern Europe as well. We have created an international resistance made up not only of émigrés of all stripes from Eastern Europe, but of Latin America and Africa as well. The *Russian* émigré community lives in a glass house, visible to all. Our émigrés have the highest profile. The very future of civilization may depend on the country which we represent.

Emigration is that state where a person loses control over his own destiny. It requires a particularly difficult kind of social adaptation. A few people may be able to continue making their living by writing. The rest are forced to retrain themselves, so as to earn a living. That brings to the surface some of man's darker instincts and sucks people deeper and deeper into conflict.

JG What about your own ideological differences with someone like Andrei Siniavsky?

VM There are no ideological differences, I assure you. I'm totally serious when I say that it is no more than the kind of fight you would expect in a shared kitchen in a Moscow apartment. Siniavsky once suggested to me and Viktor Nekrasov that his wife be made editor of *Kontinent*. Why not his mother-in-law or his son? "I should do it, not you." That's the émigré community for you.

Things were no different for German writers in the West during the Nazi period. Thomas Mann hated his brother Heinrich. They both hated Brecht, and Brecht despised them all. It's always the same. Ideology gets dragged in as the excuse for some fairly commercial dealings.

In the manuscript to his book *Hunter Upside Down,* Khenkin includes an episode in which he goes to see Rudolph Abel, the famous spy who was arrested here and then returned to the Soviets. . . .

JG Traded for Powers, I believe.

VM Yes. Khenkin was Abel's pupil. I don't know whether Khenkin kept the scene in the final version of the book, but in it he goes to see Abel, who is very depressed. Khenkin asks him what's wrong, and Abel says something like "I was called back to headquarters. There's someone in the West who has to be eliminated." In other words, he had already exposed himself. And Khenkin says, "Yes, it's a nasty business, I know." "No, no, that's not it," Abel answers. "A person has to be eliminated. That's just a job. What gets me is that they ask me to dress up as a cleaning man so I can sneak into his room and kill him with an iron hidden inside a pillow." That's what I'm talking about. They come for you with an iron hidden inside a pillow. There are no serious discussions in the magazines, no debate, no attempt to prove the facts, no. It's all so . . . shameful, shameful even to mention it.

JG I don't want to pour oil on the fire, but I do feel obliged to give you the opportunity to respond to some of what Maria Rozanova said when I interviewed her:

> We quickly set up our own personality cults: the Solzhenitsyn cult, the Maksimov cult, and the Father Dmitry Dudko cult. Then we responded to all this exactly as we had done when we were in Russia. For example, I know for an absolute fact that Vladimir Yemilianovich Maksimov detests Aleksandr Isaevich Solzhenitsyn—as a writer. He once called Solzhenitsyn a graphomaniac. Maksimov doesn't like him as a writer, and he doesn't like him as a public figure— as an ideologue. But whenever Maksimov speaks in public he begins with a quote from Solzhenitsyn and ends with a quote from Solzhenitsyn. Why? Because he has to. He has

to. That's one of the canons of Soviet behavior, one which we brought with us and which we live by to this day.

But we can go further than that. Of course, we poor souls grew up in the Soviet Union and we can't help but behave that way. But look at the First Wave of émigrés, which was untouched by the Soviet regime. You'll see the exact same thing. Their writing is Soviet. Their approach is entirely Soviet.

She then goes on to call émigrés vampires. How would you answer her?

VM To be quite frank, I don't understand why wives are being given the floor. I was under the impression that you were conducting interviews with writers. Perhaps I should ask my wife to say a few words. You have to choose. You either interview those who represent Russian literature or their distraught wives, who, after all, have reached that age when a certain condition sets in.

I should add that Rozanova and Siniavsky are up to their usual tricks—blaming their own faults on others. Everything they say could apply to themselves. They would love to set up an Andrei Siniavsky personality cult. There is ample evidence. Right from the very start she went around to all the publishers, saying choose Siniavsky or Solzhenitsyn. Why should we?

As far as Solzhenitsyn goes, once again, it's part fact and part fiction. I do not necessarily attach any pejorative meaning to the word *graphomaniac*. I call Tolstoy a brilliant graphomaniac. A graphomaniac is a person who loves to write. A graphomaniac writes everything down. He can't live without it. Maurois, for example. Writing is to me a chore. But not for Solzhenitsyn. For him it's a pleasure. He always said, "Vladimir Yemilianovich, I'd rather write someone twenty pages than make one phone call. I hate the phone." Taken out of the context a word like *graphomaniac* sounds accusatory.

As for my relations with Solzhenitsyn, yes, there is a lot about him which is alien to me. I've never tried to hide that.

JG Could you be specific?

VM Style, first off. Language is style. Language is the person. Why should one work be written one way, another in the style of, say, Dos Passos, and another in the style of Marina Tsvetaeva? Why is his *Matryona's House* written in elegant Russian, while the volume on the First World War starts out in a totally different language? That suggests to me a lack of authenticity. But the fact of the matter is, and I'm quite open about this, that Solzhenitsyn, whether we like it or not, has become the personification of Russian literature. And whether I like him or not, I'll start each of my appearances quoting him and end quoting him. When I say Solzhenitsyn, I'm not limiting myself to him alone; I'm referring to all nonconformist literature—which began with him. He has come to occupy a central point in history, and we must support him. In denigrating him, we cut off the branch on which we sit.

JG   No, I'm not asking you to do that. But beyond language, where would you find points where you and he could not be considered the same?

VM   We're not the same. Solzhenitsyn believes that the Russian people are victims. I do not. I love them. I am Russian. Russians are both executioners and the victims, just as are all peoples.

He once wrote to me saying that the émigrés from the First Wave didn't make a trip to the official visa office first. They retreated, gun in hand. To which Brodsky later replied: "Then why did they retreat? They should have attacked."

Solzhenitsyn and I have a correspondence dating back to Moscow. "How can you say it was all the fault of the ethnic minorities," I asked him. "Forgive me for saying it, but thirty thousand officers crossed over with Tukhachevsky—for the rations." And Tukhachevsky himself was a White officer. Or what about Brusilov, who had free access to the Tsar? Or dozens of members of the nobility? Or the officers, the generals? . . . Are we going to forget about them? They all went over to the Soviets, some even after they emigrated. Count Tatishchev joined the French Communist party. Sviatopolk-Mirsky joined the English Communist party the moment he got out. Look at how many of them there were! And who do you think made up the Union of Soviet Patriots?

JG   Sviatopolk-Mirsky went back and was killed.

VM   Of course he was. What did they need him back there for? Let the Moor do his duty *here*. Or Tsvetaeva's husband

Efron? What price did he pay for his return? He too was killed. He was too dangerous a witness to be kept alive. He even committed murder. It was all a terrible tragedy. Perhaps he was paying for another tragedy. After all, Reis was a human being, wasn't he? He was murdered by Sezeman, Efron, and some others—all Russian émigrés, all former Whites. With Reis's murder they bought their return to their homeland. This was the Russian nobility, the Russian intelligentsia. So I say: "Aleksandr Isaevich, it wasn't those miserable *paysans* from the collectivization. There were the Jews and others from the regional party committees, etc. But it was the peasants themselves who actually did it. The worst of the peasants, yes, but nevertheless, peasants. There's a writer named Sukonik, a very good writer. Hasn't written much lately. Lives in New York. He once wrote an article that offended everyone. He sent it to me for publication. I decided that it was too risqué, and he went ahead and published it in the *Russian Student Christian Movement Herald*. He wrote:

> I went to a certain professor of Jewish extraction. . . . [I know who it was.]
> "They say that the Jews are responsible for the Revolution," I told him.
> "Who, us?" he answers. "Never."
> Sukonik started naming names.
> "They were all black sheep," said the professor. "Nothing to do with us."

Then Sukonik went to a different professor. I know who that was too. The professor said: "Russians started the revolution? Nothing of the sort! It was the ethnic minorities." So where did the Revolution come from, the moon?

And then there's Aleksandr Isaevich's ill-conceived fondness for the rural writers. He doesn't know them. I do. I grew up with them. I was friends with them, people like Vasily Belov. They're good, talented people. But they are the kulaks of literature. Despite all their village humility, they're draped in state medals. They all serve on their district party committees. "Is that true or not?" I asked him. "Vladimir Yemilianovich," he replied. "We have to remember that. . . ." "Oh-ho," I said, "is this the new dialectic?" It's all right for some to do that. Laws that don't lie should apply to everyone, shouldn't they?

The fact is that Solzhenitsyn doesn't know those writers, whereas I ate, drank, and grew up with them. So he and I have our disagreements. He believes that *Kontinent* doesn't do enough to defend Russia and that we spend too much time on Eastern Europe. I *have* written that, if indeed we consider ourselves a great people, we should show magnanimity and be the first to shoulder the blame for everything. That is the only way to reach an understanding with those peoples who are now a part of that system—if such an understanding is possible.

JG How do you view Solzhenitsyn's belief in the need for a transitional autocracy, should the regime fall.

VM Instant democracy after the fall of a regime like ours is out of the question. People cite Germany and Japan as examples, but they shouldn't. Democracy in Germany and Japan was guaranteed by occupational forces. Without such a guarantee an immediate transition to democracy is unimaginable in a country with 116 nationalities or 114—I may be wrong—where there are a dozen different religions, including idolatry. Democracy, like monarchy, must be part of the culture; it must be instilled in a society.

JG There are those who believe that democracy is undesirable under any circumstances. They refer to democracy (*demokratiya* in Russian) as *der'mokratiya* (shitocracy).

VM I don't believe that. But 1917 showed where an unexpected turn toward democracy can lead. Lenin said that Russia in 1917 was the freest country in the world. France had military censorship. So did Germany. Russia's entire press came out against the war. There was a defeatist attitude, at least among the press. They could say anything they wanted to. The new leaders had no government experience. They were nothing more than demagogues, intellectuals. But then we're all first-rate talkers. As Aleksandr Ginzburg once said, put any one of these people in charge of even a railway station, and he'll run it into the ground. There's a crude but very accurate Russian proverb; I won't quote it exactly, but a bad dancer trips over even what's between his legs.

JG In your ruminations on the possibility of harmonious democracy after a hypothetical change of government in the USSR, you've suggested "using the country's present administrative-territorial divisions." Does that mean that you are opposed to the breakup of the Russian empire?

VM That's not what I meant. I have stated as a matter of principle that all those nations who want to leave should. What I was referring to was Russia itself, Russian national territory.

JG What about Ukraine?

VM We've made a specific statement on that point. They should decide for themselves. But I should add, and I hope you will understand me correctly, you can't call this traditional imperialism. . . . Russia is the America of the East. It was put together in exactly the same way—by territorial expansion but without overseas acquisitions. How did America expand? By spreading its culture? Who owns Texas, California? This imperialism, as it were, is an integral part of the Russian entity. . . . Russian national territory encompasses a whole wealth of other ethnic entities. How is this to be handled? It's a complicated process.

Suppose, for example, the Georgians, the Georgian intellectuals, the nonconformists want to secede. Fine. But have they given any thought to where that would take them? No. Georgia is made up of several nations. Abkhazia wants nothing to do with Georgia. Abkhazia has its own culture, its own religion, and its own language. Its people believe themselves to be descended from the original searchers for the Golden Fleece. Ajaria is Moslem and always has felt a link with Turkey. The Mingrels aren't Georgians either. Neither are the Svans.

A Georgian writer once told me, "We can't let Abkhazia go; we'd have no outlet to the sea." And that's the *intelligentsia* talking. It's the same in each of the republics. All you can say is, if you want your own independent state, you solve these matters on your own.

I have to admit that my proposal for Russian democracy is somewhat tongue-in-cheek—I made up a draft for a constitution just to see what our fighters for democracy would say. I had received a lot of mail calling my proposals totalitarian or smacking of totalitarianism. But if you've read the Swiss constitution, you will know that ours is nothing but the Swiss constitution translated into Russian. If that's totalitarian, then so be it. I'm not a political scientist. These people didn't realize that all I had done was to rewrite in my own words the constitution of one of the freest countries in the West.

JG Let me ask you briefly about *Kontinent*. How many copies do you publish?

VM It varies slightly between three and a half and four thousand.

JG Then it's increased. I remember that several years ago you said you published 1,500 copies.

VM 1,500?

JG That was several years ago at a Literary Fund meeting here in Washington.

VM We send 1,500 copies to the Soviet Union. The first issue alone was seven thousand copies. And now you can't find a single copy. It's become a rarity. The second issue dropped to three thousand. After that there was a slight increase to four thousand. But as other journals bloomed, some of our readers left us. Only to return. Ours is still four times larger than any other Russian journal in the West. A thousand or fifteen hundred copies of any Russian-language book in the West makes it a best-seller. In other words, we put out two or three best-sellers every three months. Fifteen hundred is what we officially send to the Soviet Union. We don't know how many arrive. And to Eastern Europe, as well, because it's read in Poland and Czechoslovakia, where Russian is required in school and the intelligentsia reads Russian.

JG Our time is almost up. Very briefly, whom don't you publish? You probably don't publish Edward Limonov.

VM No. I simply consider his writing provocatory. Why should I need writing like that? *Literaturnaya gazeta* publishes rave reviews of his work.

JG What about Siniavsky? You wouldn't publish him, would you?

VM Why not? By all means, any time.

JG If I send you a copy of my interview with him and Maria Rozanova would you publish it?

VM I do not need an interview with Maria Rozanova because she has nothing to do with Russian literature outside of her relation to Siniavsky.

JG What about Siniavsky himself?

VM By all means.

JG Good. I'll send it to you.

VM No, you ask him first. That's what I always say. But I will publish him. And if I don't agree with what he says, I'll add a note of my own. But I will publish him. Now, as for Limonov, I just don't consider that serious literature. Frankly, the things he does in his writings are inappropriate and unnecessary—all that anti-American pro-Soviet stuff. And when they say it's nonpolitical literature? What do they mean—"nonpolitical"? His little book manages to sling mud at Sakharov, Solzhenitsyn, and at me, as well as Radio Liberty, *Novoe Russkoe Slovo*, the Trotskyites. . . . He got everyone. How is that apolitical literature? No wonder *Literaturnaya gazeta* raved: at last somebody recognized the West for what it was! Well, I refuse to publish it. But take Sasha Sokolov. Now, there's a writer who would seem to be alien to me. But we publish everything he writes. It's quality that counts, quality!

JG I'd like to thank you very much, Vladimir Yemilianovich, for . . .

VM And about those wives . . . why should they be included just because they have their noses in the air? Stay home and mind your own. . . .

Edward Limonov

"Edward Limonov" is the literary pseudonym of Edward Savenko, prose writer
and poet (b. 1943). While still residing in
the Soviet Union, Limonov belonged to a
small, unofficial group of artists and
writers, but his work remained unpub-
lished. He emigrated in 1974 and settled
in New York, later moving to Paris. In the
relatively conservative atmosphere of
Russian letters, his books are widely
read but highly controversial because of
their graphic sexual descriptions and
often obscene language.

Books: *Eto ya—Edichka* (New York,
1979); *Russkoe* (Ann Arbor, 1979); *Dnev-
nik neudachnika, ili Sekretnaya tetrad'* (New
York, 1982); *Podrostok Savenko* (Paris,
1983); *Palach* (Jerusalem, 1986); *Molodoi
negodyai* (Paris, 1986).

English translations: *It's Me, Eddie,* trans. S. Campbell (New York: Random House, 1983); *His Butler's Story,* trans. Judson Rosengrant (New York: Grove Press, 1987); *Memoir of a Russian Punk,* trans. Judson Rosengrant (New York: Grove Weidenfeld, 1991).

Paris, December 20, 1989

JG   Let me be frank: people have asked me why I decided to interview you. I was talking to the German Slavist Wolfgang Kasack, the author of a dictionary of Russian literature. And he said: "I didn't include Limonov. Some like him, but I don't." He complained about your use of obscenities and also that what you write is nothing more than traditional nineteenth-century realism.

EL   The comments of other émigrés are nothing but a case of dogs howling at the moon. As for Kasack, let him choose whomever he likes. It makes no difference to me. I don't take that seriously.

JG   How do émigré writers establish themselves?

EL   I established myself outside the émigré community. Nine of my books have been translated into French. I was first published at the end of 1980, and since then my books have been translated into eight languages.

JG   Why outside the émigré community? The émigrés probably read your books more than anyone else's. Or don't you feel that that is the real?

EL   I never tried to write for other émigrés. I wrote my first book for publication in English. Naturally, I couldn't write it in English, so I wrote it in Russian. But I never had Russian publishers in mind. It was only later that the American publishers began to put up serious resistance. It's hard to say why. They were resisting a new breed of Russian writer, who for some reason didn't depict America in a very positive light— who didn't write as he should have. I was supposed to be satisfied, like all the other writers.

JG   How many copies of *It's Me, Eddie* have been sold?

EL   There were at least two editions, but it's hard to check how many there were. With small publishers you never know.

The first contract I signed was for about five thousand copies. Then I signed a second contract, which was also for about five thousand copies.

JG What do you have to say about the criticism or, if you prefer, the comment that what you write is nothing more than "traditional realism."

EL I agree with that.

JG You agree?

EL Absolutely.

JG Many people feel that realism is a thing of the past.

EL I can't go along with that. Do you seriously believe this is the age of modernism? No, this is an era of postmodernism which rebels against all the fanciness of the 1930s. In the 1960s there was a second wave of formalism, and then the writing world—the writing universe—returned once more to the same old realism, which is, in fact, extremely diverse.

JG Is that "writing world" Russian, French, or Western?

EL I regard the Russian world with a great deal of contempt. The books of my acquaintances, friends, and countrymen don't move me in the least. It's possible that something valuable is now being written by young people, but I haven't seen it. I don't rule it out, but to this day I have not read a single book which has stopped me in my tracks and forced me to say: "God, this is good. I wish I had written this." I haven't seen anything like that for the last thirty years. All that interests me, all that makes me feel at all envious, has been published not even by French, but by Anglo-Saxon writers.

JG For example?

EL I would like to have written some of Truman Capote's chapters or even certain of his short stories. Not everything, of course. I'm very picky. Or take Hemingway's later work. He has some unbelievable stylistic devices. I accept almost none of his novels, but I would gladly have written some passages out of them, as well as some of his short stories.

JG What if I write in my book that you are the Truman Capote of Russian émigré literature?

EL That would be untrue, because I am neither the Truman Capote nor the Henry Miller of Russian émigré literature, as the French press, as well as Americans, Germans, and whoever else, wrote after the publication of my first book. But they don't think that anymore. Now they write that Limonov has won the right to be who he is.

JG Every writer claims that right.

EL Everyone claims that right, but it has to be won. Since I live in France and am a French citizen, I make my judgments on what I read in the French press. After my first book they compared me to Henry Miller, then to Bukowski, Kerouac, and others.

JG Vladimir Bukovsky?!

EL No, Charles Bukowski. Thank God, no one has ever compared me to any Russian writers. I've been compared only to Big League writers, to those from the normal world, not émigrés or provincial Soviets.

JG Did you begin to write in the Soviet Union or in the West?

EL I began to write prose in New York. In the Soviet Union I wrote poetry. That's a part of my life and a part of my work that I don't deny. I think that I wrote unusual poems that have not faded with time. I don't know what place, if any, they should be given in Russian poetry. It's not my place to judge.

JG You entitled your collection of poems *Topics Russian* (Russkoe).

EL It was the title of a poem written in 1971. That poem was a collage of Russian literary clichés. It's an ironic title. It was also relevant because I published the collection again only in 1979, and all of the poems included in it were written in Russia. That was the reason for the title—the sense was one of great distance and humor. Of course, I use the Russian language, and I probably always will. There is still time to switch languages. On occasion I've written in English, and my first attempts weren't so bad. I could write in English. But I live in a country where French is spoken, so to write in English would be idiotic. I get translated in any case, so what's the sense of trying? I will probably never be able to write in French, since it's a difficult language for me. But my world view is mine and mine only. Let Russia do its own thing and Africa—its own. Who cares about Russian writers? They interest me so little that I'm sometimes ashamed to be associated with them. Evidently they realize that, and that realization is why we don't get along. I've remained isolated, in spite of short-lived friendships with certain Russian writers, including Sasha Sokolov. We were never friends in the true sense of the word. We were both literary outsiders of a sort. But he is, now, part of Russian literature. These days he is less and less of an outsider. In the future he will doubtless have an important place in society as the head of a certain school. But I remain an outsider.

JG Your contemporaries don't see things that way. The New York émigré critics Pyotr Vail and Aleksandr Genis said that every small to medium-sized Russian town has a group of people like Limonov and his crowd—just as they have a post office or a cafeteria. If we ignore the critical thrust of that comment, it is interesting that they perceive you as one of their own, not as an outsider.

EL That doesn't bother me much. Russia and the émigré community are a bit too provincial to evaluate and understand my work. My best reviews have always come from the foreign press—French, German, Dutch, Greek, and all the other eight languages in which I have been published. I rarely receive negative reviews in the West.

JG But isn't it rather contradictory that a person who renounces Russian literature and the Russian tradition, and who from the very beginning wrote for the West, writes in Russian all the same? How long had you lived in the West before you wrote *It's Me, Eddie*?

EL Less than two years.

JG And how old were you when you left Russia?

EL I was twenty-nine.

JG That's two years as opposed to twenty-nine. The Russian experience should outweigh the Western.

EL We're talking about the soul. Are we talking about where I belong, who I am? We may never be able to pin that down with any degree of certainty. I am telling you that I am not Russian. I was a born outsider. There are people who don't fit in with the mob, aren't there?

JG Russia is a mob?

EL There is always a crowd, even here. It doesn't matter whom it is made up of. It may be that there are several different in-groups. Some of these people know how to write books. Others do not. And then there are people like me. I write my books in Russian, but I will never belong to either Russian or French or American literature. People like us are always out-siders, walking among others, but not fitting in, bored with them in any case. And we should be gratified when they say they don't like us. Many people have not been liked, and they are always the best and brightest. As the saying goes: "you'll only get appreciated later."

JG This is not the first interview I've conducted, or even the twentieth, and everyone that I've interviewed considers him-self an outsider. I interviewed Zinoviev and he said: "Oh, I was never appreciated. Everyone acknowledges me in the West. It's only the émigré community that doesn't." Gorenstein said the same thing in his interview. Siniavsky also considers himself an outsider. If everyone is "out," who is "in"?

EL I can't answer that, John. I'm not a literary critic. I can only talk about myself, about how I feel and what I see. And I believe I have far better reasons for thinking I am an outsider than Gorenstein or anyone else. I think that Zinoviev has some grounds for considering himself an outsider, but far fewer than I. I am the pariah of Russian and Soviet literature for a multi-tude of reasons. But I am not God, and I can't look down from above and say that I am more or less of an outsider than they are. I insist on my outsiderness, or marginality, because it is evident.

JG I'm not arguing with what you say. I am simply saying that this is true of others as well, albeit perhaps truer of you than most.

EL Here we are going into the 1990s, when writers have great resources and opportunities. The publishing business is becoming more and more international. You can count the number of principal world-class authors on one hand—artists too. They are sold everywhere. At the Frankfurt Book Fair an author is marketed instantly in twenty or twenty-five countries at once. This is new and hitherto would even have been un-believable. This system, this opportunity, sustains authors like me. And I'm not the only one. Take English writers, like Law-rence Durrell, who has lived for a decade in the south of France.

Graham Greene also lives in the south of France. They don't call themselves émigrés. No one wonders why they live in France, but still write in English. Some authors are forty-five minutes by plane from London, and I am three hours by plane from Moscow. What's the difference? No one asks them: "Why do you still write in English? Why haven't you switched to French?" That would be absurd. I am convinced that that sort of thing is a remnant of the old perception of the Russian writer, who, like the Chinese writer, comes to a conference in a cap with a star on it. That's not me. I was born in Europe. I am a European writer. Turgenev lived in France all his life. Gogol lived in Rome for twenty years, but he was a Russian writer. It is a mystery to me how he could have written nothing about Rome, having lived there so long. But I live in France and write about what happens there.

A book of my short stories was just published by Ramsay. The book is entitled *Les incidents ordinaires* (Ordinary Occurrences). The action takes place in Nice, Paris, New York—everywhere but Russia. I chose those stories on purpose. But no one can take from people their understanding of the world in which they live. And the fact is that I have now lived in Paris longer than I lived in Moscow. Nabokov was once asked about his citizenship and who he considered himself to be. He answered that he was a ten-year-old American. By that he meant that he had lived in America for ten years. My life is now fifteen years removed from Russia. For fifteen years I have been a Westerner. And you can't take that away from me. There were some problems. I changed countries and readers twice. I had language problems here in France. But I never had problems with the New World. People are the same everywhere. Language is nothing. Big deal! There is something different, deeper problems of life and understanding, and these are not things that I fear in the New World.

JG "Language is nothing"—that depends on the individual writer. We were talking about Sokolov. I can't imagine him in a different language.

EL Well, I'm not like that. I'm not a folktale teller. With a great deal of energy it's possible to translate my work and preserve all its qualities.

JG I absolutely must ask you whether all of your books are autobiographical. Is Eddie really 100 percent Limonov?

EL Of course the book is autobiographical. I wrote it chapter by chapter. When I finished it, I still hadn't outgrown that stage. I was that Eddie for another year or year and a half. But we all know that for each of us every moment yields a multitude of personalities.

JG But did everything described in *Eddie* and *The Adolescent Savenko* really happen?

EL *Savenko* is more complicated because I wrote the book almost a quarter of a century after the events described. Yes, it is autobiographical, even to the extent that I preserved most of the names. At least those that I remembered. Some I simply forgot, so I had to change them. But *Savenko* is not a carbon copy of reality. It represented a version of reality that existed at the moment it was written.

JG In that regard, other writers feel differently about their books. Take Nabokov, who was a rather private person. He was driven by a sense of play. One can say the same of Borges. Your books are confessions. There are readers or critics who would call them exhibitionism. What moved you to start writing at the age of thirty-one?

EL To start writing prose? It's no coincidence that I wrote poetry for all those years. It was the only weapon I had with which to fight the world. I cannot explain that—it's the stuff of psychoanalysis. Poetry was the only way I could present myself to the world, the only thing I could sell in the way I wanted. It was something on which I could base my existence. My literary work was proof of my existence.

JG An attempt at self-affirmation?

EL Not an attempt, but an act.

JG And what if you hadn't been able to emigrate?

EL It's hard to imagine what my life would have been like. But I don't think it would have been ordinary. I left mostly because of a feeling of alienation from my homeland and countrymen. Out of a desire for a different lot.

JG I understand that, but what if you hadn't been able to leave? Would you still have written?

EL Of course.

JG Was your switch from poetry to prose a result of emigration, or would it have happened anyway?

EL The new conditions and the stress, the shock of a new reality, the troubles I encountered—although they weren't all that direct—might not have meant anything to a different person. It was the accumulation of a number of causes that made me switch to prose. You can see the roots of my change to prose in my poems of the late 1970s. The verse entitled "Russian"— not the book, but the poems that went into the collection—had whole chunks of prose in them. And the poem "We Are National Heroes," which I wrote later, also contained a great deal of prose. In other words, my move to prose had obviously already begun earlier, but it was speeded up by the effect on me of my new surroundings, my new reality. I had to make room for my new experiences. The old genre was unable to accommodate them.

JG Émigrés usually feel that they have been through something out of the ordinary. For them emigration is a shock, and they want to tell others about it. That's perfectly understandable. But it doesn't stop there. There is something about emigration that makes people write, and not just their memoirs. There are more émigré writers than one would have expected, and that is not only because many writers have emigrated. Many began to write only in the West, and that phenomenon is not limited to the Third Wave.

EL I don't know anything about that. Since 1967, until I left in 1974, I had been fairly well-known in Moscow as a poet. I really began to write when I was fifteen. Writing was never my main activity. I would stop for a while, then return to it again. At times I wrote bad poems.

JG But is writing now the main thing for you?

EL Now it's not only a way to make a living, but a means of communication with the world. That's natural.

JG Writers deprived of publishing opportunities in their homeland are, in an economic sense, like runners forced to run on one leg.

EL I don't agree at all, because I have lived in France entirely on my royalties since my very first book came out in November 1980. Not many French writers do that. They teach in universities, work as journalists, etc. There are very few people in this country, literally only a few hundred, who can live on their royalties. But I do. And I am earning more and more. I think that my books interest people because they are three-dimensional from the start. They are about America, the Soviet Union, France. We live in a big world, the world of modern man. French books, for example, are rarely bought in the United States or other countries because, in most cases, they are aimed at French readers. Their interest rarely extends beyond the borders of France.

According to *Le Monde,* only seven French books were sold at the Frankfurt Book Fair. Out of those seven, one was mine. I consider myself an international writer. Some of my books sell better than others, but almost all of them are translated into many other languages and sold in a lot of countries. Here, in France, my experiences in America were of interest as the experiences of a European in America. It was the shock resulting from the contact between European and American cultures. My first book was seen as a journey to the edge of night. It was, so to speak, "The Adventures of a European on a Different Part of the Planet." So I can't complain.

I'm making more and more money. On the whole I'm still not sold often or paid much in the United States, although the press is getting better. For example, I've sold well in Germany since the publication of my first book, and I came out in paperback in both the States and England.

JG   In terms of royalties, what country and language earns you the most in sales?

EL   That depends on the book, but for the first few years most of the money came from Germany.

JG   And now?

EL   It depends. I just sold a new book to Flammarion for a lot of money, even by American standards. That's just for the French rights. Gradually I am earning a reputation. With each book my fame is growing.

JG   Can't the opposite happen? Being prolific can result in a kind of inflation. For example, Solzhenitsyn has written so much that it's a rare individual who has read everything he's written.

EL   His problem has to do with something entirely different. He has the megalomania of the historian or the philosopher. He wants to change the world. In his writing he tries to prove that his point of view is right, and in the attempt to substantiate his claims, he writes these crazy 1,500-page books. I have never done that and never will. None of my books in Russian exceeds two hundred pages. And they are getting shorter, which proves that I am able to say what I want in fewer words. But his books are getting larger. He has different goals. He is more like a sociologist or philosopher who, for some reason—in my opinion not a very intelligent one—tries to overextend his talent and put everything he has to say in a novel. He should write essays instead of absurd books like his "Knots" or "Wheels." All of that is unbearably boring and stupid and could go as a footnote at the bottom of a page. When I write, I do not necessarily show the manuscript to a publisher. Only later do I submit my manuscripts. Once, when I had completed a book, I was asked if I couldn't give a bit of thought to a certain idea. The idea was not given to me in written form. It was just a couple of phrases tossed out in conversation. Using that idea, I wrote a pretty good book which, unfortunately, still hasn't come out.

Not all books are equally successful. I know which are better and which worse. I'm normal and don't suffer from any excessive manias. I think that as a writer I have developed normally. In other words, I started out with poetry and then switched to prose.

JG   How would you characterize your development as a writer?

EL   That's complicated. I'm not a literary scholar or a critic. I read the reviews of my books. Then I begin to understand what I do.

JG   Criticism helps?

EL   It doesn't help in the actual writing, but it does help you to define your path. It helps you to understand something, even if you do not use your understanding for many years or books ahead. But you can define who you are, at least for the time being. There was an article last year on *His Butler's Story*, published by Grove Press. It was an article by Edward Brown, and it was a pleasure to read. It wasn't just a newspaper article.

JG But Edward Brown is a Slavist, not your typical critic.

EL He's not typical, and that's why the article was so interesting. And he didn't limit himself to Slavics. I got a lot out of that article. It interested me.

JG For example?

EL For example, his claim that both books in my American cycle—*It's Me, Eddie* and *His Butler's Story*—and those of the Russian cycle—*The Adolescent Savenko* and *The Young Scoundrel*—contain anti-establishment themes. I've known that for a long time, but he somehow brought it all together. And he really showed how the anti-establishment views of the fifteen-year-old hero of *The Adolescent Savenko* carry over to the thirty-year-old man living in New York and working as a butler for a multimillionaire.

JG I remember Edward Brown at the conference in Los Angeles on Russian literature in emigration eight years ago called himself an internal émigré. Perhaps he was writing about himself, as well as about you.

Why did you decide to live in France and not America?

EL Because I didn't get the chance to publish anything in America. My first publisher was French, and that's why I came here.

JG Otherwise you would have stayed in America?

EL I would have stayed in America without a doubt.

JG In New York?

EL Yes, in New York.

JG Only in New York?

EL No place else. I love New York.

A Chronology

1860   Prince Dolgoruky in Paris writes in a book entitled *La vérité sur la Russie* that "the press [in Russia] is shackled by censors who act capriciously and according to their moods. The sole advantage derived by Russia from their activities is the establishment of several Russian presses abroad, which have been founded out of their reach because of the ludicrous severity of the Russian censorship."

1867   Dostoevsky leaves for a four-year stay in Germany, Switzerland, and Italy; fearful of debtor's prison, he is unable to return home until 1871. Turgenev publishes *Smoke*.

1868   Dostoevsky publishes *The Idiot*.

1872   Nechaev is handed over by Swiss authorities to the Russian government.

1873   Pyotr Tkachov emigrates.

1875   Serials founded: *Nabat* (The Alarm) (Geneva) and *Rabotnik* (The Worker), a newspaper for Russian workers.

1876   Pyotr Kropotkin escapes to the West.

1879   Sergei Kravchinsky flees abroad after having assassinated the chief of police in Petersburg in 1878.

1880   Georgy Plekhanov leaves for thirty-seven-year stay in Europe; the magazine *Cherny peredel* is founded in London.

1881–1884   A wave of pogroms take place in the wake of the assassination of Alexander II, further stimulating a large Jewish emigration which had already begun in the late 1870s.

1885   The Turgenev Library is founded in Paris.

1889   Kravchinsky publishes *The Career of a Nihilist* (London).

1891   Twenty thousand Jews expelled from Moscow; emigrants from the Russian Empire to the United States: 47,426.

1892   Serials founded: *Russkie novosti* (Russian News) (New York), *Russko-amerikansky vestnik* (The Russian-American Newsletter) (U.S.), *Russky mirok* (The Smaller Russian World) (U.S.).

1893   U.S. President Cleveland signs into law a bill permitting extradition of political "criminals" to Tsarist Russia over a storm of protest among Russian émigrés. Serials founded: *Progress* (Chicago) and *Soiuz* (The Union) (Paris).

1894   Sergei Kravchinsky publishes *Pavel Rudenko, Member of the Stunde* (Geneva).

1896   China permits Tsarist government to build railroad across Manchuria, creating the need for a large Russian colony on Chinese territory.

1899   Emigrants from the Russian Empire to the United States: 60,982.

1900   298,577 people are registered as exiled in Siberia; exile for life within the empire is abolished under the terms of the Tsarist penal code. Vladimir Lenin emigrates. Serials founded: *Iskra* (The Spark) (Leipzig, then Munich, then London, then Geneva) and *Russkaya zhizn' v Amerike* (Russian Life in America) (New York). Emigrants from the Russian Empire to the United States: 90,787.

1901   Maksim Gorky sent into internal exile by Tsarist government.

1902   Trotsky emigrates to London; Boris Savinkov sent into internal exile in Vologda; the Gogol Library is founded in Rome on the fiftieth anniversary of Gogol's death; emigrants from the Russian Empire to the United States: 107,347.

1903   Work is completed on the Far East railroad through Manchuria; Boris Savinkov escapes from Vologda and flees to Geneva; emigrants from the Russian Empire to the United States: 136,093.

1904   Aleksandr Amfiteatrov emigrates to Paris. Serials founded: *Skandalissimus: An Annual Humorous Satirical Scandalous Review* (Karlsruhe); *Vestnik Bunda* (Geneva). Emigrants from the Russian Empire to the United States: 145,141.

1905   After spending two weeks in prison for allowing the Central Committee of the Russian Social Democrat Workers' Party to meet in his apartment, Leonid Andreev is released but fears violence from right-wing political organizations and leaves for Western Europe; Radishchev's works are republished in Russia; Lenin and Trotsky return to Russia; of the 360 Russian students at the University of Berlin, 261 are Jewish; Lenin publishes *Party Organization and Party Literature*, and Kropotkin publishes *Ideals and Realities in Russian Literature*.

1905–1906   Pogroms in the wake of the October Manifesto of 1905.

1906   Maksim Gorky, Anatoly Lunacharsky, and Mikhail Osorgin emigrate; Leonid Andreev joins Gorky on Capri. Serials founded: *Burevestnik*, an "Organ of the Russian Anarchist Communists" (Paris); *Za rubezhom* (Abroad: A Daily Literary Political Newspaper) (Berlin); *Krasnoe znamya* (The Red Banner: A Political and Literary Magazine) (Paris). Gorky publishes *Mother*. Emigrants from the Russian Empire to the United States: 215,665.

1907   Lenin emigrates for second time; Leonid Andreev returns to Russia; Mikhail Iliin, living near Genoa, begins to contribute to émigré journals under pseudonym Osorgin; Anatoly Lunacharsky publishes *Five Farces for Amateurs,* and Leonid Andreev publishes *Darkness*. Serials founded: *Anarkhist* (Geneva); *Raduga* (The Rainbow: A Monthly Literary, Scientific, and Political Magazine) (Geneva); *Sirius* (Paris); *Russky golos* (The Russian Word) (New York). Emigrants from the Russian Empire to the United States: 258,943.

1908   Aleksandr Bogdanov publishes (in Russia) *Red Star*, and Aleksandr Amfiteatrov publishes *Twilight of the Petty Gods;* Vladimir Chertkov returns to Russia; Evno Azef is discovered to be an agent of the Tsarist *Okhranka.* Serials founded: *Russko-amerikansky rabochy* (The Russian-American Worker) (New York); *Russkaya gazeta* (The Russian Newspaper: A Literary, Social, and Political Newspaper) (Geneva). Ilya Ehrenburg leaves for Europe.

1909   Bogdanov, Bazarov, and Lunacharsky organize a party school on Capri promulgating the idea that working humanity should be a "god-building" force rather than a conspirational organization (opposed by Lenin). Serials founded: *Emigrantsky listok* (An Émigré Newspaper) (New York).

1910   German census figures record 137,697 Russians traveling or living in Germany. Serials founded: *Russkoe slovo* (New York), oldest Russian newspaper still in existence; *Sotsialist revoliutsioner* (The Socialist Revolutionary: A Quarterly Literary-Political Review) (Paris) ceases publication in 1912; *Zhurnal dlia vsekh* (A Magazine for Everyone) (New York). Emigrants from the Russian Empire to the United States: 186,792.

1911   Emigrants from the Russian Empire to the United States: 158,721.

1912   Boris Savinkov publishes (in Russia) *What Never Was;* some 5,000 students from Russia registered for study at German universities, primarily Berlin (1,174), Leipzig (758), Munich (552), Königsberg (435), Heidelberg (317), and Halle (283); Andrei Bely goes abroad to study with Rudolph Steiner. Serials founded: *Inostranets* (The Foreigner) (Paris), bimonthly newspaper; *Khleb i volya* (Bread and Freedom) (Chicago); *Mysl'* (Thought: A Political, Social, and Literary Newspaper) (Paris); *Zagranichnye otkliki* (Responses Abroad: A Social, Political, Literary, and Economic Newspaper) (Berlin). Emigrants from the Russian Empire to the United States: 162,395.

1913   The following writers emigrate: Lev Kobylinsky (Ellis), Osip Perelman (Dymov); Maksim Gorky and Konstantin Balmont return to Russia under general amnesty; emigration from Russia to the United States reaches its peak: 291,040.

1914   Lev Èllis publishes (in Russia) *Argo*. Serials founded: *Vechera* (Evenings) (Paris), monthly collection of poetry, edited by Ilya Ehrenburg; *Golos Yaponii* (Voice of Japan) (Tokyo).

1915   Serials founded: *Golos zarubezhnogo studenchestva* (Voice of Students Abroad) (Geneva); *Russky vestnik* (The Russian Herald), newspaper published in Russian by German authorities in Berlin for prisoner-of-war camp internees with a supposed circulation of 100,000 copies; *Russkoe slovo* (New York) becomes a daily newspaper. Emigrants from the Russian Empire to the United States: 26,187.

1915–1921   A wave of pogroms is set off by the belief that the Jews were to blame for war defeats; Aleksandr Amfiteatrov, Andrei Bely, and Mikhail Osorgin return to Russia.

1916   Andrei Bely returns to Russia after being called up for military service. Serials founded: *Novy mir* (The New World) (New York), with participation of Bukharin, Trotsky, and Volodarsky; *Voennaya gazeta dlia russkikh voisk vo Frantsii* (Newspaper for Russian Troops in France) (Paris), a publication of the General Staff. Emigrants from the Russian Empire to the United States: 7,842.

1917   The New York communist newspaper *Novy mir* is temporarily denied postal privileges. Ilya Ehrenburg, Pyotr Kropotkin, Vladimir Lenin, and Anatoly Lunacharsky return to Russia. Serials founded: *Russky golos* (The Russian Voice) (New York City) and *Svobodnaya Rossiya* (Free Russia) (Chicago).

1918   Founding of *Litfond*, the Fund for the Relief of Russian Writers and Scientists (New York). Leonid Andreev moves to his dacha in Finland to escape starvation. In August thirty-seven issues of *Novy mir* are confiscated by the United States government. The following writers emigrate: Aleksandr Glikberg (Sasha Chorny), Antonina Gorskaya, Igor Severianin, Gleb Struve, Aleksei Tolstoy, and Aleksandr Yashchenko. Serials founded: *Russkaya pochta* (The Russian Mail) (Chicago) and *Zhizn' i delo* (Life and Work) (New York).

1918–1922   An estimated 250,000 Russians flee to the Far East, more than half to China, mainly in Manchuria.

1919   Leonid Andreev publishes a call to the West to help save Russia from Bolshevism (*Spasite! SOS*, London); sixty thousand to one hundred thousand Russian refugees are estimated to have settled in Germany; Gorky writes his famous letter to Lenin, placing himself at the service of the Bolsheviks; the "Czech-Russian Union" is founded in Prague; the following writers emigrate: Mark Aldanov (Landau), Alfred Bem (critic), Aleksandr Bisk, Zinaida Gippius, Aleksandr Kuprin, Gizella Lakhman, Dmitry Merezhkovsky, "Mother Maria" (Elena Skobtsova), Vladimir Nabokov, family of Boris Poplavsky, Lev Shestov, Arnold Shpoliansky (Don-Aminado), Nadezhda Buchinskaya (Tèffi), Nikolai Trubetskoi, Aleksandr Vertinsky, Mark Vishnyak, and Vladimir Zlobin.

1920   Approximately 300,000 Russian emigrants are thought to be living in Germany; Pyotr Kropotkin writes an open letter to Lenin protesting the taking of political hostages and another open letter to the Eighth All-Russian Congress of Soviets defending the right of free publishing houses to exist. More than 138 émigré newspapers are founded, among them *Golos Rossii* (Voice of Russia) (Berlin), *Poslednie novosti* (The Latest News) (Paris), *Rul'* (The Rudder) (Berlin), *Novaya zarya* (A New Dawn) (San Francisco), *Russkoe obozrenie* (Russian Review) (Peking-Shanghai), *Volya Rossii* (The Will of Russia), and the journals *Griadushchaya Rossiya* (Russia of the Future) (Paris), *Sovremennye zapiski* (Contemporary Annals) (Paris), and *Teatr i zhizn'* (Theater and Life) (Riga). Russian American church groups opposed to the Soviet government form the Russian Orthodox Church Outside Russia and sever all ties with the Patriarch of Moscow; massive evacuations of White armies and followers from the Crimea to Istanbul and to Harbin and Shanghai in the Far East; Roman Jakobson goes to Prague as a translator, still retaining Soviet

citizenship. The following writers emigrate: Gleb Alek-
seev (Charnotsky), Arkady Averchenko, Konstantin Bal-
mont, Ivan Bunin, David Burliuk, Yevgeny Chirikov,
Lidia Devel (Lidia Alekseeva), Aleksandr Drozdov, Gaito
Gazdanov, Georgy Grebenshchikov, family of Yury Ivask,
Irina Knorring, family of David Fikhman (Dovid Knut),
Vladimir Korvin-Piotrovsky, Galina Kuznetsova, Sergei
Makovsky, family of Yury Mandelstam, Olga Mozhai-
skaya, family of Valery Pereleshin, Kirill Pomerantsev,
Yevgeny Raikh, Yakov Tsvibak (Andrei Sedykh), Zinaida
Shakhovskaya, Dmitry Shakhovskoy (Strannik), Ivan
Sokolov-Mikitov, family of Anatoly Steiger and Alla Golo-
vina, Vasily Sumbatov, Ekaterina Tauber, Yury Terapiano,
Vladimir Varshavsky, Semyon Yushkevich.

1921   The Russian émigré Constituent Assembly is convened in
Paris; the First Assembly of Monarchists is held in Reich-
enhall, establishing a Supreme Monarchist Council attended by representatives of seventy-five monarchist
groups; Fridjof Nansen is appointed High Commissioner
for Affairs of Russian Refugees; the Soviet government
proclaims an amnesty to its opponents, as a result of
which some 121,000 émigrés return to the Soviet Union in
1921 and 60,000 in the next nine years; the YMCA Press is
founded in Prague; Eurasianism is founded by Nikolai
Trubetskoi, Georgy Florovsky, Pyotr Savitsky, and Pyotr
Suvchinsky when they publish a collection of essays entitled *Iskhod k vostoku* (Exodus to the East) in Sofia. Organizations founded: House of the Arts (Berlin), The Russian
People's University (Paris), The Association of Russian
Writers and Journalists in Paris, the Russian Popular Li-
brary (Prague). The New Economy Policy (NEP) is estab-
lished in the Soviet Union, and a number of Russian
publishing houses are established in Berlin to service the
Soviet market. Serials founded: *Eshafot* (The Scaffold)
(Gallipoli), *Mlechny put'* (Milky Way) (Gallipoli), *Nashi dni*
(Our Days) (Constantinople), *Otechestvo* (The Fatherland)
(Paris), *Russkaya kniga* (The Russian Book) (Berlin), *Rus-
skaya mysl'* (Russian Thought) (Sofia), *Russkaya zhizn'*
(Russian Life) (San Francisco), *Smena vekh* (Change of
Landmarks) (Prague), *Spolokhi* (Berlin). The following
writers emigrate: Nikolai Agnivtsev, Nikolai Breshko-
Breshkovsky, Andrei Bely, Yevgeny Valin, Dmitry Tschi-

zewskij (literary scholar), Aleksandr Ginger, Maksim Gorky, Aleksandr Kuskian (Kusikov), Sergei Gusev-Orenburgsky, Antonin Ladinsky, Stepan Petrov-Skitalets, Aleksei Remizov, Vladimir Smolensky. Ilya Ehrenburg goes abroad with an official Soviet passport.

1922   Open letter of Aleksei Tolstoy to émigré editor N. V. Chaikovsky declaring his intention to return to Russia; the second Assembly of Monarchists is held in Paris, representing 120 monarchist groups; the "Hermitage of Poets" (Skit poètov) is established in Prague; the YMCA Press is moved from Prague to Berlin; German records indicate 600,000 Russian immigrants; Soviet government (decision of Trotsky and Lenin) deports more than 160 writers, journalists, and prominent figures from the Tsarist period; the daily newspaper *Rossiya* in Harbin is closed by Chinese government; the "Union of Russian Writers and Journalists" votes to expel all members of the Change of Landmarks newspaper *Nakanune;* repatriations: Valentin Parnakh, Ivan Sokolov-Mikitov, Mark-Liudovik-Mariya Talov; Nikolai Boycharov assassinates Aleksandr Ageev, editor of newspaper *Na rodinu.* Serials founded: *Novaya russkaya kniga* (Berlin); *Nakanune* (Berlin) becomes the only émigré newspaper officially distributed in the USSR, with an office in Moscow; *Russkoe èkho* (The Russian Echo) (Prague); *Smekhomyot* (The Laugh-Thrower) (New York); *Studencheskie gody* (Student Years) (Prague); *Zhili-byli* (Once Upon a Time) (Bizerta, Tunisia). "The Union of Russian Writers and Journalists in the Czechoslovak Republic" is founded. The following writers emigrate: Georgy Adamovich, Nina Berberova, Nikolai Berdiaev, Sergei Bulgakov, Lidia Chervinskaya, Sergei Efron, Semyon Frank, Antonina Grivtsova, Vladislav Khodasevich, Nikolai Lossky, Mikhail Osorgin, Nikolai Otsup, Viktor Shklovsky, Ivan Shmelyov, Fyodor Stepun, Marina Tsvetaeva, Boris Zaitsev; assassination of father of Vladimir Nabokov.

1923   Approximately 360,000 Russians apply for refugee status in Berlin alone; runaway inflation in Germany makes book publication very cheap; by the end of the year nearly sixty Russian émigré publishing houses are founded in Berlin alone; the New York daily *Novoe russkoe slovo* claims a circulation of 31,240 and is challenged by the communist newspaper *Russky golos*, which offers to contribute $5,000 to a charitable organization if *Novoe russkoe slovo* is able to prove it has 30 percent of that number; repatriations: Nikolai Agnivtsev, Gleb Alekseev, Andrei Bely, Aleksandr Drozdov, Venedikt Matveev, Boris Pasternak, Viktor Shklovsky, Aleksei Tolstoy; the Mladoross League (Young Russians) is established in Munich; serials founded: *Zveno* (Paris) and *Okno* (Paris); the following writers emigrate: Mikhail Artsybashev, Georgy Ivanov (according to some sources 1922), family of Kirill Khenkin, Irina Odoevtseva.

1924   Bunin gives speech on the mission of the Russian exile community; Zinaida Gippius claims that all the significant Russian writers have emigrated; Boris Savinkov illegally crosses Soviet border and is arrested; the literary circle "Daliborka" is founded in Prague; serials founded: *Rassvet* (The Dawn) (New York), *Illyustrirovannaya Rossiya* (Illustrated Russia) (Paris); eighty-six of the publishing houses existing outside the USSR are located in Berlin; the following writers emigrate: Yury Annenkov, Viacheslav Ivanov, Vladimir Veidle.

1925   Pyotr Struve estimates that 85 percent of the émigrés support the monarchists, a figure which appears to have been generally accepted; Aleksandr Kerensky banishes Mikhail Osorgin from the pages of the Berlin newspaper *Dni* (Days) for his anarchist views; "The Union of Young Poets and Writers" is formed in Paris to represent the "younger generation"; the "Russian Hearth" is founded in Prague; Russian population of Harbin, China, is estimated at 150,000; serials founded: *Perezvony* (Riga), *Vozrozhdenie* (The Renaissance) (Paris), *Rodnaya niva* (Native Field) (Harbin), *Russkoe èkho* (Russian Echo) (Berlin, refounded); the following writers emigrate: Nikolai Yevreinov and Georgy Fedotov; Boris Savinkov dies in a Soviet prison, rumored to have been thrown out a window.

1926   The literary circle *Molodaya Churaevka* is founded in Harbin; Russian poets in the United States publish a collection of verse, entitled *From America*. Serials founded: *Blagonamerenny* (The Well-Intentioned) (Brussels), *Rodnoe slovo* (Native Word) (Warsaw), *Vestnik Russkogo Studencheskogo Khristianskogo Dvizheniya* (Herald of the Russian Student Christian Movement) (Paris), *Vyorsty* (Miles) (Paris), *Ukhvat* (Tongs) (Paris).

1927   Dovid Knut claims that the capital of Russian literature is Paris and not Moscow; Vladimir Zhabotinsky settles in Paris; The Green Lamp Society is founded in Paris; serials founded: *Novy korabl'* (Paris), *Vestnik* (The Herald) (Chicago); Vladimir Nabokov writes: "In these days, when the dismal Soviet revolution is being celebrated, we celebrate ten years of contempt, loyalty, and freedom. Let us not abuse our exile, but repeat the words of an ancient warrior, as described by Plutarch: 'At night, in the empty fields, far from Rome, I erected my tent. And my tent for me was Rome.'"

1928   World conference of Russian émigré writers in Belgrade—participants, guests, and observers number 111; according to a report of the German "Völkerbund" there are 919,000 Russian emigrants throughout the world; Maksim Gorky visits the USSR.

1929   *Quiet Street* (English title of Osorgin's *Sivtsev vrazhek*) becomes a best-seller in America. A formal banquet is held in honor of Pavel Milyukov in the Paris hotel Lutèce; the next day *Vozrozhdenie* publishes a letter of Vasily Maklakov, who refuses to attend, saying that demonstratively public celebrations are inappropriate in view of the "common guilt" of the left and the right in the revolution. The third combined convention in Paris of the Russian Committee of United Organizations and the Council of Social Organizations increases its membership to 175 organizations; Lev Trotsky is exiled to Turkey.

1930   In Paris the Soviets kidnap General Vrangel's successor, General A. Kutepov; the *Solidarist* movement is formed at Belgrade conference; serials founded: *Chisla* (Numbers) (Paris) and *Color and Rhyme* (New York).

1931   Yevgeny Zamyatin is permitted to emigrate after writing a letter to Stalin; Maksim Gorky returns to Russia; serials founded: *Utverzhdeniya* (Confirmations) (Paris), *Novy grad* (New City) (Paris), *Satirikon* (Paris), *Serp i molot* (Hammer and Sickle) (New York).

1932   Russian émigré poet Pavel Gorgulov assassinates French President Paul Doumer; the Presidium of the Central Committee of the Soviet Union strips thirty-seven émigrés of Soviet citizenship, among them Lev Trotsky; Prince Dmitry Sviatopolk-Mirsky returns to the Soviet

Union; the Japanese seize Manchuria, and the Russian community there begins to move south to Shanghai.

1933   Ivan Bunin receives Nobel Prize; Roman Goul, Vladimir Korvin-Piotrovsky, and Zinaida Trotskaya emigrate from Germany to France; serials founded: *Fashist* (The Fascist) (Putnam, Connecticut), *Rossiya* (Russia) (New York), *Russkaya gazeta* (The Russian Newspaper) (New York).

1934   Petrov-Skitalets returns to Russia. Dmitry Filosofov proposes the creation of an émigré literary academy; the project is never brought to fulfillment. Filosofov also declares that émigrés who seek assimilation are "dead" to the émigré community. The "crisis" in émigré literature (and especially in poetry) continues to be a common topic of discussion in émigré publications. Serials founded: *Mech* (The Sword) (Warsaw), *Vrata* (The Gates) (Harbin), *Vstrechi* (Meetings) (Paris).

1935   Mikhail Tsetlin: "The common impoverishment of poetic talent in all literatures is no accident. . . . Poetry is 'out of step' with our time: *inter arma silent musae.* We are living in an era of wars and revolutions, so that the very source of poetry as art—the poetic 'medium' of the human soul— seems to dry up. . . . Probably, a certain 'atmosphere' is necessary—an atmosphere which is formed under conditions of spiritual quietness, in the calm of an ordered way of life. But now everything has been laid bare and rendered fruitless by tragic conflicts"; serials founded: *Na vostoke* (In the East) (Tokyo), *Vremennik* (New York).

1936   The fifth (and last) combined convention of the Russian Committee of United Organizations is held in Paris; the Council of Social Organizations increases its membership to 445 organizations; Gaito Gazdanov publishes article in *Contemporary Notes* denying that the "younger generation" of émigré writers (with the exception of Nabokov) have produced anything of lasting value; Vladimir Varshavsky: "There are plenty of writers in Russia and abroad who write a good deal, and write well, but not one has said anything so truly new and important as to how we should view our lives on the final judgment day that we might believe him the way we believe Tolstoy, Dostoevsky, and Blok"; Mark Aldanov: "In Russia . . . there was a 'vital and invigorating' literary atmosphere. As far as I can tell, such an atmosphere exists in individual émigré circles. . . . I speak here of Russian Paris (I can't say how matters stand in the 'provinces'). . . . Our catastrophe is of a different nature. . . . Russian writers abroad are not troubled by the question of a *second* profession, since they don't have a primary profession. For the émigré, literature is not a trade. It produces no income for the majority of writers, particularly the young"; Yugoslavia recognizes the Soviet government over the objections of the Russian émigré community; B. Bakhmetieff gives $1,400,000 to Columbia University to expand its Russian studies program—the Bakhmetieff Archive is now one of the chief repositories of archival materials on Russian literature in exile; Tsarist exile Grigory Zinoviev is executed in the USSR.

1937   Yevgeny Reis is murdered; Tsvetaeva's husband Sergei Efron is implicated and flees to the USSR; Parisian police announce that former White-Army General Yevgeny Miller, head of the All-Russian Military Union, has been kidnapped by Soviet agents; Sviatopolk-Mirsky is arrested in USSR; Aleksandr Kuprin repatriates and on June 18 writes in *Izvestiya* that he had "longed to return to Soviet Russia for a long time," because he "experienced nothing but anguish and separation among the other émigrés. . . . Even the flowers smell differently in the homeland. Their aroma is stronger, headier than that of foreign flowers. People say our soil is richer and more fertile. Perhaps. In any case, everything is better in the homeland!"; Semyon Frank and Vladimir Nabokov leave Germany for France; serials founded: *Russkie zapiski* (Russian Annals) (Shanghai/Paris); Nikolai Ustryalov is executed in the USSR.

1938   Former Tsarist exile Nikolai Bukharin is executed in USSR. Among the accusations leveled against Bukharin is the murder of Maksim Gorky; Aleksei Tolstoy is awarded the Order of Lenin.

1939   In April the French government unexpectedly requires registration of all foreign organizations, and Russian cultural organizations find themselves in a semilegal situation. In September "undesirable foreigners" are rounded up in France for deportation; these included Russians who had collaborated with the Nazis in Germany and also members of the pro-Soviet Union for Return to the Homeland. Aleksei Èisner and Marina Tsvetaeva return to the USSR; the Tolstoy Foundation is established in New York to assist refugees from Soviet Russia; the Parisian newspaper *Vozrozhdenie* (Renaissance) abruptly shifts from a pro-Hitler position to one loyal to the French government; serials founded: *Gran'* (Facet) (Paris) and *Chasovoy* (Watchman) (Paris); when World War II begins, the Green Lamp Society ceases to function; *Russkie zapiski* and *Novy grad* cease publication; the Prague group "Skit poètov" is closed.

1940   Vladimir Nabokov and Mark Vishnyak leave France for the United States; the Germans occupy Paris; *Sovremennye Zapiski* and *Vestnik Russkogo Studencheskogo Khristianskogo Dvizheniya* cease publication; in Paris the Turgenev library with its 100,000 volumes is confiscated and taken to Germany, where it disappears; officially registered immigration to the United States of persons born on Soviet territory: 1,812; Leon Trotsky is killed by agent of Stalin in Mexico; Sergei Efron, Tsvetaeva's husband, is executed in USSR.

1941   Number of Russian emigrants in Yugoslavia is estimated to be approximately 50,000; the following writers find themselves in cities occupied by the Germans: Boris Filippov (Novgorod), Sergei Maksimov (Smolensk), and Boris Nartsissov (Tartu); Kirill Khenkin repatriates; Ilya Ehrenburg returns to USSR; Aleksei Tolstoy is awarded first of three Stalin Prizes; Mark Landau (pseud. Mark Aldanov), Zinaida Trotskaya, Roman Yakobson arrive in the United States; German headquarters entrusts White general Skorodumov with the task of forming a Russian military unit in Yugoslavia; Marina Tsvetaeva commits suicide in Elabuga, USSR.

1942   By March 1 the Germans take 3,600,000 Russian prisoners of war; Boris Shiryaev is in Cherkessk when it is occupied by the Germans; Gennady Khomyakov taken prisoner by Germans. Hélène Iswolsky: "Our belief is that the 'disintegration of culture and personality,' which seems characteristic of the young Russian émigré authors, was partly due to the influence of the modern school of French literature; these tendencies would have probably been overcome in due time, as the 'decadent' trends of the beginning of the century have been overcome by previous generations. . . . Today, we do not find in Russian literature an author worthy of continuing the great Russian humanist tradition." Georgy Fedotov: "Marina Tsvetaeva belonged to the Moscow, and not the Paris School. Her place is there—between Mayakovsky and Pasternak. In tune with the revolution as a natural storm, she could not come to terms with communist slavery. Abroad she found poverty, emptiness, loneliness. Now she is in her native country, but we don't hear her songs. Perhaps the nightingale has been fed, but a free bird won't sing in a cage"; Tsvetaeva was already dead by the time this was written. Serials founded: *Novy zhurnal* (The New Review) (New York) and *Parizhsky vestnik* (Parisian Herald) (German supported); Valentina Sinkevich pressed into forced labor and taken to Germany; in Paris Yury Mandelstam arrested and later deported to Germany; Dmitry Krachkovsky (Klenovsky) flees to Germany; Yakov Tsvibak (Andrei Sedykh) and Vasily Yanovsky move to the United States.

1943   Roughly one million former Soviet citizens are estimated to be performing military service in the German army; Yury Felzen arrested and deported to Germany, where he evidently dies in a concentration camp; Mother Maria (Elena Skobtsova), Mikhail Gorlin, and Raissa Blokh also sent to concentration camps; the American Book-of-the-Month Club selects Aldanov's novel *The Fifth Seal* (originally titled *Nachalo kontsa*), causing heated protests among persons who still regarded the USSR as an ally; the following writers emigrate: Olga Anstei, Ella Bobrova, Ivan Matveev (pseud. Ivan Elagin); Aleksandr Vertinsky returns to Russia.

1944   The Soviet of People's Commissars resolves that Soviet citizens abroad should be returned to the Soviet Union; the Vlasov movement issues a fourteen-point manifesto, interpreted as a nonpredetermination program (*Nepredreshenchestvo*); Vasily Shulgin arrested in Yugoslavia and returned to USSR; German-supported *Parizhsky vestnik* (Paris) ceases publication; the Association of Soviet Citizens in Paris is founded; serials founded: *Russky patriot* (Paris); the following writers emigrate: Anatoly Darov, Oleg Iliinsky, Sergei Maksimov, Nikolai Nikolaevich Marchenko (pseud. Morshen).

1945 The Yalta Accords include provision for the repatriation of former Soviet citizens abroad; a group of prominent émigrés, including the last prerevolutionary Russian ambassador to France, Vasily Maklakov, pays a visit to the Soviet embassy to state that they recognize the Soviet Union as Russia's national state; U.S. President Truman directs that displaced persons be given preference with regard to U.S. immigration quotas; forced repatriation to the USSR begins; the Russian Historical Archive in Prague is closed and taken to the USSR; in the wake of the Soviet occupation of Manchuria, the Russian émigré community shifts to Shanghai.

1946 Meeting of Association of Russian Writers and Journalists in Paris to determine relationship to Soviet government; the Supreme Soviet decrees an amnesty for all Russian émigrés and offers them the opportunity to apply for Soviet citizenship; in the United Nations Andrei Gromyko complains that the resettlement of displaced persons is being conducted in such a way that "war criminals, quislings, and traitors" are being permitted to escape; Aleksandr Ginger, Antonin Ladinsky, and Anna Prismanova accept Soviet citizenship; Soviet writer Konstantin Simonov is sent to France to persuade Ivan Bunin to return to the Soviet Union. Serials founded: *Grani* (Facets) (Frankfurt-am-Main), publishing house Posev; *Ogon'* (The Flame), produced on a duplicating machine in a displaced persons camp just outside of Munich—later renamed *Znamya Rossii* (Banner of Russia); *Petrushka* (Munich); *Svobodny golos* (Free Voice) (Paris).

1947 The Union of Writers and Journalists is founded in Munich; the League of Soviet Patriots in Paris is dissolved and replaced with the League of Soviet Citizens, claiming 11,000 members; *In the Trenches of Stalingrad*, the 1946 novel of the future émigré Viktor Nekrasov, is awarded the Stalin Prize; a meeting is held of the planning committee of the Monarchist Movement Abroad to reestablish the movement; in Paris the Association of Russian Writers and Journalists votes to expel those members who had received Soviet passports; among the members who withdraw in protest from the association are Georgy Adamovich, Vera Bunina, Gaito Gazdanov, Perikl Stavrov, Vladimir Varshavsky, and Leonid Zurov; two weeks later

Ivan Bunin also withdraws from the association; in Paris leaders of the League of Soviet Citizens are rounded up for deportation to the Soviet Union; the newspaper *Sovetsky patriot* is shut down by the police; officially registered immigration to the United States of persons born on Soviet territory: 2,393; Russian Section of Voice of America is founded. Serials founded: the newspaper *Russkaya mysl'* (Russian Thought) (Paris), *Kitaisko-russkaya gazeta* (The Chinese-Russian Newspaper) (Shanghai), *Otdykh* (Rest) (Frankfurt-am-Main), *Russkoe slovo* (The Russian Word) (Shanghai). Popular novelist (and general) Pyotr Krasnov is executed (by hanging) by Soviets.

1948   Aleksei Remizov takes Soviet citizenship and wills his archive to the USSR; the Czechoslovak government ships all émigré literary archives to the Soviet Union; the Anti-Cosmopolitan campaign is launched in the USSR; serials founded: *Narodnaya pravda* (The People's Truth) (New York), *Nasha strana* (Our Country) (Buenos Aires).

1949   Officially registered immigration to the United States of persons born on Soviet territory is 4,119, among them the writers Lidia Alekseeva, Nikolai Chukhnov, Yury Ivask, Galina Kuznetsova, Iraida Lyogkaya (pseudonym), Sergei Maksimov, and Vladimir Markov; a communist government is proclaimed in mainland China, and the Russian colony in Shanghai is evacuated to the Philippines—by the mid-1950s almost all are gone; *Vestnik russkogo khristianskogo dvizheniya,* which had ceased publication during the war, is refounded in Munich; the committee Free Europe is established; Dovid Knut leaves France for Israel.

1950   The Conciliatory Commission of the U.S. Senate and House of Representatives votes to accept 341,000 displaced persons by the end of July 1951; this includes most of the remaining refugees on Tubabao. Officially registered immigration to the United States of persons born on Soviet territory is 11,050, among them the writers Olga Anstei, Nina Berberova, Ivan Burkin, Tatiana Fesenko, Boris Filippov, Elena Matveeva, Nikolai Morshen, Gennady Panin, Valentina Sinkevich; the magazine *Novosel'e* (Housewarming) moves from Paris to New York; serials founded: *Edinenie* (Unity) (Australia).

1951   Chekhov Publishing House founded; officially registered immigration to the United States of persons born on Soviet territory: 12,072.

1952   U.S. Congress unanimously passes measure legalizing the immigration of some 214,000 refugees from Eastern Europe and the Soviet Union; Truman signs a bill providing $100,000,000 for support to refugees from Eastern Europe and the Soviet Union; Roman Goul moves from Europe to the United States; serials founded: *Kolokol* (The Bell) (Hamburg), *Pod iuzhnym krestom* (Under the Southern Cross) (Buenos Aires), *Svoboda* (Freedom) (Munich).

1953   Officially registered immigration to the United States of persons born on Soviet territory: 1,832; Radio Liberty founded; Viktor Kamkin Bookstore is founded in Washington, D.C.; Igor Chinnov moves from Paris to Munich; Leonid Rzhevsky moves from Germany to Sweden; Boris Nartsissov emigrates from Australia to the United States; Valery Pereleshin emigrates from China to Brazil; literary journal *Opyty* (Experiments) (New York) founded.

1954   In the USSR Konstantin Fedin at Second All-Russian Writers' Congress claims (falsely) that Ivan Bunin had accepted Soviet citizenship.

1955   By decree of the Presidium of Supreme Soviet of the USSR, an amnesty is declared for Soviet citizens who were German prisoners-of-war or who served in the Germany army, police, or "special units"; the Committee for Return to the Homeland is founded in East Berlin with its own radio broadcasts and newspaper *Za vozvrashchenie na rodinu* (For a Return to the Homeland); Antonin Ladinsky returns to Russia.

1956   Oleg Iliinsky moves from Germany to the United States; Vasily Shulgin released from Soviet prison; Leonid Andreev's body is moved from Finland to Leningrad for reburial; five-volume collection of the work of Ivan Bunin is published in the Soviet Union; Chekhov Publishers (New York) and Vozrozhdenie Publishers (Paris) fold.

1957   *Doctor Zhivago* published in Italian, giving rise to the term *tamizdat* ("items published 'over there,' that is, in the West").

1958   The almanac *Mosty* (Bridges) created in Munich. Monarchist convention held March 22–24 in New York City. One of the speeches is given by B. L. Brazol: "Holy *Rus* is gone, replaced by the kingdom of the Anti-Christ, the black hell of the red beast, under whose clawed paw groan millions of our brothers." Boris Pasternak is awarded Nobel Prize but is forced to decline it when Khrushchev threatens him with exile; the following writers emigrate: Roman Bar-Or, Inessa Bliznetsova, Alla Ktorova.

1959   U.S. Congress passes the "Captive Nations Week Resolution"; First-Wave critic Yury Terapiano writes in *Grani* that he senses an essential commonality of approach and worldview in the poetry of the First Wave and the Second Wave; Roman Goul becomes editor-in-chief of *Novy zhurnal* after the death of Mikhail Karpovich; Andrei Siniavsky (pseud. Abram Terts) and Yuly Daniel (pseud. Nikolai Arzhak) clandestinely publish their work in the West.

1960   Lev Liubimov, deported from France to the USSR in 1947, returns for a visit to Paris: "I again felt pleasure at speaking not as an emigrant grateful for asylum, and not as a Russian with an undefined and dubious relation to his country, but as a full-fledged representative of my Fatherland who needs curry no one's favor and who knows that a great country stands behind him"; the pro-Soviet New York newspaper *Russky golos* publishes an open letter to the Russian émigré community from Vasily Shulgin, calling for a recognition of the Soviet government; the almanac *Sovremennik* (Toronto) founded.

1961   Officially registered immigration to the United States of persons born on Soviet territory: 2,352; Soviet publishing house *Moskovsky rabochy* publishes collection of stories and memoirs of Ivan Bunin.

1962   The future émigré Valery Tarsis is arrested and placed in a Soviet mental hospital after sending his manuscripts abroad for publication; Igor Chinnov moves to the United States from Western Europe.

1963   Clandestine American government assistance to a number of émigré publications is terminated; Soviet journal *Moskva* publishes verse of Vladislav Khodasevich; Soviet writer Mikhail Sholokhov in *Pravda* claims that Bunin has been almost forgotten by Soviet readers, while Gorky and Serafimovich, Bunin's contemporaries, will not be forgotten; Leonid Rzhevsky, Agniya Rzhevskaya (pseud. Aglaya Shishkova), and Yury Gertsog move to the United States; serials founded: *Al'manakh* (Caracas, Venezuela) and *Russkaya zhizn'* (San Francisco); Yury Krotkov defects.

1964   Soviet journal *Moskva* publishes two stories of Nadezhda Buchinskaya (Tèffi); two collections of the works of Arkady Averchenko are published in Moscow; Soviet journal *Nash sovremennik* (Our Contemporary) publishes verse of Aleksandr Glikberg (Sasha Chorny); Joseph Brodsky brought to trial for not having legal employment.

1965   Andrei Amalrik is prosecuted for his "anti-Soviet pornographic" plays; the first volume in a nine-volume collection of the works of Ivan Bunin is brought out in the Soviet Union (edition completed in 1968); Soviet journal *Don* publishes verse of Aleksandr Glikberg (pseud. Sasha Chorny) with a preface by L. Usenko, who does not mention that Glikberg was an émigré; *Don* republishes four stories of Aleksei Tolstoy which were first published in Paris in *Zhar-Ptitsa* (Fire-Bird) in 1922; arrest of Siniavsky and Daniel.

1966   Soviet critic V. Chivilikhin complains in *Literaturnaya Rossiya* (Literary Russia) about Soviet "imitations" of Bunin; Soviet critic A. Izotov suggests that the prerevolutionary works of Georgy Grebenshchikov could be republished in the Soviet Union, since "they have no relation to our life." U.S. Senator Robert Kennedy supposedly tells Soviet poet Yevgeny Yevtushenko that the CIA revealed the identities of Andrei Siniavsky (pseud. Abram Terts) and Yuly Daniel (pseud. Nikolai Arzhak) to the Soviet authorities; Yevtushenko claimed that the purpose of the U.S. action was to provoke the Soviets into arresting the two writers and give the Americans the opportunity to distract public opinion from the Vietnam war. Konstantin Simonov refutes rumor that Bunin had secretly become a Soviet citizen; the following writers emigrate: Leonid Finkelstein (pseud. Leonid Vladimirov), Valery Tarsis (stripped of Soviet citizenship for "actions discrediting a Soviet citizen"), Grigory Tsepliovich, and Igor Yeltsov (defects).

1967   Vladimir Nabokov's *Lolita* published in Russian in translation of author; Svetlana Allilueva, daughter of Joseph Stalin, defects to the West.

1968   Trial of Aleksandr Ginzburg, Yury Galanskov, Vera Lashkova, and Aleksei Dobrovolsky. Ginzburg is charged with smuggling out a *White Book* on Siniavsky-Daniel trial; critic Arkady Belinkov requests political asylum in the

United States; Soviet *Brief Literary Encyclopedia* pro-
nounces Nabokov a "denationalized author."

1969   Andrei Amalrik publishes in the West his essay: *Will the
Soviet Union Survive until 1984?*; Svetlana Allilueva is
stripped of Soviet citizenship; Aleksandr Solzhenitsyn is
expelled from Writers' Union.

1970   Solzhenitsyn is awarded Nobel Prize for literature; Boris
Khazanov (pseudonym): "Somewhere between the 1960s
and the 1970s it became totally clear that it was all over for
Soviet literature"; total Jewish, German, Armenian emigration: 1,388; according to U.S. Census data, 334,615
Americans declare Russian as their mother tongue; Russian Americans have thirty-one publications, twenty-five
in Russian and six in English, with a total circulation of
65,128 copies; Natalya Gorbanevskaya is committed to a
psychiatric hospital for role in publishing and distribut-
ing the *Khronika tekushchikh sobitii* (Chronicle of Current
Events); a group of Soviet citizens unsuccessfully attempt
to hijack a plane to escape to the West; serials founded:
Ami (Jerusalem) and *Mosty* (Munich); Ludmila Foster authors a *Bibliography of Russian Émigré Literature* in two
volumes, containing 17,000 entries and occupying 1,389
pages.

1971   More than 15,000 Soviet citizens leave the Soviet Union;
Ardis Publishers is founded in Ann Arbor; in the USSR
Aleksandr Galich is expelled from the Writers' Union;
Efraim Sevela and Mikhail Grobman emigrate.

1972   More than 35,000 persons emigrate; the United States
government grants Soviet Jews political refugee status. In
what is rumored to be a U.S. gesture to the Soviets on the
eve of the Olympic games, the U.S.-supported Institute
for the Study of the USSR in Munich is closed; a number
of prominent earlier émigré figures die—Georgy Adamovich, Gaito Gazdanov, Sofia Pregel, and Boris Zaitsev.
Among those who emigrate is Joseph Brodsky.

1973   Vasily Betaki, Yury Miloslavsky, Maria Rozanova, Andrei
Siniavsky, and Henri Volokhonsky emigrate, along with a
host of others, one of whom—Kirill Khenkin—even emigrates for a second time; the Soviet government becomes
a signatory to the International Copyright Agreement in
an ineffective effort to suppress foreign publication of the
works of Russian writers.

1974   Aleksandr Solzhenitsyn is expelled from the USSR; Aleksandr Galich, Genrikh Khudyakov, Edward Limonov, Yury Mamleev, and Viktor Nekrasov emigrate; the journal *Kontinent* is founded in Paris; Valery Tarsis publishes *Ward No. 7*; Aleksandr Solzhenitsyn publishes *From Under the Rubble.*

1975   Khronika Press is founded in New York; Gerald Ford refuses to meet with Solzhenitsyn; Vladimir Maksimov is stripped of Soviet citizenship; the journal *Vremya i my* is founded in Israel; among those emigrating are Viktor Tupitsyn, Aleksandr Suslov, Aleksei Tsvetkov, Konstantin Kuzminsky, and Lyudmila Shtern.

1976   Vladimir Bukovsky is exchanged for Luis Corvalan, head of the Chilean Communist Party; *Publishers' Weekly* estimates that some thirty million copies of Solzhenitsyn's books have been sold; a group of "left-liberal" émigré thinkers issue the first volume of *The USSR: Democratic Alternatives* in opposition to Solzhenitsyn and *Kontinent*; Zinoviev publishes *Yawning Heights*; Siniavsky publishes *Strolls with Pushkin*; Sasha Sokolov publishes *School for Fools*; among those emigrating are Andrei Amalrik, Anatoly Gladilin, Lev Losev, and Arkady Lvov; Mark Slonim, a prominent First-Wave literary scholar, dies.

1977   The cost of emigrating from the Soviet Union is announced as 500 rubles for forfeiture of Soviet citizenship, plus 300 rubles for a passport; Joseph Brodsky publishes *A Part of Speech*, and Boris Khazanov's *The Smell of Stars* appears; among those who emigrate are the critics Pyotr Vail and Aleksandr Genis, the future editor of *Strana i mir* Kronid Lyubarsky, Aleksei Khvostenko, Sergei Yurenen, and Aleksandr Zinoviev; deaths in the older generation include: Dmitry Tschizewskij, Vladimir Nabokov, and Mark Vishnyak. Aleksandr Galich accidentally electrocutes himself.

1978   An article in *Sintaksis* speaks of "Bolshevism as a Russian phenomenon"; in the Soviet Union a vituperatively anti-Semitic book written by Lev Korneev (*The Class Essence of Zionism*) is published and circulated on a semiclandestine basis; Aleksandr Zinoviev publishes his *The Radiant Future* and is stripped of Soviet citizenship; among those emigrating are Sergei Dovlatov and Igor Yefimov.

1979   Emigration reaches 67,000; Igor Chinnov publishes *An-*

tithesis; Maksimov publishes *A Tale of Rhinoceroses;* and Limonov publishes *It's Me, Eddie;* in the USSR the almanac *Metropole* is conceived; Yuz Aleshkovsky, Dmitry Bobyshev, and Edward Kuznetsov emigrate; among those from the First Wave who die are Father George Florovsky and Wladimir Veidle.

1980   Two new newspapers appear—*Novy amerikanets* (New American) (New York) and *Panorama* (Los Angeles); Sergei Dovlatov publishes his *Solo on the Underwood;* Vasily Aksyonov is stripped of Soviet citizenship; others leaving the Soviet Union include Fridrikh Gorenstein, Bakhyt Kenzheev, and Vladimir Voinovich; Andrei Amalrik dies.

1981   The number of émigrés drops to 22,000; Vladimir Voinovich, Lev Kopelev, and Raissa Orlova are stripped of Soviet citizenship; Aksyonov publishes *The Island of Crimea;* Aleshkovsky publishes *Kangaroo;* Korzhavin publishes *Spleteniya* (Intersections).

1982   Total emigration falls to less than 8,000; Vladimir Maksimov expels Viktor Nekrasov from the editorial board of *Kontinent;* a number of Russian émigrés are finally received at the White House, but Solzhenitsyn refuses to attend; Igor Yefimov publishes the novel *As One Flesh;* Joseph Brodsky publishes *Roman Elegies;* the linguist and literary scholar Roman Jakobson dies.

1983   Georgy Vladimov is stripped of Soviet citizenship; Aleksandr Solzhenitsyn states that "pluralism" should not be equated with moral relativism; Yury Liubimov's play based on *Crime and Punishment* is premiered in a suburb of London; among the magazines founded are *Forum* (Munich), *Kaleidoskop* (New York), *Tribuna* (Paris), and *Vstrechi* (Philadelphia); Yury Kublanovsky publishes *With the Last Sun,* and Solzhenitsyn begins his *Red Wheel;* two First-Wave figures publish memoirs: Irina Odoevtseva, *On the Banks of the Seine* and Vasily Yanovsky, *Elysian Fields;* Yury Liubimov and Georgy Vladimov emigrate.

1984   Georgy Vladimov is appointed editor-in-chief of *Grani;* Stalin's daughter Svetlana Allilueva returns to Russia; Yury Liubimov is stripped of Soviet citizenship; Mihajlo Mihajlov is expelled from the editorial board of *Kontinent;* periodicals founded include *Russkoe samosoznanie* (Richfield Springs, N.Y.), *Strelets* (Jersey City), and *Strana i mir*

(Munich); in an open letter Zinoviev declares that any cooperation with the Soviet authorities is treason.

1985   Total emigration from the USSR falls to 2,368; the Soviet government claims that there is no "objective basis" for emigration from the USSR and that the term "compatriot abroad" includes the children and grandchildren of emigrants; the journal *Vremya i my* moves from Israel to the United States; Aleksei Tsvetkov publishes *Eden,* Lev Losev publishes *The Marvelous Landing;* deaths in the older generation include Olga Anstei, Rostislav Pletnyov, and Gleb Struve.

1986   Gorbachev's policy of *perestroika* is proclaimed. Rumors begin to circulate that individual writers might be asked or permitted to return home; the Soviet magazine *Knizhnoe obozrenie* publishes a selection of Vladimir Nabokov's verse and the magazine *Moskva* his novel *Luzhin's Defense.* Among the deaths in the older group of writers: Roman Goul, Yury Ivask, and Leonid Rzhevsky.

1987   The Soviet authorities begin issuing visas to émigrés to visit the Soviet Union; Morris B. Abram, chairman of the National Conference on Soviet Jewry, announces that the Soviet government will permit thousands of Jews to emigrate to Israel within the year on direct air flights via Romania; a resolution passed by the Israel Cabinet reads: "The government of Israel believes that the status of refugees now accorded [by the U.S. government to] the Soviet émigrés whose declared goal is Israel should be abolished"; *Pravda Ukrainy* announces that Yury Liubimov can return to the Soviet Union if he so wishes; Vladimir Voinovich writes a letter to Sergei Zalygin, editor-in-chief of *Novy mir,* suggesting that *Novy mir* publish Voinovich's work, but Zalygin refuses; the Soviet poet Yevgeny Yevtushenko, in an interview granted to the West German magazine *Der Stern,* says of Solzhenitsyn: "I find it in bad taste and arrogant for a person living in the West to attack his Soviet colleagues who are still fighting for freedom. One has no moral right to do that"; Soviet authorities at the Sixth Moscow International Book Fair confiscate a number of books presented by Ardis Books, among them Sasha Sokolov's *School for Fools* and Aksyonov's *The Burn;* Voinovich publishes *Moscow 2042* (also confiscated at the book fair), a satire on Soviet society and Solzhenitsyn at the same time; Yury Druzhnikov and Boris Falkov emigrate; the First-Wave poet and memoirist Irina Odoevtseva returns to Russia; Viktor Nekrasov and Ivan Elagin die.

1988   Yury Liubimov is permitted to return to stage *Boris Godunov* in Moscow's Taganka Theater; a reading of Joseph Brodsky's poems takes place in the Palace of Theatrical Performers (*Dvorets teatral'nykh deyatelei*) in Leningrad; film producer Eldar Ryazanov states that he has been attempting to get permission to produce a film based on Voinovich's *Chonkin; Knizhnoe obozrenie* publishes an article demanding that Solzhenitsyn's citizenship be reinstated; Solzhenitsyn issues a categorical denial that he has been approached about returning to the Soviet Union or having his banned works published there; an ever-increasing number of works by émigré writers appears in the Soviet Union.

1989   *Moskovskie novosti* (Moscow News) publishes an interview with Aleksandr Yakovlev, head of a section of the USSR Academy of Sciences Institute of State and Law, who states that "flight abroad or refusal to return from abroad to the USSR" will no longer be viewed as treason under the Soviet Penal Code; Edgar Bronfman, president of the World Jewish Congress, proposes that Soviet Jews be permitted to emigrate to Israel in return for lifting the Jackson-Vannik Amendment (under the proposal would-be emigrants would be given no choice other than Israel); the United States limits immigration of Soviet Jews to the United States; Soviet publications are virtually flooded with writings by Russian émigrés.

1990   The Soviet citizenship of a number of émigrés is reinstated, some of them writers. They include Vasily Aksyonov, Vladimir Maksimov, Irina Ratushinskaya, Aleksandr Solzhenitsyn, Vladimir Voinovich, and Aleksandr Zinoviev. Russian émigré writers of all waves freely visit the Soviet Union and publish their works in large editions. Sergei Dovlatov dies.

1991   The Soviet Union ceases to exist, thus putting an end to formal exile.

Glossary of Names

Abel, Rudolph (1903–1971), spy who was arrested and returned to the Soviets in 1967 in exchange for U-2 pilot Gary Powers, 250

Abram, Morris B. (b. 1918), prominent American Jewish lawyer and educator, 293

Abramov, Fyodor (1920–1983), Russian prose writer and professor of Literature, 76, 77

Academy of Sciences, 165, 208, 212

Achair, Aleksei, pseudonym of *Aleksei Gryzov* (1896–?), Russian émigré poet in China, 5, 13

Adamovich, Georgy (1894–1972), influential Russian émigré poet and critic in Paris, 4, 9, 11, 13, 32, 33, 37, 47, 49, 128, 278, 285, 290

Afanasiev, Anatoly, Soviet historian, 21, 24, 181

Ageev, M., pseudonym of *Mark Levi,* First-Wave Russian émigré prose writer, 181, 278

Agnivtsev, Nikolai (1878–1932), poet, emigrated in 1921, repatriated in 1923, 277, 279

Akhmadulina, Bella (b. 1937), Russian poet, 36

Akhmatova, Anna, pseudonym of *Anna Gorenko* (1889–1966), Russian poet, 9, 13, 18, 26, 46, 52, 105, 106, 107, 111, 173

Aksakov, Sergei (1791–1851), Russian Slavophile writer, 155

Aksyonov, Vasily, 21, 23, 24, 69–84, 142, 221, 241, 243, 292, 293, 294

Aldanov, Mark, pseudonym of *Mark Landau* (1886–1957), Russian émigré novelist, 4, 12, 15, 61, 62, 276, 281, 283, 284

Alekseev, Gleb (1892–?), prose writer, repatriated in 1923, 277, 279

Alekseeva, Lidia. *See* Devel, Lidia Alekseevna

Aleshkovsky, Yuz (b. 1929), Russian writer, emigrated to the United States in 1979, 292

Alexander II (1818–1881), Russian Tsar, assassinated, 272

Allilueva, Svetlana (b. 1925), memoirist and daughter of Joseph Stalin, 289, 290, 292

All-Russian Writers' Congress, 287

Al'manakh, 288

Amalrik, Andrei (1938–1980), Russian émigré historian and writer, 289, 290, 291, 292

Amfiteatrov, Aleksandr (1862–1938), humorous writer, emigrated in early 1920s, 9, 273, 274, 275

Ami, 290

Anarkhist, 274

Andreev, Nikolai, pseudonyms: *G. Khomyakov* and *N. Otradin* (1908–1982), Russian émigré historian and literary critic, 16, 273, 274, 275, 276

Annenkov, Yury, pseudonym of *Boris Temiryazev* (1889–1974), prose writer, emigrated in 1924, 279

Annensky, Innokenty (1856–1909), poet, playwright, and translator, 10, 18

Anstei, Olga (1912–1985), Russian émigré poet, 16, 284, 286, 293

Apollinaire, Guillaume, pseudonym of *Willhelm Apollinaris de Kostrowicki* (1880–1918), French poet of Polish extraction, 10, 35

Apollon, a literary-artistic magazine published from 1909 to 1917 in St. Petersburg, 32, 37

Ardis Publishers, a publishing house dedicated to Russian underground and émigré literature, established by Karl and Ellendea Proffer in 1971 in Ann Arbor, Michigan, 80, 290, 293

Artsybashev, Mikhail (1878–1927), Russian writer who emigrated after the revolution, 279

Association of Russian Writers and Poets in Paris, 14

Astafiev, Viktor (b. 1924), Russian writer, 76, 77, 241

Augstein, Rudolph (b. 1923), German historian and editor of *Der Spiegel,* 132

Averchenko, Arkady (1881–1925), Russian émigré humorous writer, 8, 277, 289

Avvakum, Archpriest (1620 or 1621–1682), founder of Russian Old-Believer sect, burned at stake for heresy, 2, 44, 159, 271

Azef, Evno (1869–1818), terrorist and double agent of the Russian revolutionaries and the Tsarist secret police, 51, 52, 58–59, 274

Babel, Isaak (1894–1941), Russian writer, 71, 144, 159

Bagritsky, pseudonym of *Edward Dziubin* (1897–1934), poet, 18

Bakunin, Mikhail (1814–1876), Russian émigré anarchist, 2, 271

Balmont, Konstantin (1867–1942), Russian émigré symbolist poet, 4, 8, 10, 275, 277

Balter, Boris (1919–1974), Russian writer, 244, 245

Baratynsky, Yevgeny (1800–1844), Russian poet, 18

Bar-Or, Roman (b. 1953), poet, emigrated in 1979, 288

Bart, S., First-Wave Russian émigré poet, 9

Batshev, Vladimir (b. 1947), Russian poet and dissident, 175

Baudelaire, Charles (1821–1867), French poet, 196

Bazilevskaya, Yelena (1902–1951), First-Wave Russian émigré poet, 4

Beckett, Samuel (1906–1989), Irish dramatist who emigrated to France in 1937 and wrote in French, 109, 183

Belinkov, Arkady (1921–1970), Russian émigré literary critic, 62, 289

Belinsky, Vissarion (1811–1848), Russian literary critic, 123

Belotserkovsky, Vadim (b. 1928), prose writer, poet, journalist, human-rights activist, emigrated in 1972, has been critical of Solzhenitsyn, 231

Belov, Vasily (b. 1932), Russian writer, 76, 84

Bely, Andrei, pseudonym of *Boris Bugaev* (1890–1934), Russian prose writer, poet, and literary theoretician, 3, 9, 10, 48, 71, 72, 144, 177, 274, 275, 277, 279

Bem, Alfred (1886–1945), critic, emigrated in 1919, 9, 276

Benn, Gottfried (1886–1956), German poet and prose writer, 35, 136, 137

Benois, Aleksandr (1870–1960), Russian theater art director, painter, and ballet librettist, 4

Berberova, Nina (b. 1901), Russian émigré prose writer, poet, literary critic, 3, 278, 286

Berdiaev, Nikolai (1874–1948), First-Wave Russian émigré religious philosopher, 43

Bestuzhev-Marlinsky, Aleksandr (1797–1837), Russian writer, Decembrist, 12, 43, 62, 171, 278

Betaki, Vasily (b. 1930), Russian émigré poet, 290

Bilibin, Ivan (1876–1942), Russian painter who was an émigré in Egypt and France, 1920–1936, 4

Bisk, Aleksandr (1883–1973), poet and translator, emigrated in 1919, 276

Bitov, Andrei (b. 1937), Russian writer, 81, 245

Bitsilli, Pyotr (1879–1953), Russian émigré literary historian, 4, 6

Blagonamerenny (The Well-Wisher), a Russian émigré magazine founded in 1926 in Brussels, 271, 279

Bliznetsova, Inessa (Ina) (b. 1958), poet, emigrated in 1979, 288

Blok, Aleksandr (1880–1921), Russian Symbolist poet, 44, 48, 136, 143, 168, 281

Blokh, Raisa (1899–1943), Russian émigré poet, 12, 284

Blokh, Yakov, publisher, 52

Bobrova, Ella Ivanovna (b. 1911), poet, emigrated in 1943, 284

Bobyshev, Dmitry (b. 1936), Russian émigré poet, 26, 45, 106, 112, 292

Bogdanov, Aleksandr, pseudonym of *Aleksandr Malinovsky* (1873–1928), Tsarist émigré, political activist, and science fiction writer, 2

Bogoraz, Larisa (b. 1929), essayist, active in human rights movement, 227

Borges, Jorge Luis (1899–1986), Argentine writer, 125, 265

Borman, Martin (1900–?), Nazi party official, in 1946 sentenced to death in absentia at Nuernberg War Tribunal, 12

Boycharov, Nikolai, 278

Brazol, B. L., 287

Brecht, Bertolt (1898–1956), German émigré writer and playwright who returned to East Germany after World War II, 250

Breitman, Grigory, publisher, 51

Breshko-Breshkovsky, Nikolai (1874–1943), prose writer, emigrated in 1921, 12, 277

Brezhnev, Leonid, 1, 175, 208, 209, 214, 218, 219

Brodsky, Joseph, 21, 27, 54, 101–113, 109, 121, 135, 136, 137, 179, 181, 194, 252, 289, 290, 291, 292, 294

Bronfman, Edgar (b. 1929), President of World Jewish Congress, 294

Brown, Edward (b. 1909), American Slavist, 268, 269

Brusilov, Aleksandr (1853–1926), Russian general, 252

Bukharin, Nikolai (1888–1938), Tsarist Russian émigré, early Bolshevik leader, 275, 282

Bukovsky, Vladimir (b. 1942), Russian dissident who was exchanged by the Russian government for Luis Corvalan, head of the Chilean Communist Party, 223, 224, 231, 261, 291

Bukowski, Charles (b. 1920), American writer, 261

Bulgakov, Mikhail (1891–1940), Russian writer and playwright, 71, 72, 144, 193, 278

Bulgakov, Sergei (1877–1941), Russian émigré philosopher, 278

Bulich, Vera (1870–1953 or 1954), poet, 4, 10

Bunin, Ivan (1870–1953), Nobel Prize-winning Russian émigré writer, 3, 8, 32, 44, 61, 127, 143, 167, 168, 169, 181, 277, 279, 281, 284, 286, 287, 288, 289

Bunina, Vera, 14, 285

Burkin, Ivan (b. 1919), émigré poet, 286

Burliuk, David (1882–1967), émigré artist and poet, emigrated in 1920, 277

Butyrka, Russian prison founded in the seventeenth century, 115

Carter, Jimmy, 145

Chaadaev, Pyotr (1794–1856), Russian philosopher, 2

Chagall, Marc (1887–1985), famous Russian-Jewish painter, 4

Chaikovsky, Nikolai (1850–1926), Russian émigré editor, 278

Chalidze, Valery (b. 1938), Russian émigré physicist and publisher who was active as a political dissident in the USSR, 291

Change of Landmarks Movement (Smena vekh), a Russian émigré movement which originated in 1921 and called for the émigrés to begin collaborating with the Soviet government, 3, 5–6, 56, 277

Druzhnikov, Yury (b. 1923), Russian writer, emigrated in 1987, 294

Dudko, Father Dmitry (b. 1922), priest who renounced his former dissident activities under pressure from the Soviet authorities, 154, 162, 250

Durrell, Lawrence (1912–1990), British poet and essayist, 262

Eckermann, Johann Peter (1792–1854), German writer and Goethe's secretary, 53

Efron, Sergei (1893–1940), Russian émigré editor and prose writer who returned to the Soviet Union, where he was executed; husband of Marina Tsvetaeva, 7, 8, 253, 278, 282, 283

Ehrenburg, Ilya (1891–1967), Russian journalist and writer who lived in France, 1908–1917, and from 1921 to 1941 spent most of his time abroad on official Russian business—in Berlin, Paris, and Spain, 3, 9, 274, 275, 278, 283

Èikhenbaum, Boris (1886–1959), Russian Formalist literary scholar, 53

Èisner, Aleksei (1905–1984), Russian poet and prose writer who returned to the Soviet Union in 1939, 7, 283

Elagin, Ivan (1918–1987), Russian poet and translator, left Russia for Germany in 1943, 16, 17, 18, 19, 284, 294

Elagin, Yury (1910–1987), Russian émigré historian, 17

Èllis, Lev, pseudonym of Lev Kobylinsky (1879–1947), Russian émigré poet, literary scholar, and translator, 275

Enninger, Philip, President of German Parliament, forced to resign in 1987 after a speech considered by some to be anti-Semitic, 201

Ermolaev, Herman, Russian-American Slavist, 59

Esenin, Sergei (1895–1925), Russian poet, 18

Eurasianism, a Russian émigré movement, founded in 1921, which viewed Russian culture as neither European nor Asian, but Eurasian, 6, 27

Falkov, Boris (b. 1946), Russian writer and pianist, emigrated in 1987, 294

Faulkner, William (1897–1962), 71, 177, 193

Fedin, Konstantin (1892–1977), Russian writer, Director of the Board of the Russian Writers' Union, 53, 63, 287

Fedotov, Georgy (1886–1951), Russian émigré philosopher, 62, 279, 284

Fesenko, Tatiana (b. 1915), Second-Wave émigré writer, 17, 286

Filippov, Boris (1905–1991), Russian prose writer, poet, and editor, left Russia for Germany during World War II, 283, 286

Filosofov, Dmitry (1872–1940), Russian émigré cultural thinker, 281

Finkelstein, Leonid, pseudonym of Leonid Vladimirov (b. 1924), prose writer, defected in 1966, 289

Fitzgerald, Edward (1809–1883), English poet known chiefly for his translation of the Rubiyat, by Omar Khayyam, 71

Flaubert, Gustave (1821–1880), French novelist, 123, 124, 125, 139

Florovsky, Georgy (1893–1979), Russian émigré philosopher, 6, 277, 292

Fondaminsky, Ilya (1880–1942), Russian émigré editor, 12

Ford, Gerald, 291

Foster, Ludmila (b. 1931), Russian-American Slavist and journalist, 290

France, Anatole (1844–1924), French writer, 220

Frank, Semyon (1877–1950), Russian émigré philosopher, 62, 278, 282

Frolov, Ivan (1918–1957), Russian poet, 40, 208

Grass, Günter (b. 1927), German writer, 28

Greene, Graham (b. 1904), British writer, 263

Grivtsova, Antonina, pseudonym of A. *Gorskaya* (1900–1972), poet, emigrated in 1922, 278

Grobman, Mikhail (b. 1939), Russian poet, emigrated in 1971, 290

Gromyko, Andrei (1909–1989), Soviet ambassador to the United Nations, 13, 285

Grove Press, 268

Gruzdev, Ilya (1892–1960), Russian literary historian, 53

Gubanov, Leonid (1946–1983), Russian poet arrested in 1965 for demonstrating in support of Andrei Siniavsky and Yuly Daniel, 175

Gumilyov, Nikolai (1886–1921), Russian poet executed by the Soviet government, 9, 17, 32, 52

Gusev-Orenburgsky, Sergei (1867–1963), Russian émigré prose writer, 5, 278

Hemingway, Ernest (1899–1961), 71, 260

Herbert, Lord George (1593–1633), 43

Herzen, Aleksandr (1812–1870), Russian émigré writer and publisher, 2, 130, 181, 271

Himmler, Heinrich (1900–1945), head of SS and Gestapo, and de facto dictator of Germany after attempted assassination of Hitler, 12

House of the Arts, 277

Idashkin, Yury, 94

Iliin, Mikhail, pseudonym of *Mikhail Osorgin* (1878–1943), Russian émigré writer, 4, 274

Iliinsky, Oleg (b. 1932), poet, emigrated in 1944, 284, 287

Illyustrirovannaya Rossiya (Russia Illustrated), Russian émigré journal published in Paris from 1924 to 1939, 279

Inostrannaya literatura (Foreign Literature), magazine published monthly in Moscow since 1965, 71

Institute for the Study of the Soviet Union, established in West Germany with U.S. funding; existed from 1952 to 1972, 15, 290

Ionesco, Eugene (b. 1912), Romanian-born French playwright, 71, 246

Isakovsky, Mikhail (1900–1973), Russian poet, 86

Iskander, Fazil (b. 1929), Abkhazian prose writer and poet writing in Russian, 82, 245

Iskra (The Spark), 273

Iswolsky, Hélène, 283

Ivanov, Georgy (1894–1958), Russian émigré poet and prose writer, 4, 10, 18, 32, 33, 38, 51, 52, 279

Ivanov, Viacheslav (1866–1949), Russian émigré poet, 1, 8, 10, 13, 44, 171, 279

Jackson-Vanik Amendment (1974) to U.S. Trade Act; barred the Soviet government from receiving most-favored nation status, 294

Jakobson, Roman (1896–1982), Russian émigré linguist and literary scholar, 276–277, 292

Johnson, D. Barton (b. 1933), American Slavist, 28, 179

Joyce, James, 109, 180, 183

Kafka, Franz, 104, 180, 183, 193, 220

Kagan, Abram, 52

Kaleidoskop, 292

Kandinsky, Vasily (1866–1944), Russian painter, 4

Kapitsa, Pyotr (1894–1984), Russian physicist, 213

Karamzin, Nikolai (1766–1826), Russian writer, 271

Karamzina, Maria (1900–1942), Russian émigré poet, 4

Karpovich, Mikhail (1888–1959), Russian émigré historian and editor, 15, 61, 288

Karsavin, Lev (1882–1952), Russian émigré poet, 6

1667), diplomat and writer, emigrated in 1664, 2, 271

Kozhevnikov, Pyotr (b. 1872), Russian émigré writer, 9

Krachkovsky, Dmitry, pseudonym of *Dmitry Klenovsky* (1892 or 1893–1976), poet, 9, 16, 284

Krasnoe znamya (The Red Banner), 273–274

Krasnov, Pyotr (1869–1945), Russian White general and émigré writer, who was taken to Moscow at the end of World War II and executed, 13, 286

Kravchinsky, Sergei (1851–1895), prose writer and translator, fled abroad in 1874, traveled abroad again in 1877, fled abroad again in 1879 (without returning to Russia), 272

Kreisky, Bruno (b. 1911), Chancellor of Austria, 175

Krivenko, Lev, Russian writer, 244

Krolow, Karl (b. 1915), German poet, 35

Kropotkin, Pyotr (1842–1921), Russian revolutionary and writer, escaped abroad in 1876, returned to Russia in 1917, 2, 272, 273, 276

Krotkov, Yury (1917–1982), Russian émigré playwright and prose writer, 54, 56, 288

Krupskaya, Nadezhda (1869–1939), Lenin's wife, government and party official, 52

Krymov, Yury (1908–1941), Russian writer, 51

Ktorova, Alla (b. 1926), prose writer, emigrated in 1958, 288

Kublanovsky, Yury (b. 1947), Russian poet, emigrated in 1982, 26, 292

Küchelbeker, Wilhelm (1797–1846), Russian writer, 271

Kun, Bela (1887–1937), Communist leader and journalist, set up a Russian republic in Hungary from March to August 1919, returned to Russia and perished in the Purges, 60

Kundera, Milan (b. 1929), Czech émigré writer, 27

Kuprin, Aleksandr (1870–1938), Russian writer, emigrated in 1919, returned to Russia in 1937, 4, 7, 8, 276, 282

Kurbsky, Andrei (1528–1583), Russian political figure and writer who fled from Russia during the reign of Ivan the Terrible and launched a heated correspondence with him, 1, 271

Kushner, Aleksandr (b. 1936), Russian poet, 106

Kuskian, Aleksandr (Kusikov) (1896–1977), First-Wave Russian émigré poet, 278

Kutepov, Aleksandr (1882–1930?), Russian Tsarist general who was successor to General Vrangel as head of the Russian forces in exile during the 1920s, kidnapped and executed by the Soviets, 280

Kuzmin, Mikhail (1875–1936), Russian acmeist poet, 37, 46

Kuzminsky, Konstantin, Russian émigré poet and editor, 280

Kuznetsov, Anatoly (1929–1979), Russian writer who defected in 1969, 54

Kuznetsov, Edward (b. 1939), Russian writer who was imprisoned in Soviet Union after attempting to hijack a plane to Israel in 1970, 21, 292

Kuznetsova, Galina (1900?–1976), poet and memoirist, emigrated in 1920, 277, 286

Ladinsky, Antonin (1896–1961), Russian poet and novelist who emigrated to France through Egypt in 1920 and returned to Russia in 1955, 13, 278, 285, 287

Laforgue, Jules (1860–1887), Symbolist poet, 35

Lakhman, Gizella (1895–1969), poet, emigrated in 1919, 276

Larionov, Mikhail (1881–1964), Russian émigré painter, 4

Mamchenko, Viktor (1901–1982), Russian poet, emigrated in 1920, 11

Mamleev, Yury (b. 1931), Russian prose writer and essayist, emigrated in 1974, 57, 291

Mandelstam, Osip (1891–1938), Russian poet, died in forced-labor camp, 9, 18, 26, 34, 45, 48, 52, 107, 112, 167, 194

Mandelstam, Yury (1908–1943), Russian poet and critic, emigrated in 1920, 12, 277, 284

Mann, Thomas (1875–1955), German writer who emigrated to the United States, 130, 250

Marchenko, Nikolai, pseudonym of *N. Morshen* (b. 1917), poet, emigrated in 1944, 17

Markov, Vladimir (b. 1920), Russian émigré writer and scholar, 286

Martynov, Leonid (1905–1980), Russian poet, 36

Marx, Karl (1818–1883), 52, 146, 161, 208

Maslov, Dmitry, First-Wave Russian émigré poet, 4

Matusovsky, Mikhail (1915–?), Russian poet, 86

Matveev, Venedikt, Russian poet, 279, 284

Matveeva, Novella (b. 1934), Russian Soviet poet, 36

Medvedev, Roy (b. 1925), Russian historian, 214

Meierhold, Vsevolod (1874–1940), Russian stage director who perished during the Purges, 164

Melgunov, Sergei (1879–1956), historian and journalist, emigrated in 1923, 15, 54

Merezhkovsky, Dmitry (1865–1941), Russian poet, novelist and religious thinker, lived in Paris from 1905 to 1912, fled the USSR in 1919, 4, 8, 10, 12, 23, 127, 139, 168, 276

Metropole, 1979 literary almanac which was forbidden by Soviet authorities and published abroad, 70, 73, 78, 79, 189, 292

Mihajlov, Mihajlo (b. 1934), Yugoslav journalist of Russian extraction who became famous after being imprisoned by Yugoslav authorities for publishing his 1965 book entitled *Moscow Summer*—memoirs of time spent in the USSR, 232, 292

Miller, Henry (1891–1980), American expatriate novelist and essayist, 260, 261

Miller, Yevgeny (1867–1937?), Russian Tsarist general kidnapped by agents of the NKVD while en route to a meeting with German representatives to discuss the possibility of White Russian cooperation with the Nazis, 260, 261

Miloslavsky, Yury (b. 1946), Russian prose writer, emigrated in 1973, 290

Milyukov, Pavel (1859–1943), Minister of Foreign Affairs in Russian provisional government, editor of *Poslednie novosti*, 62, 280

Mingrels, ethnic group in Georgia, 255

Mitchell, Margaret (1900–1949), 17

Mladoross ("Young Russia") League, totalitarian political movement founded by Russian émigrés in 1923, 6, 279

Molva (The Rumor), 5

Mörike, Eduard (1804–1875), German poet and prose writer, 35

Moskovskie novosti (Moscow News), newspaper founded in 1957, 23, 294

Mother Maria (religious name of Elena Skobtsva, 1891–1943 or 1945), Russian nun who emigrated in 1919 and perished in a German concentration camp, 12, 276, 284

Mozart, Wolfgang (1756–1791), 9

Mozhaev, Boris (b. 1923), Russian writer, 76

Mozhaiskaya, Olga (1896–1973), poet, 277

Muratov, Pavel (1881–1951), Russian émigré prose writer and art historian, 3

Musil, Robert (1880–1942), Austrian writer, 140

Mysl' (Thought), 275

Nabokov, Vladimir (1899–1977), Russian émigré prose writer, 8, 12, 16, 25, 64, 110, 129, 140, 143, 148, 170, 178, 180, 182, 183, 193, 263, 264, 276, 278, 280, 282, 283, 289, 291, 293

Naiman, Anatoly (b. 1942), Russian poet and translator, 106, 112

Nakanune (On the Eve), Russian émigré newspaper published in Berlin in the 1920s, 3, 6, 51, 278

Nansen, Fridjof (1861–1930), Norwegian explorer, Nobel Prize laureate, appointed High Commissioner for Affairs of Russian Refugees in 1921, 277

Nartsissov, Boris (1906–1982), Russian émigré poet who left Russia in 1941 and settled in America, 4, 283, 287

Nash put' (Our Path), 5

Nash sovremennik (Our Contemporary), 289

Nasha strana (Our Country), 286

Nashi dni (Our Days), 277

National Labor Union (of the New Generation). *See* Solidarist Movement

Natural School, the predominant literary trend in mid-nineteenth-century Russian literature; placed emphasis on lower-class subject matter, heavily influenced by Gogol, 181

Nechaev, Sergei (1847–1882), Russian revolutionary and anarchist, murdered a co-conspirator to "bind the organization together with blood," handed over to the Tsarist government by Swiss authorities, 2, 272

Nekrasov, Viktor (1911–1987), Russian writer, emigrated to France in 1974, 56, 165, 249, 285, 291, 292, 294

NEP (New Economic Policy), the market-oriented economic policy

of the Soviet government in effect from 1921 to 1928, 5, 56, 277

Nesmelov, Arseny, pseudonym of *Arseny Mitropolsky* (?–1945 or 1946), Russian émigré poet in China, forcibly returned to Russia in 1945, 13

New Review (Novy zhurnal), Russian émigré literary and political journal, founded in New York in 1942, 15, 50, 54, 56–62, 65, 284, 288

New York Times, 247

Nikolaevsky, Boris (1887–1966), Russian émigré historian, 54, 58

NKVD (The People's Commissariat of Internal Affairs), an earlier name for the KGB, 206

Novaya mysl' (New Thought), 6

Novaya russkaya kniga (The New Russian Book), a Russian émigré magazine in Berlin in the 1920s, 6, 51, 60, 278

Novaya zarya (A New Dawn), 276

Novoe russkoe slovo (The New Russian Word), Russian émigré newspaper published in New York City, founded in 1910, 22, 167, 215, 257, 278, 279

Novosadov, Boris, pseudonym of *Boris Taggo* (1907–1945), Russian émigré poet, 4

Novosel'e (Housewarming), 286

Novy amerikanets (New American), 292

Novy grad (New City), 280, 283

Novy korabl', 280

Novy mir (The New World), 3, 31, 74, 89, 119, 243, 245, 275, 293

Novy zhurnal. See *New Review*

NTS. *See* Solidarist Movement

Oberiuty, Russian acronym for Association for Real Art, literary circle in Leningrad, 1927–30, 71, 183

Odarchenko, Yury (1890–1960), First-Wave Russian émigré poet, 11

Odoevtseva, Irina, pseudonym of *Iraida Gainike* (b. 1901), Russian poet who emigrated to Paris in

Rubezh (The Border), Russian émigré weekly magazine devoted to literature and literary criticism and published in Harbin, 1927–1933?, 5

Rural Prose, Russian literature which devotes particular attention to the Russian countryside, 75–77, 81, 84, 95–96, 181, 244–245, 253–254

Rushdie, Salman (b. 1947), author of novel entitled *Satanic Verses,* 173

Russian Committee of United Organizations, 280

Russian People's University, The, 277

Russian Popular Library, 277

Russian Social Democrat Workers' Party, 273

Russian Student Christian Movement Herald, 253

Russkaya gazeta (The Russian Newspaper), 274, 281

Russkaya kniga (The Russian Book), 277

Russkaya mysl' (Russian Thought), Russian émigré newspaper founded in Paris in 1947; an émigré magazine with this name existed during 1921–1924, 22, 32, 162, 222, 225, 231, 248, 277, 286

Russkaya pochta (The Russian Mail), 276

Russkaya zhizn' (Russian Life), 277, 288

Russkaya zhizn' v Amerike (Russian Life in America), 273

Russkie novosti (Russian News), 272

Russkie zapiski (Russian Annals), 282, 283

Russko-amerikansky rabochy (The Russian-American Worker), 274

Russko-amerikansky vestnik (The Russian-American Newsletter), 272

Russkoe èkho (The Russian Echo), 278, 279

Russkoe obozrenie (Russian Review), 276

Russkoe samosoznanie, 292

Russkoe slovo (The Russian Word), 5, 274, 275, 286

Russky golos (The Russian Word), 274, 275, 279, 288

Russky klich (The Russian War-Cry), 22

Russky mirok (The Smaller Russian World), 272

Russky patriot (The Russian Patriot), 284, 286

Russky vestnik (The Russian Herald), 275

Ryazanov, Eldar (b. 1927), Soviet film director, 294

Rzhevskaya, Agniya, pseudonym of *Aglaya Shishkova* (b. 1923), émigré poet, 288

Rzhevsky, Leonid (1905–1986), Russian writer and literary scholar, captured as prisoner of war in 1941, remained in the West, 16, 17, 287, 288, 293

Saburova, Irina (1907–1979), poet and prose writer, left Riga 1943 or 1944, 17

Sakharov, Andrei (1921–1989), Russian nuclear physicist and dissident, 55, 217, 257

Saltykov, Mikhail, pseudonym: *Shchedrin* (1826–1889), Russian satirical writer, 219, 220

Samoilov, David, pseudonym of *David Kaufman* (b. 1920), Russian poet, 245

Sarnov, Ben (b. 1927), Russian literary critic and scholar, 244

Savin, Ivan, pseudonym of *Ivan Savolainen* (1899–1927), Russian émigré poet, 4, 10

Savinkov, Boris (1879–1925), Russian writer who first emigrated in 1909, then again after the Revolution in 1918. Plotted to overthrow the Russian government and was lured into the USSR and arrested. Died in prison, 58, 273, 274, 279

Savitsky, Pyotr (1895–1968), Russian émigré poet, 6, 277

committed suicide, 4, 7, 8, 10, 11, 18, 19, 37, 45, 47, 102, 104, 107, 112, 169, 170, 245, 251, 252, 278, 283, 284

Tsvetkov, Aleksei (b. 1947), Russian poet and journalist, emigrated to the United States in 1975, 291, 293

Tukhachevsky, Mikhail (1893–1937), Russian general, 50, 252

Tupitsyn, Viktor (b. 1943), Russian poet, emigrated in 1975, 26, 291

Turgenev, Ivan (1818–1883), Russian writer, 2, 109, 130, 144, 196, 272, 283

Tvardovsky, Aleksandr (1910–1971), Russian poet and editor, 74, 245

Tynianov, Yury (1894–1943), Russian Formalist literary theoretician and novelist, 159

Ustryalov, Nikolai (1890–1938), Russian émigré who wrote that the Soviet government would be of benefit to Russia; returned to Russia in 1935 and died in the Purges, 7, 282

Utverzhdeniya (Confirmations), 280

Vagin, Yevgeny (b. 1938), Soviet dissident and editor, emigrated to Italy in 1976, 146

Vail, Pyotr (b. 1949), Russian émigré literary critic, 119, 262, 291

Varshavsky, Vladimir (1906–1977), Russian émigré prose writer and poet, 13, 16, 127, 128, 277, 281, 285

Vasnetsov, Viktor (1848–1926), Russian painter, 169

Veche, Russian émigré magazine, founded in Munich in 1981, 132, 133, 146, 170

Veidle (Weidle), Vladimir (1895–1979), Russian poet and critic, emigrated in 1924, 32, 33, 49, 279, 292

Velikanova, Tatiana, human rights activist, 223

Veresaev, pseudonym of *Vikenty Smidovich* (1867–1945), Russian prose writer, 165

Vergun, K., 6

Vernadsky, Georgy (1887–1973), Russian historian, emigrated in 1920, 6

Vernant, Jacques, 13

Vertinsky, Aleksandr (1889–1957), Russian émigré poet and "bard," emigrated in 1919, returned to Russia in 1943, 13, 276, 284

Vestnik Bunda, 273

Vestnik Manchzhurii (The Manchuria Messenger), 5

Vestnik RSKhD (Herald of the Russian Student Christian Movement), founded in Paris in 1949, 49, 162, 279, 283, 286

Viktor Kamkin Bookstore, large Russian bookstore located in Rockville, Maryland, with branch office in New York City, 287

Vinokurov, Yevgeny (b. 1925), Russian poet, 37

Vishnyak, Mark (1883–1975), First-Wave Russian writer and editor, 276, 283, 291

Vladimov, Georgy, pseudonym of *Georgy Volosevich* (b. 1931), Russian prose writer, emigrated in 1983, became editor of *Grani* in 1984, 21, 119, 122, 123, 213, 292

Vlasov, Andrei (1901–1946), Russian general who defected to the German side in 1942 and organized an army of Russian prisoners-of-war who fought against the Soviet Union. Handed over by the Americans to the Russians, who executed him, 13, 284

Voennaya gazeta dlia russkikh voisk vo Frantsii (Newspaper for Russian Troops in France), 275

Voice of America, 286

Voinovich, Vladimir, 21, 23, 25, 85–97, 119, 120, 123, 139, 161, 195, 215, 221, 292, 293, 294

Volkonskaya, Zinaida (1792–1862), poet and prose writer, expatriate, 8

Volodarsky, V., pseudonym of *Moisei Goldstein* (1891–1918), revolutionary and émigré, 275

Volokhonsky, Henri (b. 1936), Third-Wave Russian poet, 26, 290

About the Editor

John Glad is Associate Professor of Russian Literature at the University of Maryland and is the former director of the Kennan Institute for Advanced Russian Studies at the Woodrow Wilson International Center for Scholars, Washington, D.C. He is the author of *The Pronunciation of Russian* and translator and editor of numerous books of Russian poetry and fiction. He recently edited *Literature in Exile* (Duke University Press, 1990).

Library of Congress Cataloging-in-Publication Data

Conversations in exile : Russian writers abroad / edited by John Glad
; interviews translated by Richard and Joanna Robin.
p.   cm.
Translated from the Russian.
Includes index.
ISBN 0-8223-1277-8 (alk. paper). — ISBN 0-8223-1298-0 (pbk. :
alk. paper)
1. Authors, Russian—20th century—Interviews.   2. Russian
literature—20th century—History and criticism.   3. Authors,
Russian—Biography—Exile.   4. Soviet Union—Exiles.   I. Glad,
John.
PG2998.E95C66   1993
891.709'0044'08694—dc20   92-14797
                                                      CIP